My father taught me that a problem well defined is half solved. It would be foolish to be in ministry to emerging generations without carefully studying this book.

—Josh McDowell, author and speaker

Dan helps us understand issues we must address regarding the church and emerging generations. This book will help you strategize your journey out of the institution and into the mainstream of the movement.   —Reggie McNeal, Leadership Network

God is speaking to his church, and he's using those who don't even attend one to be his spokespeople. Listen up! Thanks to Kimball, new voices are directing the church toward renewal and spiritual growth.   —Michael Frost, author, *The Shaping of Things to Come*

This is a sobering read, but as Dan promises, it's ultimately a hopeful one too. We ignore those who like Jesus but not the church at our own peril.

—Tony Jones, Emergent Village

While he might not use the term, Dan Kimball is a gifted missionary-evangelist. Thoroughly christological and missional.   —Lon Allison, Billy Graham Center

Dan brings authenticity and sensitivity to the discussion by engaging people who have come to trust him as their friend. This is Jesus' way of engagement. He didn't talk about people; he conversed with them.   —Eddie Gibbs, Fuller Theological Seminary

A tough-minded, clear-sighted look at authentic Christian living in the twenty-first century.

—Leonard Sweet, George Fox University

A wonderful bridge between the real-world orthopraxy of the emerging church and the "we want to learn and understand" posture of all healthy church leaders. Dan clearly has his finger on the pulse of twentysomethings outside the church.

—Mark Oestreicher, Youth Specialties

Treats the citizens of emerging culture as people God loves rather than as enemies, targets, or customers. Essential reading for anyone serious about doing mission in emerging culture.

—Earl Creps, Assemblies of God Theological Seminary

I felt like I was sitting in a coffeehouse with Dan, having a three-hour conversation about things my heart yearned to explore. This book is beyond timely. Carry it with you into the future.   —Rudy Carrasco, Harambee Ministries

The good news is that Dan is right. More people are open to Jesus, giving us an opportunity to shed our skins of tired traditions and return to our call, a Christlike nature.

—Alan Nelson, *Rev!* magazine

With insight, gentleness, and an unswerving commitment to the wisdom of the past, Dan Kimball shows us what we don't want to see but must see if we care about the Great Commission in the twenty-first century. —Gregory Koukl, Stand to Reason

I really appreciate Dan Kimball's passion. It's important to listen to and wrestle with him in order to develop ministry models that proclaim an ancient message through relevant and flexible methods. —Efrem Smith, The Sanctuary Covenant Church

Couldn't put it down! Confronting and alarming but hopeful, this book presents real dialog with young critics of the church and offers positive suggestions for moving the church forward. —Bryce Jessup, William Jessup University

What a hopeful reminder that Jesus is not as far away from most unchurched people as church leaders think. If every church leader will heed Dan's message, emerging generations will find faith in the real Jesus through his real church.
—John Burke, author, *No Perfect People Allowed*

If you like Jesus and the church, you need to read this book. It will give you a window into the heart of a world that desperately needs Jesus and a new vision of his bride, the church. —Kevin G. Harney, Corinth Reformed Church

Every frustrated, tired, and burned-out pastor in America needs to read this book. Dan Kimball provides hope and insight for all who love Jesus and wish the church were more like God intended. —Jules Glanzer, George Fox Evangelical Seminary

Thoughtfully addresses some of the most complex issues facing the American church today. It provokes serious thinking about our responses to the hard questions about life, faith, and Jesus. —Linda Stanley, Leadership Network

The next generation is definitely looking for a less programmatic, more relational, and more missional kind of church. I agree with Dan; they want more Jesus and less religion.
—Randy Frazee, Willow Creek Community Church

Dan Kimball both points out our blind spots and gives us a clear and compelling road map for reengaging people with the good news of the gospel. This is an important book, and a great one. —Chap Clark, Ph.D., Fuller Theological Seminary

I recommend this book especially to those who think the emergent church movement is a phase. Something is wrong when people like Jesus but not the church, Jesus' body. Our job is to do something about it. —Sarah Sumner, Azusa Pacific University

THEY LIKE JESUS
BUT NOT THE CHURCH

Other Books by Dan Kimball

The Emerging Church
Emerging Worship
Listening to the Beliefs of Emerging Churches (contributor)
I Like Jesus but Not the Church (forthcoming)

THEY LIKE JESUS BUT NOT THE CHURCH

insights from emerging generations

DAN KIMBALL

ZONDERVAN®

ZONDERVAN.com/
AUTHORTRACKER
follow your favorite authors

We want to hear from you. Please send your comments about this book to us in care of zreview@zondervan.com. Thank you.

ZONDERVAN®

They Like Jesus but Not the Church
Copyright © 2007 by Dan Kimball

Requests for information should be addressed to:

Zondervan, *Grand Rapids, Michigan 49530*

Library of Congress Cataloging-in-Publication Data

Kimball, Dan.
    They like Jesus but not the church : insights from emerging generations / Dan Kimball.
      p. cm.
    Includes bibliographical references.
    ISBN-13: 978-0-310-24590-2
    ISBN-10: 0-310-24590-7
    1. Young adults — Religious life. 2. Church work with young adults. 3. Non-church-affiliated people. 4. Church renewal. 5. Emerging church movement. 6. Postmodernism — Religious aspects — Christianity. I. Title.
    BV4529.2.K54 2007
    277.3'0830842 — dc22

                                                       2006034899

Interior design by Sherri L. Hoffman

Printed in the United States of America

07 08 09 10 11 12 • 12 11 10 9 8 7 6 5 4

To church leaders and Christians
who have enough missional courage
to do whatever it takes to escape the Christian subculture
and be citizens of the kingdom rather than
citizens of the bubble (John 17:15)

CONTENTS

ACKNOWLEDGMENTS

This book is the result of many hours of wonderful conversations with those who like Jesus but not the church. Listening to the stories of people like Molly, Dustan, Maya, Duggan, Alicia, Penny, Erika, Erica, Gary, Hanna, Brad, and so many others who took the time to talk with me helped me to understand how the church and Christians are viewed from the outside. Thanks to God, some of them now like both Jesus and the church.

Also, this book was written while birthing and being part of the new missional church community of Vintage Faith Church. I received support and encouragement from so many people in this community, including Josh Fox, Kristin Culman, Tom Rahe, Fred Barnes, Steve Ruppert, Cheryl Isaacson, Shelley Pimentel, Lee Purkey, and of course my wonderful wife, Becky, to take the time needed to write and finally get this book done. I need to also mention Paul Engle, Brian Phipps, and John Raymond from Zondervan, who are always so supportive and helpful in the writing process.

INTRODUCTION
THE WORLD HAS CHANGED;
DON'T BE A WEAKLING

> The world is changed. I feel
> it in the water. I feel it in
> the earth. I smell it in the air.
> ## —GALADRIEL,
> ### FROM *THE FELLOWSHIP OF THE RING*

I am not a confrontational person. In fact, I avoid confrontation and dread even having to dispute anything. Nor do I enjoy labeling people or calling people names. But in this very unusual instance, I shocked myself. I was speaking to a group of around five hundred middle-aged pastors of a conservative denomination, and something happened to me as I talked. I started to shake because I was getting so upset and nervous, and a word that I've never even used, at least not since elementary school, just blurped out.

I called them all weaklings.

WHY I CALLED SEVERAL HUNDRED PASTORS WEAKLINGS

The focus of this particular event was on evangelizing emerging generations and on the implications of cultural changes for our methods of evangelism. During a main session, I presented the irony of how people in emerging generations are very open to talking about Jesus, though they are not interested in church. Using examples from culture, I showed how emerging generations are very spiritually minded and open. I painted an optimistic picture of the exciting times we live in, when Jesus is becoming more and more respected in our culture by non-churchgoing people. And I shared how the church is perceived by those outside of it.

I built a case for our need to think of missionaries not only as those you send overseas somewhere but also as ourselves here in our emerging culture in our own towns and cities. I then pleaded with the pastors to consider how we might spend our time and how our lives might change if we saw ourselves as missionaries. I explained that it might mean we would do what any missionary would do: be out listening to what non-Christians, especially those in their late teens to thirties, are saying and thinking about the church and Christianity. Why this age group? Because generally it is the largest segment missing from most of our churches, and so as we look at the future of the church, it's an age group we really need to pay attention to. I pleaded with them to awaken to the fact that most people in our emerging culture are not listening to us anymore. I explained that they are disappearing from most of our churches, and that we need to rethink what we are doing as church leaders in a changing culture.

I shared how I try to think like a missionary in my ministry setting. On Mondays and Tuesdays, I stay in the church office to have staff meetings and other meetings that best happen in that environment. But then on Wednesdays, instead of working in the church office or at home, I study for the weekend sermon at a local coffeehouse. I shared how I also go to another coffeehouse on Thursdays and have meetings with people there instead of in the church office.

I explained that I like going to these coffeehouses because I find myself engaging in conversations with non-Christians, primarily in their twenties, who work there or who regularly hang out there. And I shared how I don't just walk up to strangers but how instead, over a period of time, I get to know the coffeehouse workers and regulars. And as I get to know them, I get to ask them questions about what they think, and I find they are usually very willing to share their viewpoints on life, church, spirituality, and Christians. I explained that for me, listening to them and becoming friends with them has been a great and natural way to hear the thoughts and get to know the hearts of those outside the church. I shared how I even get invited to clubs to hang out and see bands, and how this also is a way to hang out with and build trust and credibility with those I'm befriending. And I shared how incredibly refreshing it is to be friends with people outside of church circles.

TOO BUSY INSIDE THE CHURCH TO KNOW THOSE OUTSIDE THE CHURCH

I concluded by telling the group that it's too easy for pastors and church leaders to get caught up in the busyness of church activities with Christians and to subtly lose touch with the mindset of emerging generations. It's too easy to get caught in our little church subcultures, and the result is that the only younger people we might know are Christians who are already inside the church. But if we go off-site, we're not just with Christians at the church campus all the time.

As I spoke about these things, I looked around and saw I was getting a lot of puzzled looks. Finally someone raised his hand and asked if the leaders and people of my church allow me to do this instead

> IT'S TOO EASY TO GET CAUGHT IN OUR LITTLE CHURCH SUBCULTURES, AND THE RESULT IS THAT THE ONLY YOUNGER PEOPLE WE MIGHT KNOW ARE CHRISTIANS WHO ARE ALREADY INSIDE THE CHURCH.

of spending time with the people in the church. Someone commented that they couldn't possibly go to a coffeehouse like that, since their church expects them to be available in the church office during the week to care for the "flock" (his word).

This caught me off-guard, so I asked if others felt the same way, and to my surprise many of them did. They felt their job as church leaders is to preach the Scriptures and stay in the church office all week long to be available for the people of the church. One person commented that non-Christians need to come to the church building and that revival meetings and "altar calls" are the way to reach them. Many indicated that it isn't church leaders' job to go out to the people; instead the people should come to us. Another commented about how "pagan" emerging generations are and how they just need to hear solid preaching, which will cause them to repent of their ways. Yet another asked me about the people I had been visiting with in the coffeehouse. "Have you sealed the deal with them?" he asked. I asked what he meant by "sealing the deal." He said, "Have you prayed the sinners' prayer with them?" To which I replied, "No, I'm just trying to be their friends and get to know them." My answer actually brought a public rebuke from this person. "Well, then you're wasting time, brother, and I will pray for you that you seal the deal with them." I could sense approval of his statement from almost everyone in the crowd and even heard an "amen" from someone.

I stood there not quite able to believe what I was hearing and felt this weird rush of blood and adrenaline through my system. My head felt a little flush, and I didn't know how to respond. I heard myself stammering, "I can't believe what I am hearing here ... This is even an evangelism conference. If there is anyone on the church staff who should want to be out of the church office and befriending and talking to non-Christians, it's you in this room. And if you are afraid to talk to your elders or the leaders in your church so that you can spend time with non-Christians during the week, then you are ... a ... a ..." I kept stammering, trying to think of the right word, and then I blurted it out: "Weaklings!"

I could see the impact of my words ripple through the crowd. I felt a double dose of nervous emotion, half of me thinking *I can't believe I just said that!* while the other half thought *I'm so glad I said that.* Near the back row an older gentleman got up, squeezed his way out of the pew, and walked out of the room, muttering something to the people he passed. Later I heard that as he was leaving, he told the people in the row, "They'll let anyone speak at this conference; I'm getting out of here!"

The session ended awkwardly, and I made my way to the person who had invited me to the conference to apologize for my outburst. Much to my relief, he said it was the best thing that had happened so far and was exactly what they needed, so he was glad I said it. He explained that so many church leaders in this denomination are losing touch with our emerging culture, and the result is the drastic dropout rate of younger people in their churches, as well as the lack of people from emerging generations coming in. I still felt bad for calling them all weaklings, but I was relieved that apparently it was something that needed to be said. I have subsequently wondered how typical and widespread this group's attitude is among church leaders across the nation.

OUR WORLD HAS CHANGED WHETHER WE LIKE IT OR NOT

In J. R. R. Tolkien's *The Fellowship of the Ring*, Galadriel, the elf queen played by Kate Blanchett in the movie, says a classic line about the changes happening in Middle Earth. She says to Frodo, "The world is changed. I feel it in the water. I feel it in the earth. I smell it in the air." I have seen this quote used by other church leaders who also feel this is true of our time: the world around us has changed, and that's why emerging generations are disappearing from most churches.

We are living in an increasingly "post-Christian" culture. America once was more of a "Christian nation" whose influences and values were aligned with Judeo-Christian values and ethics. Even most atheists had a good sense of the story line of the Bible and its main characters, and usually respected the Bible and Christian pastors. Movies and media generally taught values and ethics that aligned for the most part with the Bible.

However, the world around us has drastically changed over the past thirty years or so. In our increasingly post-Christian culture, the influences and values shaping emerging generations are no longer aligned with Christianity. Emerging generations don't have a basic understanding of the story of the Bible, and they don't have one God as the predominant God to worship. Rather, they are open to all types of faiths, including new mixtures of religions. No longer are Christian pastors and ministers the "good guys" in films and in the media. Most church leaders now actually feel embarrassed to tell people they are pastors. Some even choose titles other than pastor so they aren't dismissed by people outside the church. Some people aren't even comfortable saying they are a Christian but come up with new terms such as "Christ follower" to avoid negative and distorted associations.

We live in a quickly changing world. You might feel safe in the church world you live in, but step outside into the real world and things aren't quite the same anymore. For many pastors and church leaders, this is a scary admission. I recently met with a pastor who told me the history of his church. Back in the seventies, it was one of the dominant churches in his community, but now it's shrinking and aging. He drew an attendance graph on a whiteboard, and the line dramatically dropped downward. He expects they will be shut down in a matter of years. I wonder if this story won't be playing out in many churches, even megachurches.

I once heard someone explain that the church in America is not above what happened in Europe. European nations have truly become post-Christian nations. Their great cathedrals and church buildings once were filled with people, but now they sit almost empty on Sunday mornings and serve as tourist attractions. Far more people go through them sightseeing than actually worship there. We shouldn't think that we're above such a thing happening here. With the increasing dropout rate of people in emerging generations, it could be our destiny that in thirty or forty years, all of our recently constructed megachurch buildings, which are now filled with people, will end up as virtually empty tourist attractions. I bet in Europe they never guessed that was their future, and we shouldn't be so overly confident that it won't happen here too.

PLEASE TAKE A HARD LOOK AT YOUR CHURCH, EVEN IF IT'S A MEGACHURCH

This isn't just an issue only smaller churches are dealing with. Even though many a contemporary megachurch is packed with baby boomers, younger people are absent from so many of them. But the megachurches don't often speak of this, or they ignore it and say everything is okay. I recently met with the college pastor of a church that has well over ten thousand people. He shared that the attendance of those under thirty is rather dismal. Two-thirds of those who graduate from high school and stay in the area end up leaving their church. Yet he feels the senior pastor keeps ignoring the problem since there's so much excitement about all of the people over thirty-five who are filling the building.

> TWO-THIRDS OF THOSE WHO GRADUATE FROM HIGH SCHOOL AND STAY IN THE AREA END UP LEAVING THEIR CHURCH. YET HE FEELS THE SENIOR PASTOR KEEPS IGNORING THE PROBLEM SINCE THERE'S SO MUCH EXCITEMENT ABOUT ALL OF THE PEOPLE OVER THIRTY-FIVE WHO ARE FILLING THE BUILDING.

I just read an article by another megachurch leader saying how his church is bridging generations and impacting emerging generations. Yet I recently spoke to two people on his staff who work with high schoolers and young adults. They said that people in their twenties are disappearing and that their twenty-somethings ministry is shrinking fast. They told me they would guess that three-fourths of graduating high-school seniors leave their church as soon as they are free from their parents' making them go. That's a high percentage, and that's of those who stay in the area to go to college. Yet they felt that the church's senior leadership dismisses the trend; as long as they see *some* younger people, they think everything's okay.

I pray that those of you whom God may be using with older people would not just think everything is fine since you see some younger people in your churches. Chances are they grew up in your church. Chances are they will leave your church as they get older. Please don't ignore this elephant in the room. It may be humbling to admit the truth, but for the sake of those who live in your community, please take a hard look. Take the time to look at the demographics of the teenage and young adult population in your community. Then look at how many are part of your church or of all the churches in your area. Do some research to see what percentage of high schoolers remain part of your church after graduation. You may get a sobering wake-up call.

I'M NOT THE ONLY ONE

I understand how hard it is for pastors and church leaders to know what to do about our rapidly changing culture. It's heartbreaking and even a subtle blow to one's confidence to see one's church aging and not many people under thirty-five coming in. Granted, exciting things are happening in some churches that are exceptions to this trend, and I'm thrilled about these churches and thank God for them. I'll be sharing some exciting stories from churches that are seeing increasing numbers of people from emerging generations coming to their churches. But the overall outlook is not too good at the moment. And the implications are too important not to pay attention to it.

I have been told, "Dan, this is just your opinion because you focus on emerging generations. Not everyone feels the same way, and it's just a trend that will pass." Well, let me quote Reggie McNeal straight from the Bible Belt, who is older and wiser than me and who has been in church ministry for over thirty-three years. His book, *The Present Future*, puts these sobering words in bold: "We are witnessing the emergence of a new world.... The phenomenon has been noted by many who tag the emerging culture as post-Christian, pre-Christian, or postmodern. The point is, *the world is profoundly different than it was at the middle of the last century*, and everyone knows it. But knowing it and acting on it are two different things. *So far the North American church largely has responded with heavy infusions of denial*, believing the culture will come to its senses and come back around to the church."[1]

His words are important because they speak to pastors and church leaders who are in denial. So listen as Reggie adds some demographic information and then sounds an alarm about the disappearance of emerging generations from our churches: "The rate of disconnection indicates a dilemma far more serious than mere youthful rebellion.... The farther you go down the generational food chain, the lower the percentage each succeeding generation reports going to church.... It's more than numbers. The American culture no longer props up the church the way it did, no longer automatically accepts the church as a player at the table in public life, and can be downright hostile to the church's presence. The collapse I am talking about also involves the realization that the values of classic Christianity no longer dominate the way Americans believe or behave."[2]

> "SO FAR THE NORTH AMERICAN CHURCH LARGELY HAS RESPONDED WITH HEAVY INFUSIONS OF DENIAL, BELIEVING THE CULTURE WILL COME TO ITS SENSES AND COME BACK AROUND TO THE CHURCH."

Perhaps you are already aware of these changes. If so, I am excited and beyond thrilled that you have a heart for emerging generations; I believe too much is at stake not to have a heart for them.

A FEW THINGS YOU SHOULD KNOW ABOUT THIS BOOK

Here are a few things you should be aware of before we go farther with this book.

This book is not just my opinions. This book is the result of years of being in ministry. As a youth pastor for eight years, I had an evangelistic ministry and countless discussions with non-Christian teenagers. For the past nine years, I have been in young-adult and college ministry and have talked with countless people primarily in the eighteen- to thirty-five-year-old age range, both in the church and outside of it. I was on staff at a mega-church for many years, and I am part of a team that recently launched a brand-new church designed to be a missional church in our post-Christian emerging culture. So my observations are the result of many years in direct ministry in a variety of church contexts. I also travel quite a bit, visiting churches and talking to church leaders from all around the country. So my frame of reference for this book is not just my local context or just one church experience.

This book is not about statistics but is based on real people and their opinions and stories. Statistics and surveys can be helpful, but they miss the heart. You don't see people's faces and expressions in statistics. You don't hear their stories, and you don't hear the emotion in their voices. Statistics won't make your heart ache for those who are rejecting faith in Jesus because of their confused and distorted impressions of Christianity and the church. Statistics are just numbers. But this book is based on the comments and stories of real people with whom I have personally talked. Throughout the book, you will read quotes from people from emerging generations who are interested in Jesus but who don't go to any church. In the context of the relationships I have been building with them, I met with these people several times for extensive interviews in which they shared their impressions of the church and Christians. They also shared why they like Jesus and respect him. I hope some of the voices in this book will bring you closer to the heart and thinking of those in emerging generations. I wish you could have been present to talk with them and sense their heart. I hope their words will both haunt and inspire you.[3]

This book will likely make you feel uncomfortable. Writing this book made me uncomfortable because the comments of the people I interviewed were often rather depressing. They said some rather harsh and striking things about the church and Christianity. Listening to their impressions, I felt like I was sitting in a dentist's chair, being closely examined and judged on how well I have brushed and flossed. I initiated these conversations, asking these individuals to tell me their impressions, so it wasn't a situation in which they were coming to me to complain. They were simply answering my questions. But it was embarrassing to hear many of the things they said. In many ways, I was ashamed that the church of Jesus comes across to them the way they described. But honestly, after listening and getting to know them, I don't blame them. I think you will understand too as you read the chapters ahead.

This book will give you hope. As you read this book, you might get defensive at first, perhaps even a little depressed. But after listening to the people I interviewed, I experienced hope. Yes, they had some harsh things

WHAT IS *MISSIONAL*?

Throughout this book, you will see the term *missional.* To be missional is more than just to evangelize. Here are some ways of thinking of this term as the underlying philosophy of this book:

- Being missional means that the church sees itself as *being* missionaries, rather than having a missions department, and that we see ourselves as missionaries right where we live.
- Being missional means that we see ourselves as representatives of Jesus "sent" into our communities, and that the church aligns everything it does with the *missio dei* (mission of God).
- Being missional means we see the church not as a place we go only on Sunday, but as something we are throughout the week.
- Being missional means that we understand we don't "bring Jesus" to people but that we realize Jesus is active in culture and we join him in what he is doing.
- Being missional means we are very much in the world and engaged in culture but are not conforming to the world.
- Being missional means we serve our communities, and that we build relationships with the people in them, rather than seeing them as evangelistic targets.
- Being missional means being all the more dependent on Jesus and the Spirit through prayer, the Scriptures, and each other in community.

to say about the church and Christians, but as the title of this book implies, they are open to Jesus, and this gives me great hope.

LIVING IN HOPEFUL AND EXCITING TIMES

I believe we are in a great and wonderful period when emerging generations are open to the teachings of Jesus and even to the church. Another thing that gives me great hope is seeing churches all across the nation that are aware of the things I talk about in this book and aren't ignoring criticism of the church. They realize that they need to give both an apology and an apologetic for the church. God is doing great things as a result. Exciting things are happening in some churches in which hundreds and even thousands of people from emerging generations are being introduced to Jesus and becoming disciples. Having talked with many of the church leaders whose churches are seeing this great response, I've learned that the key thing is that they see themselves as missionaries and their churches as missional. By missional I mean that these churches don't just have an evangelism program but see their church as a mission. These churches are doing far more than just putting on concerts or hoping younger people will come to their church by adding candles, couches, and coffee. And because they are missional, they cannot default to being weaklings. It wouldn't be possible to.

I am hopeful that the Holy Spirit will use the church to reach people in our emerging culture. I hope this book will make you uncomfortable, make you think, and make you do some serious self-examination, but I hope that by the end of the book, the Spirit will make you excited about what God can do through you in your community. May we have hope and the confidence that God cares about emerging generations, and, knowing how much he cares, may we be motivated not to be weaklings.

PART 1

WHY EMERGING GENERATIONS ARE CHANGING

I PROBABLY WOULDN'T LIKE CHRISTIANS IF I WEREN'T ONE

1

Christians are hard
to tolerate; I don't know
how Jesus does it.
—BONO

I hate, hate, hate going to the gym. I am not an athlete, unless you consider bowling and shooting pool to be sports, but I do believe God wants us to take care of our bodies, so during certain seasons of the year, with good intentions, I make attempts to go to the gym for a workout. For someone like me, it's awkward enough trying to use the weights and gym equipment, but it's even more awkward because of the mirrors they have all around so you have to look at your awkward self as you fumble with the weights and equipment.

But I know it's important to go, so on this one occasion I decided to try a different gym. This one had a bunch of new hydraulic weight machines and an attendant who would show you how to use them, which worked out well for me because I didn't feel so naive and didn't have to fumble around trying to figure things out on my own. And this gym didn't have any mirrors either.

NO ##$% WAY YOU'RE A PASTOR ... PASTORS ARE CREEPY!

The instructor, a girl probably around twenty-three years old, seemed really nice. She made conversation the whole time she was showing me how to use the machines. She talked about music and how she really liked a few bands that were popular in the 1980s, such as the Cure, Siouxsie and the Banshees, and the Smiths. I was familiar with these bands and had even seen two of them live, so we instantly had a musical connection. We talked about the music scene and about other '80s musicians and bands from England that we both liked.

At the end of the loop of machines she was showing me, she wrapped up her instruction and asked me what I do for a living.

Since I don't try to hide it, I said, "I'm a pastor at a church."

Her expression changed as she took two steps backward and tripped on the leg of the machine next to her. "No ##$&& way you're a pastor. I don't believe you!"

It took several minutes to convince her I really am a pastor. She said there was no way that a pastor would ever have liked the Smiths or the Cure, and she was shocked because I seemed normal and not at all what she thought a Christian and especially a pastor would be like.

Her strong reaction made me wonder why she would think that, so I asked what she thought a pastor would be like. She said, "Pastors are creepy." She went on to say that pastors are out to "try to proselytize people to become right-wing Republicans" and that "they hate homosexuals" and that "a pastor definitely wouldn't know who the Smiths or Siouxsie and the Banshees are."

When I asked her if she knew any other pastors, she said no. Instead, her impressions came from stories she has read, from what she sees on TV, from the occasional street preacher she has seen, and from some encounters with Christians during college.

IT'S NOT JUST CALIFORNIA

You may be thinking that this woman's view would be different if that health club weren't in California. But I have lived in New Jersey, Colorado, and California, as well as in England for a year and in Israel for several months, and I've traveled enough to know that this is a widespread view. In certain areas of the country which are more conservative, such as the Bible Belt, there is a strong historical Christian presence and churches are everywhere. There is some degree of cultural respect for Christians and church leaders, and so you might not find such a strong reaction as the trainer's. But please don't assume that even in conservative areas the sentiment about Christians and churches isn't changing, especially among younger generations.

When I travel I try to find a coffeehouse to hang out in to listen, observe, and talk to (not proselytize) people hanging out there. In fact, as I was writing this chapter, I was in a coffeehouse adjacent to the University of Minnesota in Minneapolis. At the table next to me was a college-aged couple who were reading some books and talking. One of the books had the name of Solomon on the cover and some Hebrew letters, but they also had some books about magick.[4]

I politely asked about the Solomon book, and the couple said it was about Solomon and the spirits that guided him. They were friendly and eagerly opened several of the books they were studying to answer my question. They shared what they were reading and also talked about Kabbalah and showed me some diagrams of people throughout the Hebrew Bible who had guiding spirits.

Since they mentioned the Bible, I asked if they ever talked to Christians about this. They exchanged a quick glance and then with pained emotion said yes, but they warned me that the church doesn't tell people everything. They said church leaders hold back the secrets and origins of the faith from the people in their churches. Because of this, most Christians aren't aware of the origins of the Bible and of the worship of God throughout world history. This is why as soon as they talk to a Christian about any of this, they immediately are told they're wrong and are accused of being involved with demonic things.

Now, from what I could observe, the Bible condemns what they were reading as being of evil origin. But it was interesting to hear that they feel church leaders keep secrets from their churches and that the only thing they have experienced from Christians is being told right away how wrong they are.

FEELING SORRY FOR CHRISTIANS

We continued to talk about Christians, and eventually I shared with them that I am a Christian. What was interesting was that they didn't react like the girl in the gym. Instead, they gently smiled, kept looking right at me, and didn't say anything at all. Then they exchanged glances like they were having the same thought. What was weird was that their reaction communicated that they felt sorry for me. It wasn't a repulsed reaction, and

I think they didn't respond negatively because of the friendly tone of our conversation and because I had shown an interest in what they believed. When I told them I am a Christian, it felt like I had just told them I have some terminal disease and they felt sympathy for me, like they were thinking, "Oh, that's too bad. That poor, poor guy."

They were so open to dialogue, and I imagine if we had more time together, we could have compared what they were reading with the Bible and discussed why they concluded what they did. I could have explained specifically what I believe as a Christian and had a deeper dialogue with them. The couple invited me to go over to a bookstore around the corner if I wanted to read more or talk to someone who could answer more questions. So I accepted their invitation. The bookstore was larger than I expected and the manager was friendly. I took their frequently asked questions brochure and found that it said this: "We worship the Gods and Goddesses in Anglo-Saxon England, Scandinavia, and other Germanic countries *before their forcible Christianization* in the early Middle Ages." So apparently the bookstore was alluding to the Crusades and propagating the negativity of Christians' forcing their faith on others.

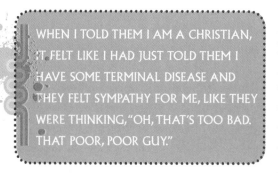

WHEN I TOLD THEM I AM A CHRISTIAN, IT FELT LIKE I HAD JUST TOLD THEM I HAVE SOME TERMINAL DISEASE AND THEY FELT SYMPATHY FOR ME, LIKE THEY WERE THINKING, "OH, THAT'S TOO BAD. THAT POOR, POOR GUY."

Now, I agree that the Bible says the worship of gods and goddesses is worshiping false gods. But I bet this young couple hadn't yet had someone talk to them about this in a loving way. They didn't react negatively to me and condemn me for not believing what they believed or for being a Christian. Rather, they treated me with respect even after they found out I'm a Christian. I relate this incident simply to show how even in another part of the country I found sitting next to me yet another example of what I'm talking about in this book.

Now, I assume that a very small percentage of the population is into magick and pagan religion. But this bookstore was right there among all the other shops, and judging by its calendar of activities, this group keeps pretty busy. Some people may think it was wrong for me even to go into their bookstore. But I hope that from my taking the time to dialogue with them, they at least had a positive conversation with a pastor who asked them questions, took the time to listen to what they believe instead of simply telling them what they should believe, and showed them respect instead of instantly condemning them, even though I don't agree with what they believe. I hope that the Spirit of God sends someone who lives near them to continue the conversation I started with them (Acts 8:29).

Whenever I go to places like that bookstore or strike up conversations with people who might be antagonistic toward Christians or other faiths, I think of the story in John 4. Jesus went out of his way to Samaria, which was a region religious Jews would normally avoid. While there, he talked with a Samaritan woman (whom a rabbi wouldn't normally talk to) who was promiscuous (all the more reason for a rabbi to avoid going near her). But Jesus did go near her, and he did talk with her, which surprised his disciples (John 4:27). I love the heart of Jesus, who spoke to people outside of the religious circles of his day. We should pay close attention to his example.

THINKING LIKE MISSIONARIES IN A POST-CHRISTIAN WORLD

The reactions of the girl in the gym and of the couple in Minneapolis really shouldn't surprise us, since we're living in a post-Christian culture. To them, Christianity isn't normal. This is really important to realize, and if you aren't sensing this in our emerging culture, you might be too enclosed in your Christian network and subculture to fully see what's happening.

If you are a baby boomer or of an older generation and were born into a Christian home, you probably have relationships with people who still share values and beliefs that are more in line with a Judeo-Christian world, and you might not see the change in emerging generations. If you are younger, were raised in a church, and surround yourself socially only with Christians, then you might not notice this as strongly either. And so it's important that we think like missionaries. Instead of viewing our towns and cities as Judeo-Christian and feeling that everyone needs to automatically adhere to what we believe, we need to act like missionaries do when they enter a different culture. When missionaries enter another culture, they listen, learn, study the spiritual beliefs of the culture, and get a sense of what the culture's values are. They may try to discover what experiences this culture has had with Christians and what the people of the culture think of Christianity. Missionaries in a foreign culture don't practice the faiths or embrace the spiritual beliefs of that culture, but they do respect them, since the missionaries are on the other culture's turf.

Maybe you're thinking, "No! This is God's turf! They need to repent and follow God, not their own beliefs! This is America!" Yes ... and no. Yes, God is the creator, and "the earth is the LORD's, and everything in it, the world, and all who live in it" (Ps. 24:1), but when missionaries enter another culture, they are in *a different culture.* God still is God, and that's why we need to be missionaries to speak of his love and salvation through Jesus. We've got to realize that in our emerging culture, we are now in a different culture and we need to view it and the people in it as a missionary would. Christians are now the foreigners in a post-Christian culture, and we have got to wake up to this reality if we haven't.

> CHRISTIANS ARE NOW THE FOREIGNERS IN A POST-CHRISTIAN CULTURE, AND WE HAVE GOT TO WAKE UP TO THIS REALITY IF WE HAVEN'T.

Perhaps you're struggling with this idea because some twenty-somethings or college students in your church don't fit this description. But do you know and interact with people in younger generations outside of your church? If not, I really believe that if you got out of your subculture, you would get much the same reaction I did with the girl in the gym or with the couple in Minneapolis.

What we have to realize as church leaders is that we aren't as respected by people who are growing up outside of the church as we were in the past. We aren't sought out as the ones to turn to for advice, and we aren't in the position of influence in our communities that we used to be in. Again, I know there are some regions where there's still a stronger positive Christian sentiment and respect for the church. But overall, from my experience talking to countless people, in particular among those who are under thirty-five years old, and especially younger people in their teens and twenties, there is a quickly growing misperception of what Christianity is, what church is, and who Christians are.

But this isn't the first time in history that there were widespread misperceptions about Christians.

CHRISTIANS WERE ONCE KNOWN AS CANNIBALISTIC, ATHEISTIC, AND INCESTUOUS

When we look at the first few hundred years of church history, we find that ancient Christians and early church leaders were also misunderstood by outsiders. For example, it was thought that:

> *The church practiced cannibalism.* Because rumors got out that Christians drank blood and ate flesh when they were taking communion, they were thought to be cannibals.
>
> *The church practiced incest.* People would hear Christians calling each other brother and sister, including married couples who now saw each other not only as husband and wife but as brother and sister in Christ. So to outsiders, hearing a married couple address each other as brother and sister implied that they were biologically brother and sister, and that looked like incest to outsiders.
>
> *The church was made up of atheists.* Most Greek and Roman religions would use a statue of their deity in their worship, and since Christians didn't have a physical representation of the God they worshiped, they were accused of being atheists.

It's easy to see how such misperceptions might come about, especially at a time when Christianity was new and people didn't know much about it. Christianity was viewed as a new sect of Judaism and as perhaps a part of the other mystery religions of that time. So the early apologists responded to these accusations in their writings. Today we aren't thought of as cannibals, atheists, or incestuous. But in our emerging culture, there are other misperceptions we need to be aware of and respond to.

TODAY, CHRISTIANS ARE KNOWN AS SCARY, ANGRY, JUDGMENTAL, RIGHT-WING FINGER-POINTERS WITH POLITICAL AGENDAS

Reading a description of Christians like the one in this subhead can make us defensive, saying, "That's not true!" But remember, you are on the inside. You know why certain Christian leaders vocalize things the way they do, even if you don't agree with them, because you understand what's behind their statements. Hopefully you aren't angry, judgmental, and pointing fingers at people, and probably other Christians you know aren't either. But we need to view ourselves the way others on the outside see us.

Also, perhaps you hang out primarily with people over thirty or thirty-five years old. Many older people outside of the church don't have as many negative impressions of the church and Christians as younger members of our emerging culture do. But, like people in the early church era, today's emerging generations don't know Christianity. They don't know the difference between Baptists, Methodists, or Episcopalians. They see the more vocal and right-wing evangelical Christian leaders being interviewed on news shows, and to many people, they represent all of Christianity. Most who have grown up outside of the church have impressions of Christians based only on television, or on occasional encounters with Christians handing out tracts and telling them they are going to hell, or on seeing Christians standing outside of rock concerts with lists of sins on big signs and shouting through megaphones that everyone passing by won't find God in the concert. (I recently experienced this very thing the last two concerts I went to.) We have the reputation of being right-wing, fundamentalist, finger-pointing, judgmental individuals. While some Christians might fit those categories, most of us don't! Sadly, the most vocal and aggressive voices that people are familiar with do.

I CAN'T BLAME THEM—I WOULDN'T LIKE CHRISTIANITY EITHER

This may sound odd, but quite honestly, I don't blame people in our emerging culture for what they think about us. If I weren't a church leader or if I weren't friends with Christians who really are following Jesus in a loving and balanced way, I would probably judge Christians and Christianity based on what I could see from the outside. And it isn't a pretty picture. Based on outside observations of Christians, there's no way I would want to become one of them. I wouldn't want to become an angry, judgmental, right-wing, finger-pointing person. I wouldn't be saying that out of rebellion against God or the church; I would simply conclude that from observations of Christians and from not wanting to change into something I wouldn't want to be like.

During the time of the early church, outsiders' perceptions of Christians weren't true. But until the early Christians befriended non-Christians, and until apologists came to explain what Christianity really was about, people didn't know better. In the same way today, people outside the church are concluding things that for the most part aren't true either, but they're making these conclusions all the same.

THE GOOD NEWS: MOST PASTORS AND CHRISTIANS AREN'T CREEPY

Most pastors and Christians are not creepy (as the girl in the gym thought) or out to condemn everyone they run into who believes differently than they do (as the couple in Minneapolis felt). I think overall, most Christian leaders are wonderful and dear people who are trying their best to follow Jesus and to make him known to others in the best way they can. Most of my friends who are pastors and Christian leaders are nothing like what the girl in the gym described.

However, I do think there are a lot of Christian leaders and Christians who need to rethink what it means to live in a post-Christian country. I do believe there are good-hearted, wonderful Christians and church leaders who don't realize how they are coming across to people in our culture today. I have met pastors, as well as read blogs and websites, who actually reinforce negative attitudes and misperceptions. But the good news is that most of us aren't like that. Most Christian leaders are not intentionally arrogant and forceful and do care how we come across to those outside the church.

But there's bad news too.

THE BAD NEWS: MOST PEOPLE DON'T SEE OR MEET THE AVERAGE CHRISTIAN OR PASTOR

When I first started leading a youth ministry, one of the students came up to me and shared how the whole youth group hated him. At that time, there were around twenty-five high schoolers in the group. I was aware there was a recent conflict between him and someone else. He told me he was thinking of not coming to the Wednesday night meeting, since no one wanted him there. I slowed him down and asked him to tell me specifically who hated him. He named two students. I said, "That's it?" and then we talked through how his perception of the whole youth group was really based on only two students, who it turned out didn't really hate him but were angry with him. We all experience this to some degree. It just takes hearing from someone that "others feel this way about you too" and you end up being consumed with the idea that the entire church or your entire office thinks about you in a certain way, when in reality it may be only one or two people.

I think at the core of a lot of the confusion is the fact that most people are making conclusions about Christians and Christianity based on a few bad experiences. But they are bad enough and reinforced enough to give the impression that this is true of all Christians. For some, it may be an excuse so they don't have to face their sin or admit that what they are doing is wrong, so they blame Christians. But I don't sense this is true of most people.

But quite often, don't we do the same? How quickly some Christians make generalizations about the gay community or liberals or whatever other terms we throw around. We need to be careful that we don't do the same thing and make assumptions about others based on a few bad experiences.

MIGHT FEEL DEPRESSING, BUT THE FUTURE IS HOPEFUL

It may be a little depressing hearing some of the things I am saying here. Yet I'm optimistic about the future of the church and the way emerging generations will respond to our efforts to reach them. But until we are out among the "natives" of the new culture, until we befriend them, earn their trust, hear their stories, understand their hearts and values, we really can't be good missionaries.

In the next chapter, I'll explain how I tunneled through the walls of Christian pop music, Christian books, Jesus trinkets, church activities and meetings, escaped the church office, and met people who like Jesus but not the church.

LOOKING AT YOUR CHURCH
THROUGH THE EYES
OF EMERGING GENERATIONS

1. When is the last time you had an encounter with someone like the girl in the gym or the couple who is into pagan magick? What did they say to you about Christians or the church? What were their impressions of Christianity?

2. If you have not had such an encounter, why do you think you haven't met anyone with viewpoints like this?

3. If you were raised outside of the church and hadn't met a Christian who represents Jesus in a good way, do you think you would like Christians? Why or why not?

WHY I ESCAPED THE CHURCH OFFICE

2

My God! What have I done?
— TALKING HEADS
"ONCE IN A LIFETIME"

In my book *The Emerging Church*,[5] I told a story about some video interviews we conducted at the University of California, Santa Cruz. The campus has a few active Christian student organizations, but when you look at the size of the university, it would be a generous estimate to say that the number of students participating in these organizations is around 2 percent. The Christian students I met kept telling me how the Christian faith is seriously attacked on campus and how they hear other students consistently condemning Christians and the church. Based on my talking with non-Christian students, I agree that this perception is accurate. I once talked to the leader of the largest Christian parachurch organization on campus, and he told me the group's primary role is to "rescue wandering and scared Christians." If you mention the university to church leaders in town, you're likely to hear assessments like, "Oh, that's such a pagan campus," and, "It's so liberal and godless up there."

LIKING JESUS BUT NOT LIKING CHRISTIANS

Knowing this about the university, our church's video team went up to the campus to interview some students. We were starting a teaching series on evangelism and wanted to hear firsthand students' thoughts about Christianity. But instead of the normal questions that some campus parachurch ministries ask, such as, "Do you believe there is only one way to God?" or, "Are there moral absolutes?" questions which, in my opinion, put people on the defensive and feel like a setup, we asked, "What do you think of when you hear the name Jesus?" and, "What comes to mind when you hear the word Christian?"

The answers were surprising and fascinating. In response to the question about Jesus, the students' eyes lit up and they smiled. When they heard the name Jesus, it was as if we were talking about a friend of theirs. We heard comments such as, "He is beautiful," "He is a wise man, like a shaman or a guru," "He came to liberate women," "I want to be like him." One girl said, "He was enlightened. I am on my way to becoming Christian." One student even said with great emotion, "I love Jesus."

What an incredible experience! On a campus with an anti-Christian and pagan reputation, students were talking about Jesus with great enthusiasm.

But when asked what they think of Christians and the church, students' responses were far different. The expressions of the same people, including the one who said he loves Jesus, changed drastically when the topic turned to the church, and we heard things like, "The church messed things up," and, "They took the teachings of Jesus and turned them into dogmatic rules." One fellow said that "Christians don't apply the message of love that Jesus gave." And then he jokingly said, "They all should be taken out back and shot."

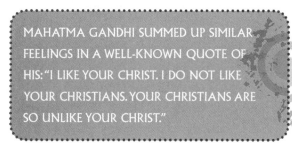

MAHATMA GANDHI SUMMED UP SIMILAR FEELINGS IN A WELL-KNOWN QUOTE OF HIS: "I LIKE YOUR CHRIST. I DO NOT LIKE YOUR CHRISTIANS. YOUR CHRISTIANS ARE SO UNLIKE YOUR CHRIST."

Yikes! What a difference between what they think about Jesus and what they think about Christians. Mahatma Gandhi summed up similar feelings in a well-known quote of his: "I like your Christ. I do not like your Christians. Your Christians are so unlike your Christ."

Now we can quickly dismiss these comments, saying, "They may like some things about Jesus, but they obviously don't know about his judgment and his comments about sin." That may be true, and we will address that later in this book. Most likely the people we interviewed have never read the whole New Testament to see all of Jesus' teachings. But what is important, and so haunting, is that they are so open to Jesus. Not only open, but they light up and smile when they talk about him. They have such positive things to say about him.

TOO CONSUMED WITH MEETINGS TO MEET THOSE WHO LIKE JESUS

Following those interviews, I did a lot of thinking. I couldn't get out of my head the difference between opinions about Jesus and about the church. I kept wondering why students feel this way. I then started wondering why there aren't many people from emerging generations in most of our churches. Could it be that we, the church, have such a bad reputation among those outside the church that it keeps them away? I knew that not all Christians are like the ones the students described in the interviews, but when we asked them if they knew any Christians, only two of the sixteen people we interviewed said they did. This was amazing to me. Most of them didn't even know a Christian personally, so their impressions and conclusions about Christians and the church were made in other ways. Could it be because we have never really engaged in conversation and relationships with them, so they form stereotypes? Could it be that when we do engage in conversation with them or "witness" to them using our typical methods, we are doing more harm than good? Having talked to enough people who have had bad experiences with Christian witnessing, I was inclined to answer yes. Maybe we in the church have been doing so much talking that we haven't really listened. Shouldn't we hear their thoughts, hear their hearts? Shouldn't we listen to why they believe what they believe, instead of jumping in to try to make them believe what we believe?

As I pondered my experiences with those outside of the church, I had a sinking feeling. I looked at my schedule as a pastor in an active church. It seemed I had become so consumed with meetings: meetings to review the weekend worship gathering, meetings to plan the next worship gathering, meetings with our home group leaders, meetings with all of the staff, meetings with leaders of ministry teams, meetings about the church budget and goals for the upcoming year. In addition, I'd block off a good chunk of time every week to study for a sermon, usually at home or in the office with my door shut so I could have it quiet. It dawned on me that all I was doing was meeting with Christians all week long. I was surrounded by Christians, and as a result, when I asked for opinions, I would get Christian answers and a Christian perspective. I knew people who had come to know Jesus in our church, but I generally hadn't met them and hung out with them until after they had become Christians.

THE PRISON OF THE CHURCH OFFICE

I looked back to determine how I got to this place. Before I was on a church staff, I worked in an office with all non-Christians. Working with non-Christians made it easy to have friendships that provided opportunities to hear the hearts, beliefs, and opinions of non-Christians, and I would share my views and beliefs with them, since we were friends. Then I became a youth pastor, and for eight years I was on the high school campus every week. As a youth pastor, I was naturally inclined to meet with non-Christian students and had the freedom to do so. But then as my role in the church shifted and I started working with adults, something changed. I subtly got sucked into spending all of my time in meetings and leading a ministry that catered to those who were already Christians. I lost contact with those outside the church who weren't Christians. Sure, I had a ton of relationships with college-aged and young-adult believers, but not with nonbelievers. I hadn't realized the severity of this disconnection because, to some degree, I still felt connected in other ways to emerging generations and the culture outside of the church, such as through music and movies. But I was so wrapped up in being busy with church that I became isolated from any true friendships with those outside of the church.

> IT WAS LIKE BEING A MISSIONARY TO THE BUDDHISTS IN CHINA BUT HANGING OUT ONLY WITH CHRISTIANS ALL THE TIME.

Having relationships only with Christians made it difficult to obey the teachings of Jesus about being on a mission for him and being salt and light to the world. It was like being a missionary to the Buddhists in China but hanging out only with Christians all the time. I started to feel convicted that I had become part of the Christian subculture, that strange bubble which little by little sucks you into it, and before you know it, you're listening only to Christian music and wearing strange T-shirts with Christian slogans on them and your conversations are peppered with Christian lingo.

I thought to myself, "Well, this is happening because I work at a church." But the more I explored this, the worse the nightmare got. I talked with volunteers in the church and asked what they do on Friday nights, who they hang out with, what they pray about, and it turned out they were just as guilty as I was. I found that younger people who had more time and freedom to socialize on weekends nevertheless were consuming time with each other, thus reinforcing the Christian bubble. I must have asked twenty or more people in my church if they had recently socialized with any non-Christian friends, and the answer was 100 percent negative. The irony is that they all worked with non-Christians. They were friendly with them at work or at school. But they didn't take it farther than that because they were too occupied with their social networks of Christians and their church activities, the very activities that I was scheduling for them. No wonder that fourteen of the sixteen people we interviewed on campus didn't know any Christians. It was making sense now that they got their impressions of us from media and the poor examples of those who proselytize without establishing relationships.

LIFE IN THE CHRISTIAN BUBBLE

Have you ever noticed that once you begin thinking about buying a particular model of car, suddenly you start seeing it all over the place? It had been out there all along, but you hadn't noticed it before. This is what happened to me. As I began looking around, all I saw was Christian paraphernalia. People carrying Christian end-times novels with them everywhere, more than the Bible itself usually. People putting chrome fish emblems on their cars. While driving on the highway, I saw a minivan that had two larger parent Christian fish emblems and two smaller children fish emblems on it. I wondered what that looks like to people who have no idea what the fish symbol means. They must think, "That family must be seriously into aquatic life." Why are we compelled to put those on our cars in the first place? You can see all types of bumper stickers on Christian's cars warning people, "In case of rapture, this car will be unmanned." Maybe you have seen the rather funny rebuttal bumper sticker: "In case you get raptured, can I have your car?" I can't blame them for saying that! We have created so many little Christian products and trinkets that just look so bizarre from an outside perspective. The more I looked around, the weirder it all looked.

Then I began noticing what most of us talk about. Generally it's the latest Christian band or concert or what's happening at church. As I recognized that we really only socialize with our Christian friends, I also recognized that overall, we are complacent about those outside the church. We aren't thinking about their eternal destiny. We aren't concerned about whether they're experiencing the abundant life Jesus offers. We are more concerned about whether there will be good snow on our church skiing trip than about the spiritual status of our neighbors and the people we work with every day. I became aware that I didn't hear much concern about those who don't know Jesus yet. We are all about making church better for ourselves and making our lives more comfortable in the Christian bubble we have created. I didn't hear much about being a voice for the voiceless or being concerned with social justice, the poor, AIDS in Africa, and other pressing needs. (I am thankful that since then the church does seem to be awakening to the AIDS epidemic and other global issues of social justice, but we still have a long way to go.) As I was awakening to the subculture I had been sucked into and was a part of, I heard and saw Christian buzz-words and phrases that suddenly sounded so incredibly corny, phrases such as "food, fellowship, and fun." And most disturbing was that when we do talk about the non-Christian world, we tend to point fingers and complain about the "horrible things going on in culture."

I didn't hear too much heartbreak for people outside the church among church leaders either. Church leaders are mainly dealing with complaints about last week's sermon or complaints that the music wasn't good enough, along with threats that people might go to another church where these things are better. When church leaders feel pressure from this kind of complaining, naturally the focus becomes having better programs, music, and activities to keep the people in their churches. Pastors face subtle pressure from Christian parents to have good youth programs to make sure that their kids stay away from the bad non-Christian kids and have the opportunity to meet other Christians. The whole thing feeds itself, isolating us from the outside world. It feels like we're building this social, spiritual, and consumeristic infrastructure, and Christians are only demanding more of it, building a stronger and thicker bubble around us, protecting us from the outside while we create this very strange Christian subculture inside. But it had happened to me so slowly that I hadn't even noticed it.

THE TRANSFORMATION FROM EXCITED MISSIONARY INTO CITIZEN OF THE BUBBLE

I have been a Christian in vocational ministry long enough to notice patterns. Let me share an observation about what happens to many believers. As I lay my theory out in phases, I hope you can get a feel for what I suspect happens quite often among us. Even though I'm going to resort to some hyberbole, I think the underlying truth is real.

Phase 1: We become Christians

Many Christians can think back to the time when they placed their faith in Jesus, understood the grace of God, and experienced the excitement and joy of learning new things from the Bible. For some individuals this may have happened when they were teenagers or even adults. Remember that burst of understanding God's grace and joy in Jesus as you told your non-Christian friends about your faith? Probably this occurred in a natural way, since you were friends rather than strangers. I recall reading that within the first year of someone's becoming a Christian, they tell approximately twenty people, from among their family and friends, about their faith and even invite them to church. This is only natural because generally everyone in a new Christian's circle of friends is outside of the church.

Phase 2: We become part of church life

As we get involved in church, we make Christian friends and participate in church activities with them. If we came from backgrounds where substance abuse or partying is the norm, we cease going into environments where we could get pulled into harmful patterns again, though we might still hang out with our non-Christian friends in healthy environments or social settings. But in any case, we tend to slowly lose touch with non-

Christian friends and become more immersed in Christian activity with our new Christian friends.

The longer we are Christians, the fewer the number of friends we have who are not Christians. Even though Christians often work alongside non-Christians or have non-Christian neighbors or sit next to nonbelieving students in class, we generally tend not to actually befriend them, or pray regularly for them, or get involved in their lives so they trust us and we can be the salt and light of Jesus to them. When I ask Christians who they went to the movies with Friday night or who they went to the beach with last weekend, it usually turns out they went with Christians from the same church. (The big stretch for people seems to be socializing with Christians from other churches, not socializing with non-Christians.) I fully understand we need Christian friendships—absolutely. We all need Christian community and we must maintain Christian community in the midst of our being on a mission for Jesus. But shouldn't it be that the longer we are Christians and the longer we walk with Jesus and understand the grace of God, the more we desire to see others experience God's grace as well? It seems incredibly ironic that as we mature and get to know Scripture better and get to know Jesus better and are transformed all the more by the Spirit, fewer non-Christians get to experience those things through relationships with us. And I'm not talking about street witnessing to strangers. I'm talking about relationships in which we dialogue and build trust with people

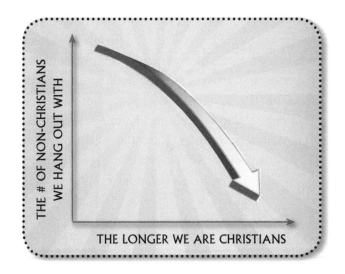

THE # OF NON-CHRISTIANS WE HANG OUT WITH

THE LONGER WE ARE CHRISTIANS

who get to know us personally. If Jesus sent us on a mission to be his salt and light to others, why is it that we have basically set up our church systems and subcultures to remove maturing people from relationships with people outside of the church?

Phase 3: We become part of the Christian bubble

Things really start changing in phase 3. As we slowly withdraw from ongoing relationships with those outside the church and focus on relationships with those inside the church, something happens. Once, it was more natural and even exciting to share life with people at work or at school, with relatives, or with neighbors. But slowly we begin to see evangelism as something the church does, primarily through events. We get more excited about going overseas to the mission field on summer trips than about the mission field we live in every day. We start to see evangelism as inviting people to *go to a church*, where the pastor will do the evangelizing and explain Christianity, instead of spending time with people and talking with them and *being the church* to them.

> WE GET MORE EXCITED ABOUT GOING OVERSEAS TO THE MISSION FIELD ON SUMMER TRIPS THAN ABOUT THE MISSION FIELD WE LIVE IN EVERY DAY.

During this phase, we stop praying daily for those who don't know Jesus and instead pray for our church's latest building project or latest program. Other than maybe at an office Christmas party that we have to go to, we rarely ever hang out with non-Christian friends or go to movies with them. For the most part, only Christians are in our circle of peers. We begin buying little Christian stickers or put metal fish symbols on our cars, and we even have a few Christian T-shirts. We set our radios only to our favorite Christian radio shows, and most of the music we listen to is Christian. We make a trip to the amusement park that has the special Christian day each year featuring Christian bands. We find ourselves regularly using Christian words and phrases and cliches, such as backsliding, prayer warrior, fellowship, quiet time, traveling mercies, "I have a check in my spirit." (Apart from the word fellowship, none of these are even from the Bible.) The transformation is complete. We have become citizens of the bubble.

Phase 4: We become Jonah

After several years as citizens of the bubble, we begin to complain and point out the terrible things happening in the culture. Like Jonah in the Hebrew Bible, who ran away when God told him to go to the wicked city of Ninevah (Jonah 1:3), we don't want anything to do with those who aren't following God as we are. Like Jonah, we even have a secret sense of delight thinking about how God will one day punish all those sinners in our towns and cities (4:5). Like Jonah, who, even after God gave him a second chance and he saw the people of Ninevah repent and cry out to God, complained about not having shade over his head and being uncomfortable (4:8–9), we complain about how well the church is providing what we want and grow numb to the fact that people all around us need the love and grace of Jesus.

We can actually get a bizarre sense of enjoyment sitting around with Christian friends talking about how lucky we are that we aren't "in the world" anymore. We get into a retreat mentality in which we think of the church as a protection-from-the-world social club. (Whether or not we actually call it that, we end up treating it that way.) We may leave the church that God used to draw us to Jesus and instead choose another church based on how good the programs are, how good the music is, or how well the church leaders perform and feed us, instead of being adults and learning to feed ourselves and being part of the church mission. Our calendars are packed entirely with church activities and meetings. Our language is ridiculously riddled with Christianese.

> WE ARE CONTENT LIVING IN OUR LITTLE CHRISTIAN SUBCULTURE AS CITIZENS OF THE BUBBLE, BUT WE DON'T EVEN KNOW IT BECAUSE EVERYONE IN OUR SOCIAL CIRCLE IS ALSO IN THE BUBBLE.

We may see those around us as lost (Luke 15:3–32), and though we might invite them to Christmas musicals, for the most part we don't think about their lostness like we used to when we prayed for them daily by name. We get more excited about the latest Christian CD or the latest Christian novel than we do thinking about how God can use us for the gospel in our own town. We even go on Christian boat cruises for vacation with our favorite Christian radio preachers and Christian bands. We are content living in our little Christian subculture as citizens of the bubble, but we don't even know it because everyone in our social circle is also in the bubble. We all view things the same way.

The sad fact is that if at phase 1 we could see ourselves in phase 4 as citizens of the bubble, we probably wouldn't even recognize ourselves. I wonder—if our phase-1 selves could meet our phase-4 selves, would we run the other way? Hopefully, the Spirit of God has transformed us into living more Jesus-like lives since phase 1.

"MY GOD! WHAT HAVE I BECOME?"

The lyrics to the Talking Heads song "Once in a Lifetime" talk about someone who has drifted into becoming something he is shocked to finally recognize. He responds by saying, "My God! What have I done?" In the same way, I looked at myself and the church subculture I had drifted into and had this experience of suddenly crying out, "My God! What have I become?"

After the horrible discovery of what I had become, I realized I needed to escape the bubble I was now in. I decided to make some significant changes so that I could be back on the mission that Jesus sent us on, rather than thinking only of the Christian subculture. I knew that I needed to escape the subculture that I had not only become engrossed in but also even helped build the walls of. I began plotting like a prisoner looking for a way to escape. I eventually began my escape by making some significant changes in my weekly schedule, which was difficult since I was serving as a pastor in a large and growing church. I planned Mondays and Tuesdays to be in the church office for meetings scheduled with staff and to take care of other things that need to happen in the office. But then I escaped by rearranging my week to be out of the office so that I wasn't receiving only a Christian viewpoint all of the time. I wanted to be in regular dialogue and build relationships with those who are outside of the church.

So I scheduled Wednesdays and Thursdays to work outside of the church office. I used Wednesdays to study for the weekend sermon. Most pastors I know lock themselves in their homes or in their offices to prepare for preaching and teaching. I decided I'd rather study in a coffeehouse where I'd be around people, with my Bible and commentaries open in full view. I also used the time to get to know the names of the staff at the coffeehouses and engage in little conversations in which they asked about what I do and what I'm reading. Little by little I gained their trust and was able to ask them what they think about Christianity and the church. I did so simply by saying that I know that the church and Christianity have a bad name generally, and that I would love their input to help me as a pastor know how the church is thought of. It has been wonderful getting input from and building friendships with those outside the church. I have never had one person say they wouldn't tell me what they thought. They love giving their opinions when you ask them. One twenty-something guy actually said with emotion, "I am really honored that you value my opinion enough to ask me."

Once I escaped, I looked for any opportunity to be around non-Christians. This meant turning things down. Hairstylists in my church often offer to cut my hair at their barbershops or salons. But I made a vow always to get my hair cut by non-Christians, since this allows me a solid half hour or more of chatting regularly with someone outside the church. I would take advantage of any opportunity I could think of to schedule time with those outside the church and befriend them. It has been an incredibly invigorating experience reengaging with those outside the church. But it took plotting an escape from the prison of the church office and the Christian bubble and tunnelling my way out. It can be done! It must be done. I can't imagine Jesus would spend his whole week surrounded by the walls of a church office.

JESUS DIDN'T WANT US TO CREATE A CHRISTIAN SUBCULTURE

I can't help but think of Jesus' prayer for his disciples: "My prayer is not that you take them out of the world but that you protect them from the evil one" (John 17:15). He didn't pray that we isolate ourselves from those outside the church. He didn't pray that we should be happy and content living inside a Christian bubble listening to our favorite worship band or Christian musician on our iPods. Instead, Jesus seemed concerned that his followers not isolate themselves from the world around them. He was concerned that we understand that evil is real and that we should be aware of the schemes of evil (2 Cor. 2:11) that would thwart us from the mission that Jesus sent us on. C. S. Lewis in his book the *Screwtape Letters* talked about how Satan's greatest deception is getting people to think he's not real. I wonder if our greatest deception in the church today is our being comfortably numb in the safety of our Christian bubble with all the Christian T-shirts and candy and CDs we find inside.

I know that we all need the refreshment and encouragement of meeting together in corporate worship and, in some smaller setting, to be encouraging each other and praying for each other. Those of us who are on a church staff need to spend time in various meetings. But is that primarily what we do? What did Jesus do? "While Jesus was having dinner at Matthew's house, many tax collectors and 'sinners' came and ate with him and his disciples. When the Pharisees saw this, they asked his disciples, 'Why does your teacher eat with tax collectors and "sinners"?' On hearing this, Jesus said, 'It is not the healthy who need a doctor, but the sick'" (Matt. 9:10–12).

Jesus spent time with those who weren't religious. He talked with them, he listened to them, he cared for them, he cried for them. He died for them. I wonder if many of us have been so busy inside our churches that we haven't really stopped to observe and listen to those outside our churches as Jesus probably would have. It's so easy to be comfortably numb in our subculture and forget about the horrific sadness of those who have yet to experience the saving grace of Jesus. It's easy to do this when we aren't in personal friendships with them. But I can tell you that when you are in authentic friendships and relationships with those outside the church, you can't forget them. Because you know them. You are friends with them. You care about them. You want them to know Jesus because of what Jesus means to you and how he has changed you. We need to have our hearts constantly broken for people, like Jesus' heart was broken. We need to look around us and see people through his compassionate eyes (Matt. 9:36). The question I have for you is, Are you in the prison of the Christian bubble? Have you become comfortably numb? Perhaps you haven't realized it, but you are there. Are you going to surrender to it, or are you planning your escape? People who like Jesus are waiting on the outside to meet you.

LOOKING AT YOUR CHURCH THROUGH THE EYES OF EMERGING GENERATIONS

1. During your week, what percentage of your time do you spend in church meetings and other Christian activities? If you're a pastor, what percentage of your time is spent in the church office in meetings or locked in a room studying?

2. What percentage of your time each week do you spend out among people who aren't part of your church, listening to them, observing them, and talking with them?

3. How many non-Christians, especially those eighteen to thirty-five years old, are you friends with and praying for?

4. Which of the four phases of being a Christian are you in?

5. Do you see yourself as a pastor or church leader of a group of people who "go to church," or as a leader and trainer of a church community of local missionaries? What could you do to have a more missional mindset?

Let me suggest a project that might help you take action. Examine your weekly or monthly calendar and ask yourself what you could remove from your schedule of church activities or delegate to someone else. Then write down what activities you could do and where you could go to be around non-Christians and simply be friends with them. It's time to escape. It's time to start having a missional heart and to think like Jesus. The possibilities are unlimited when you start thinking like a missionary again.

JESUS AS SON OF GOD AND PLASTIC ACTION FIGURE 3

I'm down with J.C. He's cool.
—MIKE DIRNT
FROM THE BAND GREEN DAY

Jesus is everywhere. I recently walked into a gas station to pay for some gas and saw some Jesus bobble-heads for sale on a shelf. I was kind of surprised to see Jesus in the gas station, but there he was, three or four of him standing in a row. As I waited to pay for the fifteen gallons I had pumped into my rusty 1966 Ford Mustang, the Jesus bobble-heads silently stared at me, all politely smiling and nodding in unison.

Not too long afterward, I visited a major clothing chain store. Near the entry was a display for the Jesus Action Figure. Probably a dozen or more Jesuses hung in nice plastic packaging that declared, "With poseable arms and gliding action!" While I stood there looking at them, a woman in her early twenties grabbed one from the rack. She enthusiastically said to her companion, "I love these!" and off she ran to the cash register with Jesus under her arm.

JESUS IS MY HOMEBOY

I saw Jesus again in another unexpected place. While standing in line at a supermarket, I saw a weekly entertainment magazine with a photo of Pamela Anderson. She was wearing a rather tight, cut-off, light-blue shirt that looked like it had an image of Jesus on the front.

Puzzled, I took the magazine off the shelf and brought it closer to my eyes. I wanted to see if that really was an image of Jesus and what the words underneath it said. Examining it closely, I could make out the words "Jesus Is My Homeboy." Suddenly I remembered that I was in line at the supermarket with people all around while I was holding the magazine close to my eyes and staring at Pamela Anderson's T-shirt. So I slammed the magazine back on the rack, awkwardly looking around to see if anyone had noticed what I was doing. When I got home, I googled "Jesus is my homeboy" and found a website which sells the shirts. The site includes a photo of Pamela Anderson wearing the Jesus Is My Homeboy shirt, as well as photos of other celebrities, such as Ben Affleck, Ashton Kutcher, and Jessica Simpson, all wearing the same shirt. So Jesus

Graphic used by permission of Teenage Millionaire[6]

is being proudly displayed and making an appearance on the shirts of several major celebrities.

JESUS IN MUSIC AND IN FASHION, AND GLOWING IN THE DARK

When I turned on MTV, I saw Jesus again, this time on Johnny Cash's video for "Hurt," the Nine Inch Nails song he covered. And Jesus is showing up in lots of other songs and in lots of other surprising places too. Both Johnny Cash and Marilyn Manson recorded versions of Depeche Mode's "Personal Jesus." Green Day wrote "Jesus of Suburbia." Singer Morrissey put out the song "I Have Forgiven Jesus." Bruce Springsteen has the song "Jesus Was an Only Son." The Violent Femmes sing "Jesus Walking on the Water." And hip-hop artist Kanye West recorded his song "Jesus Walks"; the three versions of his video even show two different versions of Jesus. Kanye also appeared on the cover of *Rolling Stone* dressed as Jesus with a crown of thorns on his head.

Another Jesus spotting occurred when I was in Portland, Oregon, visiting my brother. We walked into a gift and card store at an outdoor mall and saw Jesus all over the place. He was on a metal lunch box that had DaVinci's "Last Supper" printed on it. There were several Jesus Action Figures hanging right next to the Pee Wee Herman dolls, oddly enough. We also saw two different glow-in-the-dark Jesuses, one on a cross and one in a standing position. The store even had gift-wrap paper with multiple Andy Warhol–style portraits of Jesus on it. This wasn't even a Christian or religious store, just a major mall store that sold cards and fun gifts.

I recently read a perceptive article in the *New York Times* that observed that Jesus is becoming part of fashion in designer clothing. The article included photos showing a model wearing a sweater with the words "Jesus Loves Me" on it. Another model wore some sort of poncho with a large decorative cross on the back. I saw Jesus on a shirt (not one from a Christian store) with his arms outstretched and saying, "Put down the drugs and come get a hug." In another major clothing chain store I saw Jesus on another T-shirt, sliding on his knees in a rock-star pose. The caption on the shirt read, "Jesus Rocks!"

Jesus on T-shirts, Jesus in pop songs, Jesus bobble-heads and action figures, Jesus on TV, Jesus on the cover of magazines, Jesus on lunch boxes and wrapping paper. It seems we can't get enough of Jesus lately.

THE DILEMMA OF OWNING A JESUS BOBBLE-HEAD

With all this pop-cultural interest in Jesus, it was inevitable that someone would give me a Jesus gift. A friend of mine bought me a bobble-head Jesus as a joke. It looked pretty humorous on the speaker next to my desk in the church office. I would look at this bobble-head Jesus and pat his head with my finger. He would stand there bobbing away and smiling, like all bobble-heads do. But an unsettling thing happened. As I met with people in my office, depending on how conservative they were, I would take the bobble-head off the speaker and hide it in my desk. I was torn. It was definitely fun to have around, but I kept thinking, Jesus, the Son of God, Messiah, King of Kings and Lord of Lords … a bobble-head? Is this good? Is this bad? Should I keep the Jesus bobble-head? Should I think it's funny? It is funny, but should I feel guilty that I think it's funny? Should I enjoy the lightheartedness of it? I didn't know. I went back and forth thinking about it. Eventually I couldn't live with the tension and guilt any longer, so I gave the Jesus bobble-head to the administrative assistant in our office. Jesus now sits out in the lobby by her desk so she can live with the guilt of it. He's still nearby, but at least he's not staring at me anymore as I sit at my desk.

THERE'S SOMETHING ABOUT JESUS

Something about Jesus fascinates us. Whether we want him on our dashboards or on our T-shirts or in the lyrics of our songs, he has become something of a pop icon in our culture. As Mike Dirnt, the bassist for Green Day, says, "I'm down with J.C. He's cool." How ironic that at the same time pop culture is producing Jesus paraphernalia, Christians have also created a subculture of Jesus paraphernalia. Walk into many Christian bookstores and you'll likely find them flooded with all types of odd Christian trinkets and Jesus things. I was just in a Christian bookstore and saw pencil sharpeners with Jesus' name on them, Jesus bracelets, Jesus sun visors, plastic sunglasses with Jesus' name on the frames, frisbees with Jesus' name on them, little rubber balls with Jesus' name on them, lots of T-shirts and Jesus coffee mugs, and even sandals that leave the words "Jesus Loves You" behind you in the sand as you stroll the beach. It's almost impossible to tell sometimes which Jesus paraphernalia comes from Christians and which comes from pop culture. To be honest, I like the non-Christian paraphernalia more than most of the rather cheesy Christian paraphernalia out there.

What makes all of these products and all of this attention to Jesus interesting and even exciting is that, combined with all the interest in and respect for Jesus among many people, it is becoming easier to talk about Jesus. Most people today, whether in the church or outside the church, believe Jesus is a good person who has some sort of spiritual insight. When Pamela Anderson explained why she gives money to the homeless, she answered, "If I refuse one of them, I'd be like, 'Oh my God. What if that was Jesus?'"[7] I have no idea what she believes, but even if she isn't following Jesus, she still has some respect for him. It is increasingly common to hear comments like this one from Moby, the musician: "I really love Christ, and I think that the wisdom of Christ is the highest, strongest wisdom I've ever encountered."[8] Albert Einstein, who was not a professed Christian, still respected Jesus like so many people in emerging generations do today. He once said, "I am a Jew, but I am enthralled by the luminous figure of the Nazarene.... No one can read the Gospels without feeling the actual presence of Jesus." Over and over again we see an awareness of Jesus and a respect for him in all areas of culture.

"WHO DO YOU SAY I AM?"

In Matthew 16:15, Jesus asks Peter a critical question. "'But what about you?' he asked. 'Who do you say I am?'" This is a question we need to ask. Many people today say they like Jesus, but who is this Jesus they are talking about? Even if you walked into a Christian bookstore and asked Christians what they think of Jesus, you might wonder what Jesus they are talking about. It seems the Jesus of the Bible isn't always the same as the Jesus we see in either pop culture or in the Christian subculture. I think we see glimpses of him in both, but to me it's a bit scary to realize what version of Jesus we are creating in both of these worlds.

In one extreme of the Christian subculture, we have trivialized Jesus to fashionable T-shirts, bumper stickers, coffee mugs, and strange paintings in Christian stores. We often hear Jesus referred to as our buddy and our friend. We have focused so much of our worship of Jesus into concert events with large video screens and flashing lights and fog machines. Christians may not think of Jesus in a trivial way, but looking at what we produce in the Christian subculture from the outside can certainly give that impression. We sing about him and our love for him in our churches, but I wonder if we were to ask people in church to list all of the things they actually know about Jesus, how long the list would be beyond "he loves me" and "he died for my sins." I am overstating things a bit, generalizing to make a point. But I wonder how much we have turned Jesus into a shadow of who he really is according to the Bible. Yes, he loves us and he died for our sins, but there's so much more to him and his teachings.

On the other end of the Christian spectrum, the more extreme fundamentalist camp has made Jesus out to be an angry avenging figure. Instead of having compassion and love for sinners, he has only anger and points his finger at their sins to condemn them. This Jesus probably votes only for one political party and has strong opinions on all types of things outside of what he said in the Bible, including on the role of women in the church, what type of music to listen to, and which Bible version to use. This Jesus is talked about a lot in terms of his judgment and coming in the clouds to separate the goats and the sheep. A favorite response from this group to those who disagree with them is Matthew 10:35, where Jesus said, "For I have come to turn 'a man against his father, a daughter against her mother.'" Sometimes there is even a hint of delight in their voices. Again, I'm exaggerating to make a point, but nevertheless this Jesus is out there too.

Christians have quite a variety of opinions about what Jesus is like. We think Jesus holds to the same beliefs we do. We probably think he believes worship and preaching should be like the worship and preaching at our church. If we stress social justice in our churches, we feel Jesus would stress that too. If we stress global evangelism, we feel Jesus would want us to put the most effort into that. Calvinists would probably bet Jesus is a five-point TULIP enthusiast. We generally think of Jesus as having the same temperament and personality as we do. For the extrovert, Jesus is outgoing and ready with plenty of jokes and laughs. The introvert will think of Jesus as being more serious, deep, and introspective. It's so fascinating to hear the differences between Christians' ideas about Jesus.

And then there's the pop-culture Jesus. This Jesus is the friend who stands up for the poor and needy and is a revolutionary for the oppressed. This Jesus focuses his message on love and not hate. This Jesus doesn't really judge, except when it comes to religious hypocrites. As long as you love other people and are happy, this Jesus is happy. He is a wise teacher, a guru. He is fashionable and a pop icon, and so wearing him on your shirt or saying you are into him is acceptable. He is right up there with other religious figures of our day, figures such as Martin Luther King Jr., Mother Teresa, and the Dalai Lama. The pop-culture Jesus has a mystical connection to God, and he may have even been resurrected from the dead, though people don't give much thought to what that might mean for day-to-day living. The pop-culture Jesus is the loving, hypocrite-hating man of peace who taught us not to judge others.

Quite a variety of Jesuses are appearing on the stage today.

SO WHO IS "VINTAGE" JESUS?

In this book, I don't intend to get into a theological discussion of who Jesus is, since there are volumes and volumes of scripturally based books that do that. The point of this book is to examine what others think of Jesus and of the church so that we can think like missionaries, understanding emerging generations better and speaking more effectively with them about the gospel. But I think it might be helpful for readers to know what is in my heart and mind as I dialogue with people about "vintage Jesus."

I am convinced that Jesus was a revolutionary, but there is much more to him than that. Jesus taught about loving others, but there is much more to him than that. Jesus looked out for the outcasts and fringe groups of society, but there is much more to him than that. These are all things about Jesus that people in emerging generations respect. But there is so much more to him than these things.

When I think of Jesus, I think of the triune God, who eternally exists in three persons—Father, Son, and Holy Spirit—coeternal in being, coeternal in nature, coequal in power and glory, all three persons having the same attributes and perfections (Deut. 6:4; 2 Cor. 13:14). These terms may sound technical to people, but these ideas are so incredibly hard to grasp that technical words sometimes convey them better than emotional responses. I think of Jesus as the one who was conceived by the Holy Spirit and born of the Virgin Mary (Luke 1:26–31). He was a Jewish rabbi (John 1:38), a teacher who astonished people with his insight and his authoritative teaching (Matt. 7:28–29). I think of his heart breaking with compassion for people (Matt. 9:36) and how he wept for people, even for those who rejected him (Luke 19:41). I think of the Jesus who was an advocate for the poor, the marginalized, and the oppressed (Luke 4:18–19; Matt. 19:16–30; Luke 14:13; Matt. 25:31–46). I think of the one who stood strong against the religious legalism of his day (Luke 20:19–20). I think of the one who not only drank wine but also provided it (John 2:1–11). I think of the one who didn't just sit in a holy huddle or point out the wrongs of culture but hung out with sinners and ate with them (Matt. 9:10). I think of the Jesus who was tempted and understands temptation yet was sinless (Heb. 4:15; 1 Peter 2:22). I think of the Jesus who was sent by God because of his great love for humanity to take on our sin (John 1:1–2, 14, 29; 3:16–21). I think of the Jesus who accomplished our redemption through his death on the cross as a substitutionary sacrifice and then was bodily resurrected from the dead (Rom. 3:24; 1 Peter 2:24). I think of the Jesus who appeared to his disciples and said that they have a mission not to create an inwardly focused community and to complain about the world but rather to go out and with the power of the Spirit live missional lives, bringing the light of Jesus to others (Acts 1:8). I think of the Jesus who sees the church as his bride (Rev. 21:2, 9) and loves the church, even when we disappoint him. I think of the Jesus who ascended into heaven and is now exalted at the right hand of God, where, as our High Priest, he intercedes for us and serves as our advocate (Acts 1:9–10; Heb. 7:25; 9:24). I also think, soberly, of the Jesus who will one day come again to judge the living and the dead (1 Peter 4:5; Rom. 14:9; 2 Tim. 4:1). Jesus is our friend and the friend of sinners, but he also is a righteous judge who will hold us all accountable one day for how we lived our lives. We must have a balanced view of Jesus, being careful not to swing to one extreme or the other.

The reason I am writing this book, and the reason I continue to go out of my way to meet, befriend, hang out with, and talk with those who like Jesus but not the church is because I so desire for others to experience the full Jesus, not just the good teacher or the friend but also the Lord of Lords and King of Kings and the Savior who changes lives.

"I MISS JESUS"

I think the most haunting and memorable part of Lee Strobel's book *The Case for Faith* is his description of meeting with Charles Templeton. Templeton was one of Billy Graham's partners and close friends in the early days of his ministry. He was a powerful preacher and evangelist like Billy Graham. But Templeton ended up doubting his faith and eventually abandoned it altogether. Not only did he abandon it, but he became a major critic of Christianity. He wrote a book called *Farewell to God: My Reasons for Rejecting the Christian Faith*. Templeton was eighty-three years old at the time Strobel interviewed him and asked him for his assessment of Jesus.

> "In my view," he declared, "he is the most important human being who ever existed." That's when Templeton uttered the words I never expected to hear from him. "And if I may put it this way," he said as his voice began to crack, "I … miss … him!"
>
> With that tears flooded his eyes. He turned his head and looked downward, raising his left hand to shield his face from me. He shoulders bobbed as he wept.[9]

This is so incredibly sad. Charles Templeton had rejected Christianity, the church, his faith in the Bible, and his former vocation of preaching and evangelism. But at the end of his life, when asked about Jesus, he broke down and wept, saying how much he missed Jesus. Something about Jesus transcends Christianity and all that Charles Templeton had rejected. Jesus grabs hold of people, and it's hard to just ignore him or not think of him once you get to know him. This is why I have so much optimism and hope for people in emerging generations. Most of them haven't yet been fully introduced to Jesus. Though they might know a few stories about his life, they don't know his teachings, and they don't know the fullness of his love and passion for people, including them.

LISTENING TO THOSE WHO LIKE JESUS BUT NOT THE CHURCH

In the next chapter, you will meet several people who aren't part of a church but are open to Jesus. They are intrigued by him and love talking about him. Yes, they might have more of a pop-culture view of him, and no, they might not mention his lordship or future judgment, but I have hope for them and for so many others like them because I have seen people who like Jesus but not the church end up putting their faith in him and believing that he rose from the dead and is their Savior, not just a wise man or prophet.

I believe Jesus cares for those who like him but don't like the church. He wants them to know him more fully and to trust in him and believe he rose from the dead. He wants them to understand that the kingdom of God is now on this earth, not just coming in heaven after we die (Mark 1:15). I believe Jesus wants them to understand what the church really is and not just make assumptions about it. I think Jesus wants the church to offer an apology to people when needed, and I think Jesus wants those who like him to forgive the church if she has wounded them. But I know that Jesus wants them to experience the church and to be part of his bride, a supernatural community. We miss out when we are not part of his church. That's what motivates me to be all the more passionate about reaching them. I believe that when we pray for them and view them the way Jesus does — with compassion — we may have our hearts moved as well. Let's meet some of them now in the next chapter and hear what they say about Jesus.

LOOKING AT YOUR CHURCH
THROUGH THE EYES OF
EMERGING GENERATIONS

1. What are some ways you have seen Jesus appear in pop culture?

2. Does the rising interest in the pop-culture Jesus excite you because of the potential for initiating conversation with others, or do you see it as a threat to the gospel and the biblical Jesus? Why?

3. How do you picture Jesus? How much does the way you imagine his temperament and personality resemble your own?

4. What would Jesus say if he were to walk into your church's weekend worship gathering? Imagine him sitting there during the whole service. What would he think about it? What would Jesus think about a Christian concert or a Christian bookstore? What observations do you think he would make?

5. Try this yourself or as an experiment with people in your church. Write the name of Jesus on a piece of paper, and then underneath that write words to describe him. Then see how many of your descriptions you can verify in Scripture. How many are really only your own thoughts of what he is like?

MEETING THOSE WHO LIKE JESUS

4

Jesus, Jesus, Jesus,
Let all heaven and earth proclaim.
Kings and kingdoms
Will all pass away,
But there's something about that name.

—BILL AND GLORIA GAITHER
"THERE'S SOMETHING ABOUT THAT NAME"

he lyrics of the gospel song "There's Something about That Name" are so true. When you speak about Jesus, something happens, and the rising fascination with Jesus in today's emerging culture reflects that. What a wonderful development to be able to talk to people about Jesus in a positive way and not be embarrassed. We may be embarrassed about Christianity, but we don't have to be embarrassed about Jesus.

In this chapter, I will introduce you to some of the individuals you will be hearing from in this book. They will be sharing what they think of Jesus and why they respect him and believe he was an important spiritual leader. Quite often, once they started talking about Jesus, it was hard for them to stop. They found it natural to do so and felt free to tell me what they think of him. But they also will be talking about why they don't like church and most Christians. They will share how the church and Christians come across to them and the experiences they have had with them.

> WE MAY BE EMBARRASSED ABOUT CHRISTIANITY, BUT WE DON'T HAVE TO BE EMBARRASSED ABOUT JESUS.

FOCUSING ON WHAT THEY DO KNOW ABOUT JESUS

I have this uneasy feeling that some Christian leaders might not regard the comments you will read worth listening to. If you are in that group, I hope this book changes your mind. It's important to listen to them because you will find people making the same comments in your towns and nearby cities. And even though they don't know everything about Jesus and what he said about repentance and sin, we can appreciate their respect and admiration for what they do know about Jesus.

I met most of the people I'll be quoting from *after* I escaped the church office. And I didn't set out to proselytize them; I simply met them to befriend them, enjoy their company, and ask their opinions. I still hang out with them, even though our interviews are done and even though not all of them are coming to church or have put their faith in Jesus. I see them as friends, not as evangelistic targets. And they aren't people I randomly walked up to on the street to survey. They are individuals with whom I have developed relationships. I spent long periods of time with each of them, asking questions, hearing their stories, and listening to their opinions. Building trust and establishing relationships paved the way for dialogue with them.

The people I quote in this chapter aren't the only people I have talked with. I spoke in-depth with others specifically for this book, and I am constantly asking questions of people I meet about their views of church and Christianity. Also, keep in mind that the perspective and thoughts of this book are based not only on the people I quote from but also on years of ministry, traveling, and living in a variety of places.

WHY I CHOSE THE PEOPLE YOU'LL MEET

I chose to talk with a wide spectrum of people in their late teens, twenties, and early thirties, each with different backgrounds, education, and interests. Some had church experience growing up. I chose them because there is an increasing number of people who grew up in a church but then left the faith when they hit their late teens. Others had no church background at all. For this book, I focused on using quotes primarily from those in their twenties, rather than those in their late teens, because they are old enough to reflect on what caused them to leave the church or to get their negative impressions of the church. Also, because the number of people in their twenties who are part of a church is extremely low, I wanted to focus on people in this age group.[10]

When I asked each of those I interviewed if they were interested in being part of this book and in having the opportunity to speak to Christian pastors and leaders across the country, they all immediately said yes. So this is their chance to express to those of us who are in Christian leadership how we come across to them and what their viewpoints are. They were all aware of why I was asking these questions and were eager to share with us their impressions of Christianity and the church. Yet they were also eager to state why they respect Jesus and hold him in high esteem. They all gave me permission to use what they said in this book.

MEETING THE PEOPLE YOU WILL HEAR FROM IN THIS BOOK

It's important that you know I talked with many more people than you will meet in this book. You will also be hearing from a few people other than those I'll introduce you to in this section. But here's a sampling of comments that represent the thoughts of so many outside the church about Jesus.

Alicia, molecular biologist, 24 years old

> *Jesus, to me, is an all-loving, perfect, prophetic person. I don't even know where I gathered this information from. Maybe some from television, some from reading.*
>
> *When I think of Jesus, I have always thought of him as the same person as God. On the same team. I once heard somewhere that Jesus is God in human form, and I thought, that's so interesting. Dear God ... Dear Jesus — same thing. I didn't see any problem with that.*

Alicia is twenty-four years old and a graduate of the University of California, Santa Cruz, with a degree in molecular biology. At the time of the interviews, she was working in a biotechnology firm researching antibodies. She grew up in the Midwest and was not raised in a church. She did have some church exposure while in her late teens, when she was dating someone who became a Christian while they were dating. She then moved from the Midwest to Santa Cruz to attend the university. I met Alicia when she was working at a coffee shop and going to school. She saw me studying and meeting people each week at the coffee shop, so we began talking and got to know each other. After she graduated and got the job at the biotech company, we kept meeting at the coffeehouse where she used to work. She came to our church several times, as a result of our friendship and discussions. Alicia is environmentally conscience and very intelligent. She just moved back to the Midwest to be nearer to her family. She doesn't attend any church there but respects and likes Jesus.

Duggan, coffee shop manager, 30 years old

Jesus was a great teacher. A caregiver. A carpenter. A human being. Approachable. He was the everyday man who lived among others and understood the trials and tribulations of what it takes to put food on the table. But at the same time, he was able to organize groups of people and was a great leader. Jesus was a voice of peace and hope and an inspiration to many people.

Jesus had a lot of moral conviction about the goodness of human beings. Instead of seeing darkness in people, he saw goodness. Turn the other cheek; if your brother sins against you, forgive him. He believed in people.

Duggan is a thirty-year-old manager of an independent coffee shop. He is a true Santa Cruzian, born and raised here, and is into bicycle riding and surfing. He's an extrovert who makes people feel like they are his best friend. He is talented in dealing with customers in the coffee shop. Duggan is Irish and as a child went to a Catholic church on holidays. When he was thirteen, his dad gave him some religious writings from several faiths—a Bible, the Koran, the I Ching, and so on—and encouraged him to read them and seek his own spiritual direction. I met Duggan in the coffee shop. We first began talking about music and bands that we liked, but this eventually led to a discussion about Jesus and faith issues. He has come to our church worship gathering, and I even had him speak to our church to give his perspective as someone outside the church. He is open to coming to church more, but at this point he doesn't attend any church, even though he respects and likes Jesus.

Erika, graduate student, 23 years old

Jesus is someone I really respect. His teachings hit you at a very personal level.

Jesus is a man whose actions, story, and life are very powerful. He obviously had some sort of intense spiritual connection to God.

Erika is a twenty-three-year-old college graduate with a degree in environmental studies. She is heading off to graduate school to get her masters degree in landscape architecture. Erika grew up in a denominational church, where her parents brought her but didn't put any pressure on her to be part of the church. At fourteen, she stopped going entirely, primarily because she felt the church focused too much on the negative things about the world and she was more optimistic. Erika is a bright and energetic person. She lights up a room when she walks into it and is cheerful and upbeat. I met Erika through a friend of hers who is part of our church. Her friend still hangs out with her and arranged for us to connect and talk. She lives out of town now, attending university, but she comes to our church worship gatherings on special occasions, and she is always so receptive and friendly and encouraging. Erika likes Jesus but is not part of any church.

Dustan, college student, 27 years old

I believe Jesus, historically, lived. It is cool to think that he really lived among us. I respect what he stood for and how he went against the establishment with his message.

Jesus was probably spiritually enlightened, charismatic, and compassionate. He was driven to help people find inner peace.

Jesus taught really good things to people about love and how to treat others as yourself.

This one is a little personal for me. Dustan is twenty-seven years old and grew up in a Baptist church in Santa Cruz. When he got to high school, he switched churches and became part of the high school ministry I was leading. He became a leader in the youth ministry and influenced others. Since he was in student leadership, I spent quite a bit of time with him during his high school years. However, as you will hear later, he ended up leaving the church in his senior year and has not returned. He no longer thinks of himself as Christian. He recently decided to go back to school and is getting his degree in psychology from a local university and plans on being a counselor. Dustan bears an uncanny resemblance to Elvis Presley when Elvis was healthy and in his early twenties. During the years I was a willing prisoner of the Christian subculture, I didn't see Dustan too often. But after I escaped, I made the effort to rekindle our friendship, and he has been receptive to meeting, talking, and hanging out together. He doesn't attend any church but respects and likes Jesus.

Penny, advertising manager, 35 years old

I hold Jesus to be a wise man. Jesus was inspirational and pure. He was a wonderful man with great lessons to teach about love, acceptance, and peace.

Jesus was someone who lived out his message and wasn't a hypocrite like many modern religious leaders. Jesus stood out among the others of his time.

I believe 100 percent that Jesus walked the earth, and that because of his teaching, he sent a lot of people's gray matter spinning.

I believe there has to be a God. Not believing would make no sense. We are here for a reason.

Penny is thirty-five years old and works at a newspaper as an advertising director. She is a lesbian, having realized during her teenage years that she is gay. Penny was born and raised in England. She had some church exposure in her elementary school years at an Anglican church, but that experience was, for the most part, neutral in shaping her thinking about church and Christianity. I got to know Penny through a friend who works with her. There was an article in her newspaper about Christianity and homosexuality, so initially we met to talk about that, which led to a friendship. Penny is someone you can talk to easily for hours about all types of things — art, music, clothing. Many times when I met with her I couldn't believe how quickly the time went by. She doesn't attend any church but respects and likes Jesus.

Gary and Erica, young married couple, 31 years old

Jesus stood for strength and character. He plowed the path to do right. He was more than a Gandhi; I believe he was raised from the dead. Jesus was a fusion of the power of good and flesh that had a message for people to do what is right and loving.

Jesus was a charismatic and motivating man who taught some revolutionary and beautiful philosophy. He told people that they could change. He was so giving and so loving.

Gary and Erica are recently married. I was even part of their wedding. They both are thirty-one years old. Gary is the lead singer in a local band and works in a print shop. Erica has a BA in psychology and is working as a counselor in a residential treatment facility for substance abuse and mental illness. They both are into vintage clothing and rockabilly music, and they look like a couple from 1956. I am quite envious of their clothing and vinyl record collection.

Gary grew up in church but stopped going when he was a teenager. He felt that the church pastor was using the Bible to express his angst and his agenda. Erica grew up outside of the church. Her parents did not go to church and didn't take her. I met Gary at a clothing store he was working in. He told me he was in a rockabilly band, so I went to see his band play, and we became friends. Gary and Erica don't attend any church but respect and like Jesus.

Maya, hairstylist and beautician, 27 years old

Jesus was powerful and a good leader. People trusted him, and trust is very important.

Jesus gave so many people hope. He gave people hope that there is a life after this, but more importantly, he gave people hope in this life. He told people that things don't have to be the way they are and that they can change.

Jesus was kind of like a pirate—a modern thinker who led a rebellion against religion that was corrupt.

Jesus was a Messiah. He was a good leader who came to help a lot of people. Jesus was someone who had something important to say.

Maya is a twenty-seven-year-old hairstylist who works at a local salon and used to cut my hair. I've known her now for about four years. We chatted for hours while she cut my hair, and we would hang out sometimes. She has been over to our house for dinner. She gave our daughters their first haircuts. While she was growing up, Maya's parents brought her to church sometimes on Easter and Christmas. She grew up in a relatively affluent town up near San Francisco and moved to Santa Cruz to pursue her career. She has a passion for psychobilly and rockabilly music and has on her arm one of the coolest tattoos I have ever seen. I am tattooless, but if I ever got one, it would be like hers. She does not attend any church but respects and likes Jesus. Recently, to my great sadness, Maya moved to Austin, Texas. However, we stay in contact. Now I'm getting my hair cut by someone she recommended, and the new person is also someone who likes Jesus but not the church.

WHAT CHURCH ARE THEY NOT LIKING?

You can see there is quite a diversity in background among those I listed, yet their thoughts about Jesus are similar in that they like and respect him. You will hear from others in this book as well, but I think those I've introduced you to are representative of people in our emerging culture. The important thing to pay attention to is the consistency of what they say about Jesus. They all have such wonderful things to say about him. But as you will see, their thoughts on the church and Christians are far different. If you get discouraged by their comments on the church, please turn back to this chapter to be reminded of what they say about Jesus.

Generally, the church that they don't like isn't really the biblical church. They might say what they think of the Sunday morning church service, but the biblical church isn't just the meetings we have on Sundays. The biblical church is the people. They might describe an individual Christian or two (or several) who have wounded them, but the church of Jesus is not defined by an individual. The biblical church is the whole group of all who follow Jesus in all times and in all places (Acts 9:31). The biblical church is also the local church, a specific community of followers of Jesus in a given place and time (Acts 5:11; 1 Thess. 1:1). But when a few followers of Jesus don't act the way the head of the church, Jesus, would approve of, people assume that this is representative of all churches and all Christians. They don't see the church as something beautiful and precious to Jesus, as his bride (Eph. 5:25–27). They usually only see the ways the bride acts and sometimes doesn't honor the groom. Most of the comments made about the church are about experiences they've had with members of the church. But looking at it from their perspective, it's hard to blame them for coming to the conclusions they do.

GIVING AN APOLOGY AND AN APOLOGETIC FOR THE CHURCH

Criticisms and misperceptions of the church should matter to all of us, even if the criticisms are against a branch or denomination of the church that we have nothing to do with. The criticism is still about the church, and we are all part of the universal church. When part of us misrepresents Jesus, we all are misrepresented. If part of us is misunderstood, we all are misunderstood. So the next six chapters aren't about specific churches or Christians that have hurt people or misrepresented Jesus; they are about how "we" are seen and how "we" have hurt and misrepresented Jesus. We are all family and are all in this together.

In some cases, we will need to tell people we are sorry for how we as the church have acted. We may need to apologize on behalf of the church to those who have been hurt by us or who have had Jesus wrongly represented to them. In other cases, we may need to give an apologetic for the church. We may need to clear up misperceptions about us, much like the early church had to give an apologetic when they were accused of cannibalism, incest, and atheism. As you will read, not all of the perceptions about us are correct. But just because they aren't correct doesn't mean there aren't good reasons we are seen the way we are.

WHAT'S AHEAD IN THE FOLLOWING CHAPTERS

The next six chapters summarize six misperceptions of the church and Christians that are commonly held by those who like Jesus but not the church, misperceptions that keep them from wanting to be part of any church. No matter who I talked to, these misperceptions kept coming up. As you read, try not to get defensive, but ask yourself if what they are saying is true. They all developed their opinions from personal experience. By understanding the why behind their opinions, we can better understand the people expressing them, and then we can see how to be more effective as missionaries in today's emerging culture.

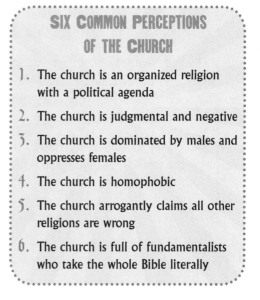

SIX COMMON PERCEPTIONS OF THE CHURCH

1. The church is an organized religion with a political agenda

2. The church is judgmental and negative

3. The church is dominated by males and oppresses females

4. The church is homophobic

5. The church arrogantly claims all other religions are wrong

6. The church is full of fundamentalists who take the whole Bible literally

THE COMPANION BOOK, *I LIKE JESUS BUT NOT THE CHURCH*

In this book, I won't try to answer all of the questions and criticisms of people in emerging generations. Instead I will address church leaders and suggest how the church might respond. However, in a companion book, *I Like Jesus but Not the Church: Following Jesus without Following Organized Religion*,[11] I answer these misperceptions and criticisms (see appendix 2). The companion book is for anyone, not just church leaders, and specifically shows how we can respond to criticisms. It's a book you could give someone who likes Jesus but not the church, or to someone who needs answers to their own doubts about the church.

As you turn the page, get ready to listen to what emerging generations are saying and thinking about the church and Christians. Be ready to feel uncomfortable, embarrassed, challenged, and even upset. But also be ready to be energized for the mission we have ahead of us as we go out to give an apology and an apologetic for the church. Be ready to be energized to be the church among those who like Jesus but not the church.

LOOKING AT YOUR CHURCH THROUGH THE EYES OF EMERGING GENERATIONS

1. You have read brief backgrounds on some of the people who like Jesus but not the church. If you were writing this book, who would you approach in your community to ask what they think of Jesus and of the church?

2. Of the six common perceptions covered in this book, which are the same as what you would hear in your community? Which are different?

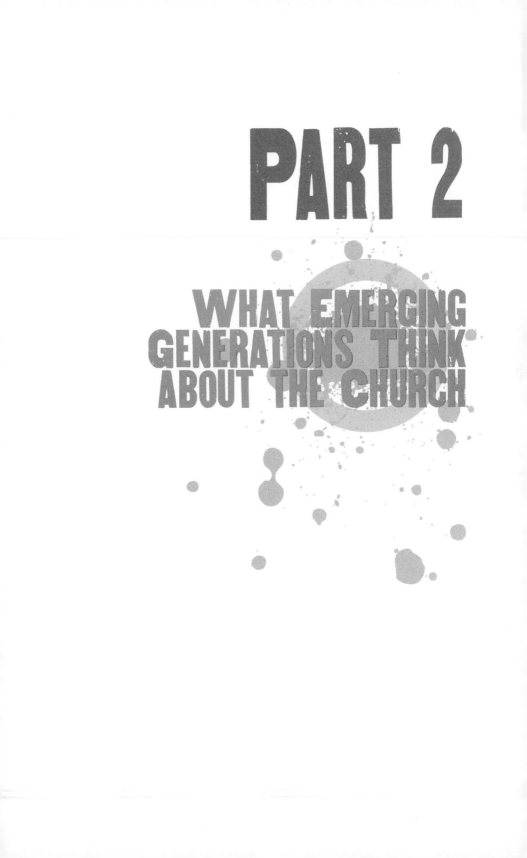

PART 2

WHAT EMERGING GENERATIONS THINK ABOUT THE CHURCH

THE CHURCH IS AN ORGANIZED RELIGION WITH A POLITICAL AGENDA

5

I don't think there's anything wrong with the teachings of Jesus, but I am suspicious of organized religion.

— **MADONNA**

Today I met with a friend for lunch at a restaurant. One of the waitresses, in her early twenties, has a waiter-customer friendship with him, since he frequently eats at that restaurant. When he introduced her to me, he explained that he knew me from his church. She responded in a friendly manner, mentioning how she is a very spiritual person. My friend then asked if she goes to church, and she politely responded with what has almost become a cliche: "No, I don't go to church. I am very spiritual but definitely not into organized religion."

I can't count how many times I have heard the words organized religion to describe the church. When the word organized is used in this manner, it's certainly not meant to reflect positively on the church. The irony is that it's used in the context of a growing openness to being spiritual. This waitress had absolutely no problem sharing that she was *very* spiritual, but she made it clear that she distanced herself from organized religion. Spiritual, yes; organized religion, no.

Quite often when I ask people who say something like this to me how they would define organized religion, they're caught off guard. I suspect they haven't really thought through what they mean by it. But as I dialogue with them, what they say fits a pattern we need to listen to, because it's such a significant reason why so many are repelled by the church. As we listen to what the people I interviewed for this book have to say, ask yourself, "If I were looking at it from the outside, would I see my church this way? Are these valid criticisms of my church?"

THE FIRST REASON WHY THEY SEE THE CHURCH AS ORGANIZED RELIGION

There are three primary reasons why people today see the church as organized religion. Here's the first: *I can relate to God without all of the unnatural structure the organized church would impose on me.*

Alicia, the twenty-four-year-old molecular biologist, exudes joy and intelligence when she speaks. Many of the things she says about the church are rather biting, but her tone and expression reveal not even a trace of anger or sarcasm. She speaks from a gentle and even concerned heart, so please take that into consideration as you read her comments.

> *Why do I need church? It isn't necessary. I have a relationship with God, and I pray a lot. But I don't see the point of having to add on all these organized rules like the church leaders think you should do. It feels like they take something beautiful and natural and make it into this complex nonorganic structure where you now have to jump through hoops and do everything in the way the organized church tells you to. It seems to lose all its innocence when it becomes so structured and controlled.* ALICIA

Alicia really isn't saying anything new, but it's being said more often today. Her comment shouldn't surprise us, since most people at some point in their lives seek out the eternity that God places in their hearts (Eccl. 3:11) and sense God's invisible qualities in creation (Rom. 1:20). Most people understand that they can pray to a caring and personal God if they want. I have talked to many people who aren't part of any church, and most say they pray all of the time and take prayer seriously. That would be a natural thing, if God is God and if people sense him and want to know him. They are missing what the Scriptures reveal about God and salvation and Jesus, but nonetheless they have a natural desire to get to know God. I rarely meet an atheist anymore. Virtually everyone believes in some sort of God or higher spiritual being.

SPIRITUAL, YES; CHURCH, NO

You might think that if emerging generations believed in God, they should naturally want to come to a church to seek him. But we have to remember that more and more individuals in our emerging culture have not grown up in a church. Most don't see the church as a place they would naturally go to seek God and spiritual growth. Instead, they have no problem going on with their lives and praying to and developing a relationship with God on their own. Second, the negative impressions and stereotypes that emerging generations have of Christians and the church keep them away. Mostly they practice their own forms of worship and prayer. Some choose to look into other faiths or create mixes of world faiths, but most people I've met are more like Alicia. She believes in God, is respectful of and open to Jesus, and maintains a personal faith of sorts. But it ends there. People see the church as a place that would wreck personal freedom, and as a foreign and unnecessary thing. It would be like you or me saying that we need to go to a Buddhist temple to be spiritual. We wouldn't think to go there, and those outside the church don't think to go to church today either. They don't equate the church with spirituality. In fact, it's probably the last place many would even think to turn.

People outside of the church who see the church as organized religion believe that church leaders will try to control them by dictating how and when they should pray. Many also feel that church leaders will organize their faith the way church leaders think it should be. They fear that organized religion will also try to control how they think, dress, and act. No one has ever told me that they are against becoming like Jesus or being conformed to the ways of Jesus; it's the ways and thinking of the organized church that they don't want to conform to.

A good example is Gary, the drummer in a rockabilly band who also works in a print shop. Gary is respectful of Jesus and thinks highly of him. He has a church background because his parents forced him to go to church on and off when he was growing up. By age sixteen, he stopped going entirely. When I met with Gary, he repeatedly told me how he prays all of the time. He is even fond of using the Lord's Prayer. But he doesn't go to church because he doesn't want to be part of an organized religion.

> *I call the church "organized religion" because if I am praying on my own,*
> *whenever I want, there is such freedom in that. But then I go to a church*
> *and someone is there to say, "Stand up now," "Sit down now," "Sing this*
> *now," "Listen to me now," "Do what I say now," "Act like this now." It's*
> *kind of like a religious Simon Says. Why go through all that when it can*
> *be much more natural praying and talking to the Good Lord* on my own*
> *without all that extra control?*
>
> * Gary used the word Lord quite often.

Gary is representative of people today who resist becoming part of a church because they feel they would lose the purity and simplicity of praying as they want to. They feel that church leaders would box in how they express their spirituality, cluttering it with rules and strangling it with restrictions. They don't want to be controlled in their spirituality. Of course, church leaders understand that asking people to stand up or sit down or respond in other ways is merely to help guide people's worship. As I've probed this issue, I've discovered that emerging generations are really concerned about lifeless and unexplained ritual. A lot of people actually said that wouldn't mind tradition or ritual as long as it's not lifeless, dull, and routine, quenching the beauty and naturalness of their prayers.

THE SECOND REASON WHY THEY SEE THE CHURCH AS ORGANIZED RELIGION

Here's the second reason why people in emerging generations see the church as organized religion: *The church is about hierarchy, power, and control with a political agenda.*

Gary shared with me the defining moment at age sixteen when he decided he wanted no part of church:

> *The preacher was giving a sermon, and it just didn't feel right to me. Instead*
> *of talking about Jesus, it seemed like this guy was giving his own personal*
> *ideas about things, and it was just annoying. He even was getting angry at*
> *certain points, and it felt more like a politically oriented message where he*
> *was using God's name and the Bible to voice his own angst.*
>
> *I just decided this is wrong and got up and walked out. Haven't been*
> *back since. That's not what church is supposed to be. It's supposed to be*

about Jesus and his teachings about love and being a better person. So why waste my time going to hear these guys working out their own issues and venting their political agendas to their churches, rather than focusing on the Lord? I can do that on my own.

GARY

These days, mentioning Christianity and politics stirs up strong feelings because some think church leaders are out to persuade their churches of their personal agendas against certain moral wrongs. Emerging generations have a strong sense that most churches are fundamentalist and are influencing the government in ways they're not comfortable with. You hear criticism of how the "right-wing fundamentalist Christians" are trying to sway political leaders with their influence on voters. Alicia made this comment:

I don't trust the church. All you ever see is men who have their own political agendas basically brainwashing the people in their church that if they don't believe the same things the church leaders do, and vote the same way, they are going to hell. Church shouldn't be about politics. It's all about organizing their religion to control people to conform them to their viewpoints and mix that in with spiritual faith. What is sad is how many people sit there and never question it.

ALICIA

This issue stirs up hot emotions. But if you met Alicia, you would see a gentle spirit. She never raised her voice when she said this. Rather, she said it out of sadness.

If you are a church leader, you know that most churches don't have political agendas. But on the outside, the impression is that we do. You also know that not every church leader believes that certain cartoon characters or children's toys are gay and campaigns against them. But when a national Christian leader or pastor makes statements along these lines, they immediately become national news and understandably get joked about on late-night television, and the perception that churches are driven by agendas is heightened and even mocked.

Gary had this to say about the contrast between the political agendas of church leaders and what he feels Jesus was about:

> *The church has taken Jesus, who was a carpenter, a man of simplicity, and made him into an organized religion ... a business, a corporation. He's been butchered by some churches and even used in politics, so they try to get you to vote a certain way.* **GARY**

Many people think church leaders not only have political agendas but also use Jesus to promote them. But the reality is that it's generally politicians (not church leaders) who are the ones who use the church and Christians for their agendas and to gain votes. Many Christians, especially conservative ones, get swayed by politicians who push churchgoers' "hot buttons." My prayer is that Christians will discern when any subtle political manipulation is occuring. We need to regain the respect of others by showing that Christians vote intelligently and thoughtfully and not just out of fear or manipulation. And we need to show that it's primarily the politicians, not the church, that equate Christian faith with a specific political party. Most people think it's the church that uses politics, not politicians who use the church. As a result, we in the church have become stereotyped as being blindly obedient to one political party.

We also need to remember that many of the founding fathers of our "Christian nation" were deists, didn't believe in the inspiration of the whole Bible, and had slaves. Since some American Christians are vocal about getting back to our "Christian roots" politically, we need to be careful not to forget this. When you examine them, some of our roots turn out not to be that Christian. So making a case for a "Christian America" comes across as the church mixing religion and politics.

WE ARE KNOWN FOR WHAT WE'RE AGAINST, NOT WHAT WE'RE FOR

I will mention this again in the next chapter, but when I talk to those outside of the church, I find that we in the church are known more for what we stand against politically than what we stand for spiritually. How sad, since we should be known for being churches that passionately love God, love each other, and love people. We should be known for being followers of Jesus, serving him, each other, and our communities. We should be known for helping the needy, looking out for the marginalized, and being good neighbors. Instead, when people hear about Christians or church leaders in local and national media, either we come across as smug and angry, pointing fingers at others, or we come across as being so cheery, smiling rehearsed smiles, that we seem artificial.

These are lasting impressions. No wonder people have distorted impressions about us. The next time you see Christians interviewed on TV or read about them in your newspaper, imagine seeing them through the eyes of people outside the church. If this were all you saw of Christians, what would you think?

THE THIRD REASON WHY THEY SEE THE CHURCH AS ORGANIZED RELIGION

Here's the third reason why they see the church as organized religion: *The church is made of leaders who function like CEOs and desire power and control.*

In many churches, particularly the larger ones, our use of language furthers the impression that the church is organized religion. For most of church history, the primary titles used for church leaders were pastor or minister or even reverend. These titles reflected the role of a shepherd, which is what the word pastor means. Shepherds care for and nurture their sheep and even notice if one is missing. But in the 1980s, churches began applying business principles to the church. Pastors and leaders began using some of the language and metaphors of the business world, including

"Assistant Pastor? Please ... my title is 'Vice President, Worship Operations.' "

Cartoon by Nick Hobart from *Leadership* journal. Used with permission.

adding business descriptions to our titles, such as executive pastor, senior pastor, chief financial officer, executive assistant to the senior pastor, the elder board, management team, and others.

To most baby boomers, this made sense. They wanted their churches to be led smartly and efficiently, and titles related to people's values and culture help people understand roles in a church. A business executive might appreciate knowing that his or her church has an executive pastor who runs and manages the staff and administration of the church. We also have to admit that whatever we choose for our titles reflects our values and how we want to be seen by others, as the cartoon on the previous page illustrates.

I recently read an article in a business magazine that featured the rise of megachurches and big business in the church world. In the photos in this article, the pastors' clothing, demeanor, and poses all fit the corporate image. To those who value churches functioning as corporations or businesses, as many baby boomers did, this was fine and made sense. But in our emerging culture, this can come across very unlike Jesus, since it equates the church with big business and only reinforces the idea that the church is organized religion.

> *Church leaders seem to focus more on acting like businessmen raising funds to build bigger buildings for their own organized religious corporations than they do on taking the time to teach about social action for the poor. I think Jesus would have cared more about raising money for the poor than building yet another minimall church with comfortable seating and wide video screens so you can see the CEO pastor all the better and bigger.* ALICIA

I fully understand the need for building new church buildings that are well equipped, and that most churches have good motives for doing so. God uses buildings for his kingdom and for spreading the gospel of Jesus. But what if you don't know the hearts of the pastors and church leaders? What if you saw only the elaborate buildings on large campuses? What if you saw only the fancy business suits and power ties and demeanor of the pastors of large churches being interviewed on television? Megachurch pastors usually have a high-drive personality type, which is then perceived as the norm for a pastor or a Christian leader. What if you saw only these bits and pieces from the outside and didn't really know the heart of these pastors and leaders? What would happen if you went to talk to such a pastor? Here's what happened when a thirty-something woman did that very thing:

> I went to visit a church office, and it felt more like going to a lawyer's office or something. I had to get by the receptionist, who then had another secretary buzzed on a phone intercom. Then I had to sit and wait like I was visiting a president of a major corporation. When I finally walked through the office, it felt more intense and uptight than the broker's office I worked in. I felt more like I was an interruption than someone seeking spiritual guidance.
>
> A THIRTY-SOMETHING WOMAN'S IMPRESSION AFTER A CHURCH VISIT

I just talked to a twenty-nine-year-old drummer in a band (not Gary) who is part of a large church and even gives his tithes to it. He found it incredibly disillusioning when he tried multiple times for more than a month to make an appointment with one of the pastors, and it wasn't even the senior pastor. He was peeved and commented to me something like, "They take my money but don't even have time to see me." I understand the dilemma; it isn't easy to meet the needs of everyone in a growing church and meet with all the people who want to talk. I am a full believer in Ephesians 4:11–12, which teaches that church leaders should equip others for the work of ministry so that the paid staff don't have to be the only ones that people see. But in this case, a person's impression of the church as organized religion and a business have only been reinforced.

DO YOUNGER LEADERS IN YOUR CHURCH HAVE A VOICE?

A major question we need to address is whether younger leaders have a place of leadership and a voice in our churches. So often only older leaders have most of the authority. Of course, older leaders have wisdom and experience, but what about influencers and shapers who are younger? Musicians writing the songs that influence people at a national and global level are primarily in their twenties. The creativity and innovation of people in their twenties and thirties are used in the marketplace and in the music world, but are they given a place to help shape the church? How easy is it for a young leader to be in a place of influence and innovation in the church? This is an important question, because if you aren't creating ways for younger people to be shapers and influencers and to bring innovative ideas, you will squelch their hearts and minds and only reinforce the idea that we are a hierarchical organized religion. People in their late teens to early thirties have so much optimism and idealism and zeal. Historically, we see people of those ages starting all types of movements and new ways of thinking. Calvin was twenty-six when he wrote his *Institutes of the Christian Religion*. Bill Hybels and Rick Warren were in their early twenties when they started innovative churches that changed the face of the church in America. But quite often we don't listen to younger voices, and we miss the great ideas they have to offer that could help the church. We need to listen to them and have a place for them to express their ideas and be involved in leadership at a high level. In many churches, even small churches, we set up hierarchical structures that dampen any younger person's desire to help bring innovation and change at a higher level.

Erika, who is in environmental studies pursuing a masters degree in landscape architecture, has a bubbly personality, and as she talked about Jesus, her enthusiasm was evident, especially when she talked about Jesus' teachings about love and caring for the poor and needy. But as she talked about the church and its leaders, her expression changed. She is highly sensitive about the church being organized religion.

> *Church has so many levels of hierarchy. It seems like a presidency, with the pastor being the president and wielding power over his people.* — **ERIKA**

Erika isn't alone. Many people seem to think that the church today has leaders who set up church structures so they can get power and control people. This outside perception that the church is like a business adds to the impression that it's organized religion, something they don't want to be part of. Late Senate Chaplain Richard Halverson puts history into perspective with this observation: "But historians of religion like to say that Christianity was born in the Middle East as a religion, moved to Greece and became a philosophy, journeyed to Rome and became a legal system, spread through Europe as a culture — and when it migrated to America, Christianity became big business."[12]

> "HISTORIANS OF RELIGION LIKE TO SAY THAT CHRISTIANITY WAS BORN IN THE MIDDLE EAST AS A RELIGION, MOVED TO GREECE AND BECAME A PHILOSOPHY, JOURNEYED TO ROME AND BECAME A LEGAL SYSTEM, SPREAD THROUGH EUROPE AS A CULTURE — AND WHEN IT MIGRATED TO AMERICA, CHRISTIANITY BECAME BIG BUSINESS."

WHAT CAN WE LEARN FROM THIS MISPERCEPTION?

Rather than ignoring false perceptions of the church, we need to address them and take them seriously. How can we address the misperception that the church is an organized religion with a political agenda?

We can be organized without being organized religion

We all need organization — in our schools, hospitals, and even in our automobiles. Our laptops and cell phones have organized mother boards and circuit boards. Our bodies are highly complex with circulatory, nervous, digestive, skeletal, and other systems all organized to function together. So we absolutely need organization in life.

Speaking about religion as organized, however, stirs up criticism and negative reactions. Why? Because the Christian faith is a relationship with a living God, with a church family, and with other people. But in any relationship or family, organization is necessary. For example, a family meal requires organization to pick what gets cooked for dinner, to determine the cooking process, and even to make sure enough chairs are placed around the table. Likewise, a church family needs to be organized. In reality, I don't think being organized is what stirs criticism. Rather, the criticism comes from how we come across to people through our attitudes, and how we communicate how we are organized and how we practice our faith.

In the epigraph to this chapter, pop singer Madonna says she doesn't find anything wrong with the teachings of Jesus. (I would love to have a conversation with her to see what she means by this.) But she says she is suspicious of organized religion. Yet Madonna is into an organized religion

in Kabbalah. I have read books about Kabbalah, visited the national organization's website, and received their emails. I can confidently say that they
are an organized faith. But they are careful how they project it. So it is
organized, but not "organized." I believe people don't mind if religion is
organized in a healthy way.

Erica, Gary's wife, said this about organized religion:

> *Organized religion in concept is fine and not wrong in itself. There is a need
> for structure and well-thought-through leadership and what a church does.
> I don't mind that. But what I do mind is when a church organizes for the
> sake of controlling and manipulating people, like in politics. We are not in
> the Dark Ages anymore. We don't have to just sit and blindly obey religious
> leaders trying to control us like they did back then.* ERICA

If we are trying to develop a healthy view of our need to be organized,
we can give examples from the Bible, such as Jesus organizing the disciples
or Jesus setting up the Passover meal. He did these things to facilitate
ministry, not for control. Other classic examples include Exodus 18, where
Jethro, Moses' father-in-law, put an organizational structure in place so
that more people could be ministered to and so that Moses wouldn't suffer
burnout. Or consider Acts 6:1–7, where the early church needed to create
an organizational structure so that more people could be ministered to.
Communicating the underlying reasons for scriptural examples of organization may help to minimize negative connotations. It starts with clearly
communicating these reasons to people inside our churches so they can
share them as they talk about church leadership to those on the outside. In
this way, we can help to break stereotypes.

The danger of nonorganic organization

In our church, we are trying to establish a culture in which the pastors
and staff are not seen as higher than anyone else organizationally. It's too
dangerous to let the whole CEO, top-down mentality creep in, creating
organized religion in a bad way. It's also dangerous to be giving power
and control to only one pastor. Power and control can corrupt even good
people. When a church develops an elite sort of leadership, it can easily

create a culture of organized religion. So we ruthlessly avoid the super-leader mentality as much as possible. In fact, we try to go to the other extreme by constantly stressing we are servants of the people and volunteers of the church. We strive to establish an Ephesians 4:11–12 culture in our church, in which the majority of the people, not just the paid staff, will be organized, in the good sense of the word, to care for, shepherd, know, and guide people in the church. We strive to create a culture and structure in which the paid staff focuses on empowering people for ministry. If we are successful in doing this, then those who are a regular part of the church should have most of their needs met, since the church is functioning as a community not dependent on the paid staff and higher levels of leadership. We won't have to battle levels of hierarchy, since the leadership is spread out, making access to decision-makers all the more easy. We still have structure and levels of leadership, but leadership's goals are to see people owning, sharing, and developing the vision of the church using their gifts, personalities, and skills.

Preacher focused or Jesus focused?

Think of how you set up leaders in your church worship gatherings. Generally churches put them in the spotlight in the central focal point of the room, which is understandable, since people need to see leaders when they are speaking. In recent years, however, especially in larger churches, we have added the video projection of the preacher on large screens. When we do that, we just need to be all the more careful that we balance that by constantly communicating that the church is not about the communication skills and charisma of the preacher but about Jesus.

Even the placement of the pulpit demonstrates our values. Prior to the Reformation, people didn't have access to the Scriptures, and corrupt church leaders misused the Scriptures for their advantage. To counteract that, Reformation preachers began placing their pulpits way up high with pulpit structures around them in order to stress the authority of the Scriptures. It made sense then because of what was occurring culturally. But in today's emerging culture, the high pulpit of the Reformation only emphasizes that the preacher is the focus. You can't even see a Bible usually, and the elevation of the preacher reinforces the hierarchical, man-made feel of organized religion. And this isn't just a large-church issue. I was in a very small church once, and I was amazed that the preacher stood behind a pulpit quite a distance from the people, rather than standing closer to them in such an intimate setting.

In our church, we do whatever we can to lessen the sense of separation between paid staff and the people. In the worship gatherings, we've placed a large cross where the preacher normally would stand. When I preach, I stand below the cross and off to its side a little. I'm on a small elevated stage so people can see me, but our desire is to make it clear who is most prominent in the room. It's Jesus, not the preacher. We also have the worship band set up below the cross and not at the center of things. We want to promote that this is not a man-made religion, that we are serving Jesus here, that the leaders aren't putting on a program in which they are the centerpiece. Jesus is the centerpiece. I was recently at a church where there were three thousand people, mainly in their twenties and thirties. They placed the platform in the center of the room, rather than at one end. It was elevated so that people could see, but having it in the center made the preacher distinctively less distant from the people. The members of the worship band set up in the corners of the stage, all facing inward so as not to draw attention to themselves. Whether you're a small church or a megachurch, you can find ways to communicate that your church is not about the paid pastors or about a separation between the pastors and the people.

Vintage home church or large-scale theater church?

Don't underestimate the power of your seating arrangement. The way you set up seating for your worship gathering can establish a culture of an organic family type of spirituality instead of organized religion. We've really gotten far from the "vintage" church meetings of the early church, which met in homes. They had leaders and teaching, but the culture of the home church made it easier to have a sense of family and community. Today, we have giant spaces with theater seating and spotlights on the stage. In smaller churches, we have pews that are locked into one position facing the front, where the preacher and leaders stand. I'm not saying we need to go back to having only house churches again. We live in a different time and culture. But we need to think about how our meeting spaces emphasize our values.

In our church, we still have large weekend gatherings and hope to see God use them to help hundreds and thousands of people in our community trust in Jesus and become his followers. Not all of what we do can be done in homes, because we are far too big to meet in a home all together. But in addition to the large weekend gathering, we really stress home communities that meet in homes midweek as the way to really connect and form true community. These communities are different from cell groups or small groups; we are trying to define them instead as minichurches. Then on the weekend, all these minichurches meet together for a larger worship gathering. Even in these larger meetings, churches can break up the room so it's not just rows and rows of chairs facing one direction. I've been to a church that took out all the pews and set up couches and comfortable chairs in the room. When you walk in, the setting really shouts out community and family instead of controlled seating and organized religion. I've been to another church of several hundred people mainly in their twenties that set up their space like a coffeehouse with little tables and chairs, and the pastor spoke from the center of the room. Again, spaces like these attempt to break down hierarchy and stress vintage values of family and community even in large meetings. When you study church architecture, for over 1300 years the church didn't have pews or rows of chairs. When they brought them in, it changed the dynamic of worship and the meeting. I'm not saying that seating people in rows is automatically bad. If God is growing your church to a large size, you might not have any choice but to sit in rows. But if that's the case, it just means being all the more strategic in how you teach that the church is an organic family and explain how the larger meeting fits within that. But I know it can be done. I have seen very large churches whose people sit in rows, and yet it's obvious that their values and teaching don't promote hierarchy and organized religion.

On a satirical Christian website there's an article making fun of the movie-theater-church approach.[13] A photo in the article shows a movie-theater complex which was turned into a church facility. You pull into the multiplex cinema, drop your kids off in the nursery, and then choose from "Thirty Sermons Now in Progress." Another photo in the article shows ushers tearing corners off of people's bulletins as they enter the theater, as if the bulletins were tickets. Please understand, I know of many wonderful and growing churches that meet in movie theaters and in theaterlike buildings. We just need to make sure that as we meet in movie theaters, we are teaching that church is not a movie or a play that we passively sit and watch as others perform for us. We need to stress all the more that church is an organic missional family, not merely a Sunday performance.

From the homeless Son of Man to theater seating and video screens

Imagine being twenty-three years old and interested in Jesus. You have been reading about Jesus' life, how he had a heart for the poor and lived a nomadic life, teaching from hillsides, walking with fisherman, and moving among outcasts and beggars and the lame. How he went into the temple and turned out the money changers. How he would get away to quiet places to rest and pray. You've been picturing Jesus wearing sandals, walking on dirt paths, talking with people.

You've also been reading how the early church met in homes in an informal familylike way, how they formed relationships in these smaller

Image used with permission of larknews.com

home gatherings and prayed for others as they went about their mission together. You've been reading how the early church had meals together in these homes, and you imagine that there must have been a lot of dialogue during these meals. You get these wonderful images of "vintage Christianity," picturing how the church must have functioned back then.

Now imagine walking into a typical worship gathering today: pews all formally in rows with organ music going and people in suits and ties or even robes up front. Or comfortable movie-theater seats facing a stage in a large theaterlike setting. Large screens with PowerPoint projection. Loud bands playing pop music with lighting and fancy sound systems. You would be quite shocked, and it would take some getting used to after reading about the life of Jesus. You probably wouldn't be able to even remotely connect what you've read about Jesus and the early church to what we have turned church into today. Please understand, in our church, we do use PowerPoint, pop music, videos, and lighting. But we are constantly trying to balance that by teaching what church and worship are so that we aren't defining them to people by these things.

These things do make a difference

Just two weeks ago I was stopped in the hallway of the building where our church meets. A twenty-year-old told me that recently she had prayed in the worship gathering to become a Christian. I asked what led her to that, and it turned out that it began with relationships first. After she came to trust the people she had relationships with, she decided to come to our worship gathering. She went into great detail about what she observed in the room and how the very first thing she noticed was the central placement of the cross. She shared how she was glad to see Jesus up there (and she motioned with her hand to the cross) and that I was down there (she pointed to where I preach below the cross). To her, that was important and played down any idea that we are a man-made organized religion focused on the leader. And she also observed from the room setup that it was clear we are a community of "Jesus followers" (her words).

Please don't feel I'm making judgments about churches that have pews or theater seats, video screens and lights, or whose preachers preach from high platforms. God works in all types of ways in all types of settings. For the purposes of this book, I am only relaying what some people outside the church are observing and are saying influences their thoughts of the church as an organized religion. The larger your church is, the more attention you may need to pay to this.

Strangling your church in organization

Another way the church comes across as organized religion is by building an infrastructure that strangles the church and doesn't allow healthy change, younger people to have a voice, or the empowerment of younger leaders. I recently spent time in a church which is growing older and not seeing many younger people coming in. As I came to understand their leadership structure, I was amazed. For simple decisions, you might have to go through two or three committees, and it could take over a month to get a simple answer about something. The organization and committees and decision-making process of this church are strangling it with bureaucracy and control. I keep asking them, "Why do you need this committee to decide that?" and the answers, seriously, have been, "Because we always do it that way," and, "The committee is in charge of that." No wonder there aren't too many younger people coming into this church. They have tightly set up the structure not to allow, or at best to discourage, new ideas and younger voices to participate. I can only imagine the frustration of energetic, younger people who try to get involved or make changes in this church, only to be deflated by all the organization and committees. Such churches only reinforce the idea that the church is an organized religion, rather than a community of gifted people serving together on a mission.

We can empower younger leaders without bureaucracy

I have talked with larger churches that are doing great things for God with leadership made up mostly of people who are baby boomers or older. As I talk to younger leaders on staff in these churches, as well as with the people in them, I am generally told that younger leaders don't have much of a voice. They usually serve in niche generational ministry roles but aren't brought up to the higher levels of influencing and leading the whole church. The incredible irony is that it is this very age group that is shaping our culture through music, media, and new ideas, but the church shuts out their influence and creativity. So as the church makes decisions, younger leaders don't have much voice in the direction the church takes. If that's how it is for younger leaders, imagine how it is for people in emerging generations who aren't on staff and desire to have a voice in the church or share new ideas. Again, the irony is that most larger churches that have a ton of baby boomers in them were started by younger pastors and leaders with fresh voices and innovative ideas. They understood that the culture was changing and designed their churches to have a culture of change. But now many of these very church leaders are older and are limiting younger leaders from doing what they did when they were younger. Younger people in the church need to be able to bring new ideas to the older leaders; if they can't do so, the church comes across to them as organized religion with no sense of freedom or organic change, and emerging generations feel more disconnected from the culture of the church.

Churches that want to bridge this leadership gap can find ways to do so. A church might want to make sure it has one or two younger elders on its elder board to serve as younger voices and to represent younger people. A church could set up a leadership training structure in which people, regardless of age, are trained in their area of giftedness and are invited to serve in all areas of the church in all areas of leadership. I would suggest that we need to go beyond just involving younger people in youth or young-adult ministries; I would suggest having them in all types of ministries. We can be constantly asking younger people to be part of the decision-making process for the whole church. They might have the ideas that your whole church, not just your youth or young-adult department, desperately needs. We need not only to make it easier for them to be involved but also to show them that they are needed in all areas of the church and that we respect their opinions regarding the direction of the church. It's sad how often I have met growing, capable, enthusiastic younger leaders who had to leave their churches because there was no room for their voices. The older upper leadership controlled things, and though younger leaders could lead ther specific areas of ministry, they could not have influence in the larger church. So many get frustrated and eventually leave. The church then gets older and older because it doesn't empower younger leaders or create a culture for them to thrive in.

We can bring life and meaning to rituals seen as controlling or lifeless

Some of the misperception that the church is organized religion has to do with our worship gatherings. Many churches have become dull and ritualistic, and people from emerging generations see them as structuring and controlling how people worship, rather than guiding worship. Through the centuries, the church has guided people in corporate worship with many beautiful directions and procedures; for example, directions to stand, or recite a prayer, or read a responsive reading. These "rituals" can be so beautiful and meaningful. But when they come across as lifeless or joyless and aren't explained, they seem to sap the life out of relational worship. It can feel like the leaders are forcing people to do these things.

I believe emerging generations are actually appreciative of ritual and using worship practices from throughout church history. But we do need to explain them and practice them with life and meaning or, as Gary said, they can come across as a Simon Says type of controlled worship.

We can be sensitive to our use of the pulpit for personal agendas

We need to preach and make strong stands on issues the Bible clearly teaches on, but at the same time, we need to be careful of how much our biases and opinions slip into our preaching. We need to be careful to avoid saying, "Jesus thinks this …" when we really don't know what he thinks, subtly using God and Jesus to back our opinions. I am convinced that emerging generations are open to hearing hard things that go against the culture. We should not be afraid to show how Jesus said some strong things. But when we do so with even a hint of a stinky attitude or a bitter or angry heart, we come across as simply pushing our own agendas and reinforce the misperception that the church is organized religion.

We can lead without the trappings of the corporate world

Remember the woman who visited a church and felt like she was in a lawyer's office rather than in a spiritual leader's office? What vibe does your church office communicate to visitors? How many calls, emails, reception-

THE CHURCH IS AN ORGANIZED RELIGION WITH A POLITICAL AGENDA

ists, and other hoops does a person have to go through to make contact with someone in leadership?

How about titles for church leaders? If we are using titles such as senior pastor or executive pastor, have we ever paused to ask why we use those terms? If there is only one pastor on staff, why use the title senior pastor? How do the titles we use come across to people who don't equate corporate business with spiritual leadership? What does your church bulletin look like? What does it communicate graphically? How often does the name Jesus appear in your bulletin or other church literature? Or is your bulletin filled with information about programs and the names of your church staff, but Jesus is hard to find? Will emerging generations, who are respectful of Jesus, see Jesus in your church culture? Or will they see and hear more about the church leaders than about Jesus, who ultimately is the leader of the church leaders (Eph. 1:22; 5:23)?

These are all little things, but in an emerging culture that criticizes the church for being a business and organized religion, they all add up. While numbers of people may think nothing of business titles, the use of such titles for spiritual leaders doesn't sit well with members of our emerging culture and reinforces the perception that the church is organized religion. In our church, we use the title "pastor" in everything we print, but we don't label our roles in hierarchy or seniority. We are definitely structured with organized leadership, but we avoid displaying the hierarchy in our titles. On my business cards, I don't even put anything other than my name, along with the church name and information. I don't see the need to promote titles and ranks when ministry is about relationship. I have been to an emerging church that even calls all of their volunteers "staff." It seemed odd and confusing to me when I visited there, since the church had around 250 people and I must have met twenty or more who introduced themselves as staff. I met so many staff, I couldn't believe it. But then the lead pastor explained that the church wants to promote the value that volunteers are as important as paid staff. And who is being drawn into this church? People from emerging generations, many from outside the church. We don't call our volunteers staff, but we do everything we can not to create a feeling of corporate hierarchy.

THE TRUTH WITHIN A CLICHE

We are living in a wonderful time when there is so much openness to Jesus and even his countercultural teachings. But some of the trappings we have added to our faith can get in the way of Jesus and his teachings. He came to free people from the organized religion of his time, when the religious leaders had become stuck in legalism, power, control, and other trappings of religion. As corny as it sounds, Jesus came to say it's not about religion; it truly is about relationship.

And it's not only about an individual's relationship with God. It's also about a relationship with a community of faith. When we enter a church community, we are submersed in a wonderful, messy communal relationship with God. Yes, we need organization, as any family does. But not the sort of organization that strangles the church, promotes legalism, and turns a family into a corporation. We can move from being perceived as functioning as an organized religion to being seen as an organic community:

> The church is an organized religion with a political agenda
>
> → The church is an organized community with a heart to serve others

I hope that, having read some of the comments from emerging generations in this chapter, we will be able to take an honest look at how we might be reinforcing the negative concept of the church as organized religion. Little things make a big difference. May we make it easy for people from emerging generations who are looking for Jesus to see him in our midst.

LOOKING AT YOUR CHURCH THROUGH THE EYES OF EMERGING GENERATIONS

1. How would you define *organized religion?* How do you see your church being organized in a good way? How is it organized in a bad way?

2. What are some examples of ways churches today add to Scripture their own agendas or political leanings? Does this ever happen in your church? How?

3. Are there any rituals or worship practices in your church that have become mundane or are not explained to people? How can you make sure that the organized parts of your services come across as relational, vibrant worship of God?

4. Imagine a stranger visiting your weekend worship gathering. What would a visitor observe that clearly points to Jesus as the reason you are gathered? How often would Jesus' name be mentioned? Would a visitor perceive in a negative way that your church has adopted business attitudes or titles that sound like organized religion? If so, what are some examples? What should you do differently?

5. This may be a hard question to ask yourself, but based on what you subtly and unintentionally communicate, would people describe your church as Jesus-centered or as senior-pastor centered?

6. What values does your weekly meeting space communicate to those in our emerging culture?

7. How easy would it be for a twenty-five-year-old to get involved in the life of your church in a significant way? How many hoops would they have to jump through? Can you honestly say you respect someone of that age who is walking with God, and would help them discover their gifts and empower them as a leader in your church? How are you building younger leaders into your church?

THE CHURCH IS JUDGMENTAL AND NEGATIVE 6

I did grow up in a church, but now I am a Buddhist.
When I became a mother, I wanted my daughter to have a
spiritual upbringing. However, I didn't want her to become
like the Christians in the church I knew. They were always
so negative and complaining about everything, and I
wanted my daughter to be in a positive environment.
I became Buddhist since they are a much more loving
and peaceful people than those in the church.

— JENNINE
OWNER OF A BEAUTY SALON

I couldn't believe what I was hearing. Maya, the girl who usually cut
my hair, had moved to Austin, so I was trying out another salon. I
ended up chatting with Jennine, the owner of the salon, who is in
her early thirties. As she was cutting my hair, she asked me where I work,
so I told her about the church I'm part of. I eventually asked her about
her spiritual beliefs, and she shared that she is a Buddhist, and not just a
casual one. She takes Buddhist spirituality very seriously, meeting once a
week with someone to train her in Buddhism and meditation. That's not
what caught me off-guard, since an increasing number of people seem
to be drawn to some form of Buddhism. Rather, it was her next comment, quoted in the epigraph to this chapter, that got me. She shared that
she became Buddhist because she desired a spiritual upbringing for her
daughter, and she decided that Buddhism would be better for her than the
church because the Christians she knew were always negative, complaining, and making judgments about other people. She wanted something
more positive and loving for her daughter.

What an insanely wild thing to hear. She viewed Christians as negative, judgmental, and complaining people. Aren't we supposed to be known

for the opposite? Shouldn't we be living a joyful life, despite our circumstances? Aren't we the ones whom others should see bringing hope and encouragement to those around us? Jesus said, "I have come that they may have life, and have it to the full" (John 10:10). He didn't say he came that we may become negative, judgmental, and complaining. Galatians 5:22–23 says, "The fruit of the Spirit is love, joy, peace, patience, kindness, goodness, faithfulness, gentleness and self-control." Jesus tells us we are to be salt and light (Matt. 5:13–16) to others, so they will see something in us that draws them to himself. But Jennine experienced the opposite. She was not only repelled from the church but also drawn toward Buddhism because Buddhists had a better reputation than Christians.

"I HATE WORKING ON SUNDAYS, BECAUSE THAT'S WHEN THE CHRISTIANS COME IN"

Now, I wish I could say this is an isolated incident, but it isn't. In my interviews for this book, as well as in all sorts of other conversations, this negative impression popped up again and again. When I recently spoke to several hundred youth workers and asked them to list some of the perceptions they feel people outside of the church have of Christians, the words judgmental, critical, negative, and condemning were all shouted out multiple times. At another conference I just spoke at, I was talking to a member of the conference staff. He told me that he's been escaping the church office to hang out and study at a coffeehouse in Dallas a few days a week. As he became friends with some of the people working there, he heard them say how they hate working on Sundays. He asked them why, and they told him that there's a church nearby and that the Christians all flood into the coffeehouse on Sundays. The employees hate working that day because the Christians complain more than other people do, have poor attitudes, make more of a fuss and are particular about things, and don't tip. This is how we are known in our culture today. Why is this happening?

WE ARE KNOWN FOR WHAT WE'RE AGAINST, NOT WHAT WE'RE FOR

Maya cut my hair for four or five years, giving me numerous opportunities to speak with her about Christianity, church, and faith. She'd had some church experience in her childhood years because her family attended occasionally at Easter and Christmas. She'd always felt there is a God, and she told me that Jesus was "powerful, a good leader." She said, "I trust him." She hadn't thought a lot about Christianity or church until a close friend of hers became a Christian. Then not only did she have to think about it, but Christianity became a negative thing to her:

> Before my friend became a Christian, you could talk to him. It was normal. He became a Christian after he met a girl, and then through her got converted. But after his conversion, you couldn't talk to him anymore. Every conversation was about condemning something about my lifestyle. All he did was keep telling me all the things I was doing wrong. I shouldn't be smoking. I shouldn't be drinking. He didn't like the way I dressed or the music I listened to. I was mad at the church for turning him into this kind of very negative person.

It may be that her friend expressed extreme views because he was a new Christian or perhaps because of the influence of the culture of his church. But in any case, his comments and attitude conveyed to Maya that this is what happens when you become a Christian. Here's how this experience impacted her even several years later:

> You ask why I don't go to church? Why would I want to become a negative person like most Christians are? That's why. The world is negative enough without having the church make me more negative. I saw what it did to someone very close to me, and I don't want to become like that.

Once again, I wish this were an isolated incident, but it isn't. The question I want to raise is, Why do we in the church focus so intensely on the negatives? Why is it that people on the outside know us only for what we stand against? I repeatedly heard in all the interviews for this book that we are people who pick out all of the negative things in the world and then protest them. Here are a couple of those comments:

The church is a group of judgmental mudslingers. They seem to really like picking fights with others. Whether it is homosexuals, or other religions, or even with each other. That's the weirdest part. Jesus said to love one another, but you're always hearing how the church even fights among themselves and with other denominations. But this isn't anything new. Look at the Crusades. The church has always been an angry bunch.

GARY

I wish church leaders would be more empathetic and kind to other people who don't necessarily believe exactly what they do. From what I've experienced on campus and see on television, they seem to like telling others that they are going to hell when you don't agree with them. I have had Christians who try to evangelize me actually judge me without even knowing me and tell me where my eternal destiny will be. Not the kind of people you want to hang out with on a Friday night, are they?

ERIKA

This unflattering perception of the church and Christians comes from seeing Christians protesting on the streets with large signs telling people they are going to hell. It comes from reading about various things Christians protest against, such as the teaching of evolution in the schools, or the removal of the Ten Commandments monument from a courthouse, or homosexual marriage. It comes from seeing Christians on television crediting God for natural disasters to punish sinners, and from being approached by Christians who ask leading questions to witness to them, putting them on the defensive and invading their privacy.

I was contacted once by the local university to help be a peacemaker in a situation in which an overzealous Christian confronted the gay and lesbian group on campus. The group was sitting at a table in a public area of the campus taking sign-ups for their various activities and meetings. The Christian publicly confronted them and told them that if they continued, they would be going to hell. The Christian made no attempt at establishing a relationship but simply walked over to their table and began an argument. I was told this scenario was witnessed by dozens of college students who were nearby. Once again, an incident reinforced the negative stereotype of Christians. I had to do some damage control and let the group know that this is not the normal Christian approach.

IF ALL PEOPLE SEE IS THE NEGATIVE, THEY WON'T KNOW ANY DIFFERENTLY

Recently I was in the airport in Dallas waiting to board a plane when I spotted a young man in his twenties wearing a black T-shirt with the word *intolerant* in large capital letters on the front. Below the word, the shirt said, "Jesus says," which made it look like Jesus was being quoted as saying, "Intolerant." It also said, "He is the way, the truth, and the life." When I spotted this shirt, I thought, "Uh oh." I was afraid to look at the back of it, but I didn't have a choice. As the young man got ready to board the plane, he turned and I saw that the entire back of his shirt listed in big bold letters: "Islam is a lie! Homosexuality is sin! Abortion is murder!" Everyone nearby noticed the shirt. While we were standing in line to board the plane, I watched people's faces as they read the shirt, and I kept wondering, What if a Muslim is reading this? What if someone was wearing a "Christianity is a lie!" shirt? Imagine the emotions we would feel about that. What if someone who is gay is reading this shirt? That person might be open to dialogue, but instead all they get is the impersonal blasting of these messages on the shirt. What if a mother and her young child read this shirt? The mother might not want her seven-year-old reading those messages, and then having to explain to her child what they mean and why the person is wearing it. Or imagine just anyone in the neutral setting of an airport reading these types of things. I didn't see anyone high-fiving the guy or giving him a wink of approval. You could see people rolling their eyes and imagine what they were thinking: "Those Christians ... They're pretty messed up and angry."

I was rather embarrassed at how this fellow chose to make his beliefs known. I battled in my mind, wondering if I should say something to him. Now, I am theologically conservative and pro-life. But I totally disagreed with the way this guy was communicating these beliefs. I asked him what kind of church he was from. He said, "A Bible-preaching Bible church." (I think those were his exact words.) He was friendly, smiling as he talked.

"Are you a Christian?" he said.

"Yes, I am."

"Praise God!" he said.

And then I gently said, "I wouldn't be wearing that shirt though; I think it repels people from the message rather than drawing people to Jesus."

He kept smiling and said, "Well, we can't hide the truth, and if one person repents as a result of this shirt, it's worth it."

My adrenaline began flowing, and I said, "Have you ever known someone to repent as a result of the shirt?"

"No," he said, "but that's the Holy Spirit's job. Our job is to get the message out there."

I realized a quick conversation wasn't going to change his mind. At this point, I was blocking people behind me from going past me in the aisle of the plane, and I didn't feel like getting into a debate while holding up the line, so I ended the conversation. I just said, "Thanks for talking," and moved on to my seat.

Again, this story illustrates a way that many people come to see Christians as judgmental finger-pointers and how such a negative stereotype gets reinforced. This young man forced his shirt on people by wearing it in public. He felt that the message needed to get out there, but shouldn't we be the message? Shouldn't we be building friendships with people so they see the message living in us? Then after we've gained their trust, we'd have the credibility to dialog about these things. We would present the message to others better if we were demonstrations of the love of Jesus. I'm sure he had good intentions, but to me, wearing an overtly condemning T-shirt seems like a cop-out and a cheap way to tell people about Jesus and his teachings, a way that only reinforces the perception of Christians as negative and judgmental.

THE DAY I TORE SOME PAGES OUT OF A BIBLE

I get nervous telling this story, because it might offend some people. But I'm hoping you'll hear the heart of what I'm saying. I was sitting in a coffeehouse talking with someone who worked there. We had established a friendship over some months, and on this day he actually asked me a question about the Bible. He knew very well that I'm a pastor, and we had talked about church and Jesus before. But on this day, I felt the time was right, so I asked him, "Would you like a Bible?" I was so thrilled that he responded positively, after all my months of praying, that I said goodbye and drove straight back to the church office to get him one.

At the office, I jumped out of my car, actually ran inside, and grabbed a Bible from the box of new believers' New Testaments that the church gives away at events. Then I jumped back in the car and drove right back to the coffeehouse. When I parked, I thought I would first look at this new believers' Bible to get a sense of what was in it. I was pretty surprised by what I found. Throughout the Bible there were large highlighted boxes with commentary about the Scriptures. That was fine in and of itself, but the commentary wasn't fine. For example, I found a box that said something like, "Now that you're a Christian, you won't have sex before marriage anymore." It was in a place where the Bible speaks of sexuality, but the heading of this box and the wording in the text were all about what you shouldn't be doing. My friend was living with his girlfriend, but that was not the issue he was asking about. Handing him a Bible that had a highlighted box telling him he is sinning in this area was not what I wanted to be doing at this point. I wanted him to read the life of Jesus to get to know Jesus' story and his heart. But I still wanted him to have a Bible, and I thought that maybe he wouldn't notice if it jumped from 1 Corinthians 6 to 1 Corinthians 8. He will just think Christians skip numbers or something. So I ripped out that page.

Please understand me! I was not ripping out the page because of what the Scriptures say there. I ripped out the page because of the commentary in the highlighted box.

I then skimmed through other sections and found the same thing over and over. The commentary in another highlighted box talked about how homosexuality is a sin. Another talked about drinking and getting drunk. I couldn't believe how much of this kind of commentary the editors of this new believers' edition of the New Testament chose to include. It was mainly about all the negative things we aren't supposed to do. I ripped out about four pages and then finally gave up. I drove back to the church office and got a normal Bible without the commentary.

Remember, my friend had never read the Bible before, so he didn't know that the highlighted boxes are not part of the Scriptures. He would assume that the Bible is about only these negative things and that what's most important in the Bible is what is highlighted in these boxes.

EMBARRASSED NOT BY THE BIBLE BUT BY WHAT WE DO WITH IT

Again, please understand what I'm saying here. I was not embarrassed by the Scriptures, and I wasn't trying to hide them. But I was embarrassed about giving my friend this particular Bible because all of the negative commentary would distract him from reading about having a positive relationship with Jesus. I wanted his experience of reading the Bible for the first time to be about who Jesus is. I wanted it to be about inner heart issues rather than select outward actions. I wished the editors of this new believers' Bible would have highlighted the joys and first steps of following Jesus. I am all for telling people about sin. But we should do it the right way and at the right time. As a person's relationship with Jesus deepens, we should allow the Holy Spirit to convict and the process of sanctification to occur.

A junior high pastor recently told me about a non-Christian junior higher who attended the youth meeting. The young teen said, "You Christians really hate homosexuals, don't you?" That's the first impression this seventh-grader had of the church. He didn't say, "You Christians really know how to love other people," or, "You Christians really take seriously caring for the widows and the poor," or, "You Christians really have strong marriages." Nope. Once again the impression is about something we stand against, rather than what we stand for. And if the impression people get is that we are negative, complaining, judgmental people, no wonder people don't want to become Christians.

WHAT CAN WE LEARN FROM THIS MISPERCEPTION?

Perhaps you're thinking that I'm soft or afraid of proclaiming the truth or am promoting only the positive-thinking part of Christianity. I want to assure you that isn't what I'm saying at all. I know that some churches go to the other extreme and rarely mention sin. They may never talk about judgment and may teach only things that make people feel good, ignoring all the talk about sin and repentance in the Bible. Rather, I'm calling for a balance here, desiring that Christians and the church become known for what we are for, not just for what we are against.

So how can we address the misperception that the church is judgmental and negative?

We must know how and when to talk about sin

I am convinced that emerging generations actually want to be told about sin. That may sound weird, but I have been in enough conversations to say that they do want to be informed about the ways of Jesus and the teachings of the Bible, even the ones which require repentance and change. Regularly in our church I see so many on their knees in repentance, speaking with God, confessing sin, asking the Spirit of God to change them. Just a few months ago, we spent an evening talking about the importance of following through on Matthew 18 and Galatians 6, where we are taught to confront sin in other believers. We even gave people little cards on which we asked them to write the names of Christians that they would invite to hold them accountable to walk in the ways of Jesus. It gave these other Christians permission to speak to them if they see symptoms of their straying into sin. Two weeks ago, we spent a whole message teaching on what repentance is. So I fully believe in repentance and in recognizing sin and confronting other believers. Absolutely. But how and when we do it makes all the difference.

Maya makes a relevant comment about this:

> I actually would want to be told if I am doing something that God wouldn't like me to. I want to become a better person and be more like Jesus. But that isn't how it feels coming from Christians and the church. It feels more like they are trying to shame you and control you into their way of thinking and personal opinions about what is right and wrong, rather than it being about becoming more like Jesus and a more loving human being.

Maya actually wants to be a better person and wants to become more like Jesus. She may not fully grasp what that means, but she is open to it. Though she shared how a Christian came across negatively and pointed out her sins, she wants to change to become more like Jesus. But that's the key! If we go around pointing out sins and being negative and shaming people, the reaction will usually be negative. But if we share how we can become more loving and more like Jesus by changing in certain ways, then it is accepted as a positive thing. I love the way Peter approached those in Solomon's Colonnade in Acts 3:19. He says, "Repent, then, and turn to God, so that your sins may be wiped out, that times of refreshing may come from the Lord." He speaks of repentance as "refreshing." I believe we can speak about all truths and not be afraid of talking about sin and repentance. But how, to whom, and when makes a huge difference.

Whom are we to judge and how are we to do it?

What about the overwhelming criticism that we are critical and judgmental? I will address the issue in terms of Jesus' being "the only way" in chapter 9. Regarding judging others, we need to be clear on some biblical guidelines. Jesus taught his disciples, "Do not judge" (Matt. 7:1). But I believe Jesus was saying that God is most concerned with our hearts and the attitude with which we judge other people. He explains, "For in the same way you judge others, you will be judged" (v. 2). Though Paul told the Christians in Rome not to judge one another (Rom. 14:13), he also taught the Corinthians to judge sinful believers and to leave people who were outside the church to God (1 Cor. 5:12–13). Matthew 18:15–20 and Galatians 6:1 indicate that we are to lovingly confront other Christians on sin issues. But the pattern here is judging *Christians*, not those outside of the church. As sin-tainted human beings, Christians will gravitate to and participate in sin. So we need other Christians to lovingly hold us to our walk with Jesus and to being holy. As I described earlier, in the church in which I serve, we try to foster a culture for doing this. But it's a culture designed to help overcome infection. What do I mean? The church is a body, and so if a foot gets infected with sin, then for the health of the whole body, all of the members of the body need to work together to restore the foot to health. Because we are all vulnerable to temptation, we need each other to be healthy, and so it makes sense to look at confronting sin in the church this way. We should be judging within the church in a loving, graceful, humble manner with the goal of restoring the infected part of the body. But when it comes to persons outside the church, we are to leave judgment to God. We should be telling people about Jesus and his saving grace rather than judging and condemning them.

Let me add this important qualification: we should be careful not to make judgments based on personal opinions rather than on the clear teaching of Scripture. I have talked to many wounded younger Christians who left the church because they were confronted in a legalistic way about extrabiblical things. While Scripture says we should not get drunk (Eph. 5:18) or become addicted to alcohol (Titus 2:3), nowhere does it say we can't drink. Yet how easy it is for some to make extrabiblical judgments on this divisive issue. Tattoos and piercings are another big issue in some circles. I have heard some older Christian leaders speak of tattoos as sinful and even occultic, subtly mocking those who get nose rings or other piercings. But the fact is that one cannot make a biblical case against tattoos today. The marks on the skin referred to in the Hebrew Bible (Lev. 19:28) were related to pagan religious customs of the people who surrounded ancient Israel. These marks honored dieties who were believed to preside over the dead. Today tattoos are about personal artistic expression. They generally have personal meaning but are not about honoring pagan gods. If Christians mark themselves with idolatrous religious symbols, that would be different. But many tattoos on Christians are artistic expressions of their faith, quite often Christian symbols or Bible verses. Yet I have heard some church leaders make both harshly and subtly critical remarks condemning tattoos. Imagine being a younger person hearing these negative and judgmental comments based on personal opinions, not scriptural teaching.

"Those lost and confused tattooed and pierced young people"

A few years ago, when I was the young-adult pastor at a church, a fellow in his twenties who was becoming part of our young-adult ministry expressed interest in becoming a member of the church. He had lots of tattoos and several piercings. I went with him to the church's membership class. During the class, the pastor teaching it began talking about the mission of the church and how "we want to reach the confused and lost young people who hang out downtown and have those tattoos and piercings." I looked over at the guy I was with and he was looking right at me with this questioning "what the heck?" look. At the break, I talked to the pastor and told him how he had come across with his comment. The pastor felt bad. Because he was older and had strong opinions about these things, he didn't realize how he was coming across to someone who has tattoos or piercings. Unfortunately, when we make careless comments based on personal opinion, people can easily get the impression that we are judgmental and critical of others.

When I first started going to a church, I was told all secular music is bad. Not knowing any better, I threw away all of my secular music. Since then, I realized that I had taken an action because of someone's opinion rather than because of clear scriptural teaching. I have since bought most of those albums back, with the exception of some I felt weren't quite edifying.

Once when I was speaking at a camp, I talked to a girl about twenty years old who was in tears. She had been told by the senior pastor in her church that she shouldn't wear black because it's depressing. She explained that she loved black clothing and dressed in a somewhat gothic fashion, but she was wounded by this Christian leader's judgment of her character based on what she wore. Let me clarify that it had nothing to do with immodesty. Most gothic-styled clothing involves many layers, practically hiding every square inch. But she was hurt, and now she was torn because she felt she could be committing a sin for wearing black clothing.

In some cases, Christians need to be approached in a concerned manner if their clothing crosses the line of sexual appropriateness or if their music really is inappropriate for a follower of Jesus. But in such a sticky situation, we need to check whether our concern is based merely on preference and opinion, or on Scripture. I know a guy who was told by a church leader that he should not wear a Mickey Mouse watch. The leader felt that Christians should not support Disneyland, so therefore it's wrong to wear such a watch. This young man in his early twenties, who was new in the faith, wanted to do the right thing, but he was confused by the judgmental comment of a Christian who was basing his criticism on his own opinion rather than on the clear teaching of Scripture.

Younger people notice our critical and judgmental hearts

I mention some of these examples because overstepping our boundaries can cause people to conclude that all Christians are negative, judgmental, and complaining. In my conversations with those in their twenties who have left the church, I often hear that they felt church leaders or people in the church had judgmental attitudes and critical spirits. People notice when we bicker among ourselves. I have heard Christians ripping apart other Christians over whether they believe in a literal twenty-four-hour, six-day creation account and over other secondary issues. I'm not talking about Nicene Creed types of core doctrines but secondary issues such as the gift of tongues, women in ministry, end-times scenarios, and other similar issues on which wonderful godly people have different viewpoints. When we obsess on these things, our hearts can become bitter and opinionated. And guess who watches this? The younger Christians in our churches, and then those on the outside of our churches wind up hearing about these things. Younger Christians see our critical and judgmental hearts, and then we wonder why they leave the church and turn to Buddhism or other options.

Perhaps we need to evaluate ourselves a bit and ask God to convict us if we are stumbling blocks because of our critical spirits or judgmental hearts. And it isn't just what we say in the pulpit that our children take note of but our words and attitudes in our homes. They hear the conversations we have in restaurants after church services, in which we criticize the sermon or another leader or someone in the church. At work, non-Christians hear us when we make unloving comments about people or issues. Maybe we should first evaluate our own lives and then look at our sermons. What do we preach on? Good news or negative news? When we talk about repentance, is it with glee that people will face God's wrath and anger? I'm not kidding. People who focus so much on God's wrath come across like they're happy that people will suffer one day. Instead of having a broken and humble heart, they can come across with the attitude "I'm glad I'm saved, and too bad you aren't and will be punished." Why do we communicate that repentance is almost a punishment instead of a way of being cleansed and refreshed before a holy God (Acts 3:19)?

The Spirit transforms them to be like Jesus

I recently heard the story of someone with a musical background who became a Christian. He had a heavy-metal haircut and dressed in black leather jackets and other clothing that fit with the genre of music he liked.

His style was part of what made him unique. He became a Christian and was fully accepted into the church and embraced as a new believer. But after about two or three months, the subtle hints began. "Maybe it's time you stopped wearing an earring." "Maybe you shouldn't wear clothing like that." "Maybe should cut your hair to be more normal." Little by little this person, not knowing any better, conformed to these comments and changed the way he looked.

This person eventually lost his uniqueness, which had nothing to do with being transformed inwardly as a disciple of Jesus and everything to do with conforming to what this particular church thought a Christian should look like and act like. It was clear that to be accepted in this church long-term meant fitting into the cultural vibe of the church. He was accepted as a convert but then had to quickly fit the cultural norm. I was told that he did change totally, and that as he did so, he also lost contact with his non-Christian friends, whom he fit in with in that musical subculture. Imagine being one of his friends, knowing he became a Christian and then seeing how he adopted the dress code of the church. They probably couldn't help but imagine that becoming a Christian means losing your uniqueness and conforming to a church subculture. Hopefully, they could see his life being transformed by the Spirit, but still it would be hard not to equate the church and Christianity with a fashion code to obey. I know not all churches would do this, but the question is, What code, spoken or unspoken, does your church have? Maybe it doesn't have anything to do with fashion, but what subtle standards, spoken and unspoken, does your church have that have nothing to do with Scripture?

As I listened to this story, my heart ached. It seems that in many of our churches, we get excited about someone coming to the faith, but then we subtly make it clear that for them to be fully accepted, they need to conform to our church's culture. I'm sensitive to this because I went through a similar experience, a story which I share in *I Like Jesus but Not the Church*. It's a weird, hard thing for a new believer when we set these extra standards of acceptance that have nothing to do with sin and everything to do with the church subculture. We should leave the job of transforming people to the Holy Spirit, even letting them keep their uniquenesses, and instead spend our time loving them and accepting them in our church community.

I believe that in God's timing, people will change as the Spirit changes them. The churches that I have seen that are well-populated by emerging generations are by no means holding back talking about sin. When the pastors and leaders teach, they say hard things, calling for repentance and calling out sin, but the context is love. When there are relationships and trust-building, emerging generations respond well to being told about sin and repentance. Jesus had lots to say about sin and was concerned about the hearts of people. In our church, we devote many of our worship gatherings to giving people time to pray and evaluate whether they are astray in any area of sin. So I don't advocate holding back when it comes to talking about sin with younger people in the church, but I am saying that we should do it at the right time with the right attitude. We should guard our hearts and lips against pouring out criticism and judgment, leaving the judging of those outside the church to God.

We need to focus more on what we stand for

With all the criticism against the church for being negative and judgmental, why not turn the whole thing around and put some effort into showing what we stand for? Jesus taught that we should be a people of salt and light. Salt is a flavor that causes someone to want even more of it. Light is a guide and a source of warmth that people are drawn toward. What's interesting is that churches attended by emerging generations usually have a strong emphasis on bringing the love of Jesus to others. You see many emerging churches concerned not only with local and global social justice but also with taking action. This is a really refreshing and positive thing that counters the negative.

I just visited the websites of several growing churches I know of which have emerging generations participating in them. I wasn't surprised by how easy it is to see that they are involved in compassion projects both locally and globally. One has a link called "Africa" right on their home page and shows how the church is involved with orphanages there. More than just a once-a-year summer missions trip, their involvement occupies several pages. Another website has several pages about their involvement with a recent hurricane disaster and how they helped on-site with construction projects. Another website prominently displays the church's involvement with deaf children in South America and helping out with children's ministry in refugee camps in Algeria. Another has a promotion for local involvement in teaching immigrant children English. Yet another church site features a written philosophy of being involved in racial reconciliation in their urban area.

You can easily see how these churches are taking stands on local and global action. They are becoming known for trying to make a difference in others' lives. I can say that many emerging churches are also taking action in local service projects. I know a church that volunteers to help clean their city streets and parks. Another church repainted graffiti walls in their town with no charge to the city. I know a church with a half-time paid staff person dedicated to organizing local churches to together be an agent of change and light in their community wherever it is needed. They organize all types of community-service and compassion projects. In these churches you will find people from emerging generations who are seeing that Christians are not just critical and negative but are taking action to help the community and the world.

Those who like Jesus but not the church think of Jesus as one who stood up for the poor and oppressed. They have tremendous respect for him because of that. Our churches need to stand up for the poor and oppressed too, because we have a biblical mandate from Jesus to bring justice to those who are experiencing oppression. But we will also earn the respect of those outside the church for doing so. Today, one of the first questions many people new to our church ask isn't what denomination we belong to. Instead it's, What are we doing for the poor? What are we doing in response to the AIDS epidemic? How are these things part of the life of our church and not just something we do once a year? Those who like Jesus but not the church are watching to see if we are taking the poor and oppressed as seriously as Jesus did.

> TODAY, ONE OF THE FIRST QUESTIONS MANY PEOPLE NEW TO OUR CHURCH ASK ISN'T WHAT DENOMINATION WE BELONG TO. INSTEAD IT'S, WHAT ARE WE DOING FOR THE POOR? WHAT ARE WE DOING IN RESPONSE TO THE AIDS EPIDEMIC?

We can teach our churches to be salt and light

We can use preaching to foster a culture of being salt and light in daily life. We can teach people in our churches that their attitudes impact those outside of the church, and show them what it looks like to live their lives as ambassadors for Jesus (2 Cor. 5:20). We can teach people the importance of breaking out of the Christian subculture so that we can regain our reputation as a people of goodness and love rather than of critical bitterness. Unless we are creating cultures in our church in which people see themselves as missional in their day-to-day worlds, unless we challenge Christians to break out of the Christian bubble, only the loudest, often-negative voices will be heard. We can move from being perceived as judgmental and negative to being seen as positive agents:

The church is judgmental and negative →

The church is a positive agent of change, loving others as Jesus would

Though I stress that the church should be a positive agent of change, I know that it's the Spirit of God in the church who does the changing. I also fully recognize that loving others as Jesus would may mean talking about sin, repentance, and judgment, so I'm not suggesting that we only "love" people. But love involves relationship. Love involves time. Love involves telling people about God's abundant goodness and his "awesome works" (Ps. 145:6–8), and not just about his wrath and judgment. Love involves holding our tongues and being wise in the way we act toward those outside the church, having our conversations be "full of grace" and "seasoned with salt" (Col. 4:5–6). Love is more than passing out a tract or holding up a sign and feeling that our job is done because we've let others know about Jesus.

We live in a time of great hope, as positive change is slowly taking place in many churches. More and more churches are taking seriously the global AIDS crisis and getting their churches involved. More and more churches are jumping in to help when disaster strikes. Perhaps one day when people think of Christians and the church, they will think about how we help the needy and compassionately get involved both locally and globally. Maybe they will think of us as gentle rather than abrasive, even with those we disagree with. Hopefully they won't be able to dismiss us as being cold, negative, and judgmental. But this transformation requires leadership to set the example. I believe the church will follow if leaders set the pace and foster a culture of being salt and light, of being loving instead of judgmental and negative. The more we focus on what we stand for instead of what we stand against, the more we will line up with Jesus and his teachings about the kingdom of God, and the more we will be seen as a people who believe in truth and love.

LOOKING AT YOUR CHURCH THROUGH THE EYES OF EMERGING GENERATIONS

1. If you were to look at the sermons of your church over a period of time, would you say they are more positive or negative in tone and content? If they are positive, how would you say sin and repentance are addressed so that you aren't going to the extreme of ignoring them?

2. What is your congregation's attitude toward those who hold beliefs different from yours on secondary doctrinal issues? How do you talk about other denominations?

3. How is your church known in your community? How do you think people in your town would describe your church and the people of your church? Do they even know you exist? What are you known for? Would your church be missed in your community if it went away? How would it be missed?

4. Are there any ways your church is involved in compassion and social justice projects both locally and globally, demonstrating that the church is a positive agent for change in the world? If not, what can you do about it?

5. If you were to ask those you associate with daily, both inside and outside your home, whether your talk is judgmental and negative or loving and positive, what would they say?

6. You may say that you are loving and accepting, but if someone came in to your church and began following Jesus, can you honestly say that that would be your foremost concern, not what they look like or how they dress or whether they drink or smoke or what language they use?

THE CHURCH IS DOMINATED BY MALES AND OPPRESSES FEMALES

7

> I feel the church is very sexist, yet I don't believe that Jesus was sexist. From what I have observed, women in the church basically sit on the sidelines and are only able to work with children, answer the phones, be secretaries, and serve the men. They seem to be given no voice. The church seems pretty much like a boys' club for adults.
>
> **— ALICIA**

A boys' club for adults." That's how Alicia describes the church, feeling that men dominate it and women are stifled and held back. Alicia isn't part of any church, yet even with her limited exposure to churches, this is what she has observed and felt about how the church views women. And even with her limited knowledge of Scripture, she senses that Jesus would want women to have more options than just becoming secretaries and children's workers in the church.

This is yet another major issue for emerging generations. How does the church treat women? Does it value and respect them? What roles can women have within the church? As people outside of the church look at us, many think of us as a boys' club, concluding that the church teaches that females are not as valued and respected as men are. This conclusion keeps many people away who might otherwise trust the church enough to enter into community with us.

WRITING THIS CHAPTER MAKES ME NERVOUS

I feel a nervous tension developing in my body even as I type this sentence. My neck is aching a little, and it rarely does that. I'm picturing church leaders who hold to a complementarian view (ministry roles differentiated by gender) of women in ministry. Most are wonderful godly people who use the Scriptures to back their viewpoint, and most highly respect women. Yet they hold that women should not be involved in most teaching ministries in a church nor serve as pastors or elders. At the same time, I'm picturing those who hold to an egalitarian view (equal ministry opportunity for both genders). Most egalitarians are also wonderful godly people who use the Scriptures to back their viewpoint, and most highly respect women. They hold that women can be involved in all of the teaching ministries within a church and serve as pastors and elders.

I've learned there is quite a difference of opinion on this theological issue. Because I get to speak at a lot of places around the country, many times I ask the church leaders attending, "Who in this room believes women should be elders and pastors?" and usually around half of them raise their hands. I then ask, "Who here thinks women shouldn't be elders and pastors?" Generally, the other half raise their hands, and usually there are a few no-votes who seem to be wondering what I'm asking this for. After everyone sees this split of opinion in the room, I then jokingly say, "One of you is wrong!" But then I say, "Look at each other. You all love God. You all desire to serve Jesus. You each study the Scriptures and pray about this issue and ask the Spirit to guide you. Yet you've come to different conclusions. Perhaps this isn't such a cut-and-dried issue as you think." Everyone usually laughs and smiles and agrees, but that doesn't always mean that they feel that generous outside of the room.

Writing this chapter makes me nervous because, sadly, I have witnessed and read some very heated arguments between church leaders and other people within the church concerning the role of women. I know that a diversity of people will be reading this book and that their theological presuppositions will probably determine how they read this chapter. I'm not going to try to resolve this issue by defending either the egalitarian or the complementarian viewpoint. I'm not going to try to convince you to change your viewpoint. However, I am going to ask you to take a fresh look at the attitude with which you communicate within your church whatever your viewpoint is.

I hope that the mission Jesus has sent us on to emerging generations will override divisive and critical attitudes toward those who hold different viewpoints. May our mission also override pride or any traditions that might prevent us from taking a good look at how we function and come across to people in our churches. So many see the church as a male-dominated place that oppresses females. I hope you will hear what they have to say in order to understand why they think that. Ask yourself, Is anything they're saying valid? Is there anything we can change in our churches without compromising our views so as not to be a stumbling block to individuals who are open to Jesus but not the church?

Egalitarians might wonder why they are reading this chapter, since they probably aren't getting much criticism from the emerging culture on this issue. Complementarians will find this chapter more challenging. But I don't believe that anything I suggest in this chapter compromises either viewpoint. Remember, the goal of this book is to examine how we come across to emerging generations. I'm not suggesting we need to change our particular viewpoint because of the emerging culture, but I am asking that we be sensitive to how we come across to our culture on this issue.

MY INITIAL OBSERVATION ABOUT WOMEN IN THE CHURCH

I grew up outside of the church, so I had no viewpoint on this issue. In fact, I didn't even know it was an issue. The one church I attended consistently for a year in England was a tiny church with a male pastor, but half of the attendees were women, and everyone seemed to jump in naturally to help do everything. So I didn't even think about the roles of men and women in the church. When I came back to America and started looking for a church, I visited several. That's when I noticed from an outside perspective that most churches seemed very male dominated. I remember the odd feeling I had when I attended one church and it struck me that there were no female ushers. Being accustomed to seeing both male and female ushers in theaters for movies and plays, I found this a little puzzling. Quite honestly, the all-male ushers in this one church looked and acted like intense Secret Service or CIA agents. They wore dark suits and ties and were even signaling each other across the room with hand signals. Then I noticed that the bulletin listed only men as the pastors and elders. I didn't even know what an elder was, but I couldn't help noticing that no women were listed. The same was true of the teachers of the adult Sunday school—only men.

During the worship gathering, most everything was handled by men. A man gave the announcements. A man led the singing. There were women in the choir, and there was a female backup singer, but they played supporting roles to the male leader. A man preached. Men took the offering and served the communion. There was a baptism, and sure enough, another man handled the baptism. I sat there reflecting on how I was just back from living in England, where Margaret Thatcher was the prime minister. She was conservative and female, but she had the huge responsibility of leading the whole country. People seemed to give her a lot of respect, and she gave speeches and reports that global leaders listened to. I had a female doctor and trusted her to teach me about my health. I had several professors at Colorado State University who were females and great teachers from whom I learned much. But I didn't see any female names in that church bulletin. I remember thinking it odd. Women could be recognized as wonderful teachers and leaders outside the church, but I didn't see them being recognized as such inside the church, unless it was with children or other women.

Remember, at this time I was not a churchgoer, and I noticed these things on the very first visit. People in emerging generations also notice whether we have women in leadership roles. Don't underestimate this. Our viewpoint of women in ministry may be so ingrained in our particular church culture that we forget to look at how it comes across to people outside the church and outside our understanding of what we believe and why.

LITTLE THINGS MAKE A BIG DIFFERENCE

Perhaps you're thinking that we don't need to care how people see us, because, after all, we only need to remain true to the Bible. It's true that we must be faithful to the Bible. But keep in mind that it's not just our practices that people object to but also our attitudes. Remember that I'm presenting reasons why emerging generations are avoiding most churches and what they observe about us. If we care about them, we must take their comments seriously.

Let's begin with some words from Erika:

The church has to understand the feelings of women, and not only what it feels like to be a female in the church but a female in the job marketplace, a female in politics, a female anywhere in a male–dominated society. I can't imagine that Jesus would not pay a lot of attention to this and make sure the church understands what females feel and respects and honors them.

ERIKA

These are wonderful words of wisdom. I believe Erika is dead-on when she says that Jesus would pay attention to how females feel both in the church and in society in general. Erika grew up in a church but left it in her teens because she felt it focused too much on negative things. She is an optimistic person, and she is studying landscape architecture, which is about making positive change in our environment, so I can see how she wouldn't fit in a church that focused on the don'ts and on how terrible the world is. Her experience growing up in a church impacted her so much that she has not felt the need to return. She may have given up on the church, but she has not given up on Jesus. In fact, she brought Jesus into our conversation quite often. She has a boyfriend, and she even expressed that she has no bent on women's rights or women's liberation. But when I asked her during our conversations why she isn't part of a church, the role of women surfaced strongly several times.

America was birthed primarily from a male–dominated European society. So the church naturally is rooted from there. However, in our society today, there are great steps being made of seeing females as more equal in the job market and other places. So I certainly would think that the church would be doing the same, but it doesn't seem to be. I have only seen and heard about churches shooting down women who both aspire in their faith and then desire to be in church leadership.

ERIKA

The issue, as Erika's comments illustrate, is a lot bigger than just women in the church; it's about women in society. Even though Erika hopes that the church will catch up with advances in society, please notice the heart of what she's saying. She's expressing sadness that if a woman grows in her faith and wants to help lead the church, she is shot down and restricted because she is a female. However, Erika made it clear that she doesn't have an agenda:

> *I am not a feminist or women's rights advocate! All I am saying is that the church better respect and treat females with equality and dignity for who they are, and allow them to contribute in major ways to the church. What a shame it is for churches to be shaped only by the men, when females have so incredibly much to offer.*
>
> ERIKA

What she's saying is important because I have heard many dismiss female opinions on this issue simply because the ones expressing the opinions are females. I heard one church leader dismiss a female's voice on this because she was just a "female libber, so of course she is going to complain about the role of women in the church." Exploring it further with Erika, I discovered that her views are also based on what she has sensed from talking to others who grew up in the church.

Listen to another opinion on this:

> *When I look around, I see only male priests and ministers. If you're a female, is your only choice to join the Catholic Church and become a nun?*
>
> GARY

Females may be more disturbed by this issue than males, but by no means are only females thinking this about the church. In almost every conversation I had in the interviews for this book, the topic eventually came up with both males and females. I witnessed the same feelings, the same impression that the church is male dominated and that females aren't given the same respect as males. The conversations raise some valid points. Alicia, whom I quoted at the start of this chapter, made this fascinating comment:

> *When I think of God, I think of God being both motherly and fatherly. Fathers seem more conditional with their love. Mothers are more caring and nurturing. I see Jesus very much like a mother, in terms of him caring for and nurturing and accepting people. But I don't see this in the church. It is*

mainly male leaders, so of course they will be more one-sided and have a male deity and ignore more of the motherly side of God and Jesus. ALICIA

I think we need to pay attention to her insight. We can say that God is Spirit (John 4:24), not a gender. We know that both male and female are created in the image of God and patterned after God (Gen. 1:27). Both man and woman are created in the image of God, not just one of them, showing that God has male and female characteristics. The Bible contains around 170 references to God as Father, so we know that God wanted us to view him as protector and provider and as having the characteristics of a good father. So we approach God and call him Father, since this is how even Jesus prayed and how Jesus spoke of God (Matt. 6:9). Jesus spoke of God as Father more than 150 times. In John 10:30, Jesus says, "I and the Father are one." So Jesus himself came in the form of a human male revealing God the Father.

I personally make it clear that the Bible teaches we are to see God as Father, and I am not moving away from that here. God wants us to address him and see him as Father. However, we can also see where God describes himself with female characterstics in metaphors and poetry. Isaiah 66:13 says, "As a mother comforts her child, so will I comfort you." In Isaiah 42:14, God says, "But now, like a woman in childbirth, I cry out, I gasp and pant." Jesus even uses the metaphor of a hen when he says in Matthew 23:37, "O Jerusalem, Jerusalem, you who kill the prophets and stone those sent to you, how often I have longed to gather your children together, as a hen gathers her chicks under her wings, but you were not willing." I mention these Scriptures to show that God himself used the beautiful characteristics of females to describe himself poetically. So we should ask ourselves, As a church, are we reflecting the wholeness of God and the fact that human beings, both males and females, are created in God's image?

I MENTION THESE SCRIPTURES TO SHOW THAT GOD HIMSELF USED THE BEAUTIFUL CHARACTERISTICS OF FEMALES TO DESCRIBE HIMSELF POETICALLY. SO WE SHOULD ASK OURSELVES, AS A CHURCH, ARE WE REFLECTING THE WHOLENESS OF GOD AND THE FACT THAT HUMAN BEINGS, BOTH MALES AND FEMALES, ARE CREATED IN GOD'S IMAGE?

THE CHURCH IS A BRIDE, NOT A BOYS' CLUB

It's ironic that the church is seen as a boys' club when Scripture calls the church the bride of Christ (Rev. 19:7). Of course, there are several other metaphors used for the church, including a body (1 Cor. 12:12–27; Col. 1:18), an army (2 Tim. 2:3–4; Eph. 6:10–17), and others. But since a boys' club isn't one of the metaphors for the church but a bride is, and since God created male and female in his image, doesn't this mean we need to have both male and female characteristics, opinions, and input reflected in our churches? We can certainly make sure there are both males and females represented to help shape what we do and who we are as a church. We need to be aware not only that the Bible shows the value of males and females but also that emerging generations are looking for the leadership of a church to show the value of both males and females.

I'm not saying you need to change your particular theology because of the culture. In fact, I know of emerging churches that hold a complementarian view and have hundreds, and in a few cases thousands, of younger people in them. I also know of emerging churches that hold an egalitarian view and have hundreds and even thousands of younger people in them. What do these churches have in common? No matter which theological view they hold, they all are sensitive in how they go about honoring, respecting, and empowering females within their view. They are sensitive to how they come across in their practices and attitudes.

Let me suggest a few ways that the church can be sensitive to how we come across to the emerging culture.

WHAT CAN WE LEARN FROM THIS MISPERCEPTION?

Many readers who are complementarians may find that some of these suggestions go against their nature, church culture, and traditions. But instead of dismissing what's said here, please be open to honest self-evaluation. As you read these suggestions, evaluate your emotional response by asking whether your reaction is shaped by your feelings and church subculture or on a thoughtful study of Scripture. I am convinced that those who hold a complementarian view can still go far beyond what most churches do and still not go against their theological beliefs on this.

We need to have a balance of males and females

For those in churches that already have females in leadership positions, most of the suggestions in this chapter don't apply to you. However, if your primary leaders, pastors, or elders are female, I would encourage you to make sure that you reflect balance in your leadership. If your primary leaders and pastors are females, do you balance them with male representatives? And of course, if your primary leaders are males, do you balance them with females?

Also, it's important that complementarians be respectful of egalitarians, and egalitarians be respectful of complementarians. People will quickly pick up on our attitudes toward those in other churches or denominations, so we really need to demonstrate grace and respect for one another.

We need to have a well-thought-out understanding of the Bible

A major reason why people feel the church is dominated by males and oppresses females is because of the way we explain our view of women in the church. I am saddened and often dismayed by the way many churches explain the role of women in the church. I'm talking primarily about the complementarian side here, because they are the ones who are limiting the roles women can play. Don't we need to be able to explain the reasons for our restrictions? Since this is such a divisive and sensitive issue, we should be able to clearly and intelligently articulate our position. However, in my experience, the answers church leaders and the people of the church usually give when they say that women shouldn't teach or be pastors are based more on church subculture than on Scripture. And when they do use Scripture, they generally just shoot off verses taken out of context. Not being able to give clear, intelligent, and compassionate reasons is detrimental to emerging generations. We owe it to them to be able to explain what we believe. Some of the Scripture passages about women and the church, at first glance, seem rather bizarre, so it helps if we put ourselves in the place of those outside of the church to see how these passages come across to them.

Imagine you're an intelligent, twenty-seven-year-old, female college graduate trained as a pharmacist, lawyer, or high-school English teacher.

You're well rounded, a reader, and culturally savvy. Say you've become interested in Christian spirituality and pick up a Bible only to be confronted with verses like these:

> Women should remain silent in the churches. They are not allowed to speak, but must be in submission, as the Law says. If they want to inquire about something, they should ask their own husbands at home; for it is disgraceful for a woman to speak in the church.
>
> —1 Corinthians 14:34–35

> A woman should learn in quietness and full submission. I do not permit a woman to teach or to have authority over a man; she must be silent. For Adam was formed first, then Eve. And Adam was not the one deceived; it was the woman who was deceived and became a sinner. But women will be saved through childbearing—if they continue in faith, love and holiness with propriety.
>
> —1 Timothy 2:11–15

Imagine thinking, What the heck is this? Women must be silent? Women can't teach a man? Women will be saved through childbearing? Is this a joke? Do Christians really believe this?

MOST CHRISTIANS ARE NOT PREPARED TO ANSWER THESE QUESTIONS

I have talked to enough people and church leaders to know that most of us are not really prepared to give good explanations of these passages. We may quote these verses and give weak explanations using Christian cliches, but are we really ready to go into the cultural context of these passages? Are we ready to make some sense of what seems ridiculous at first glance? And we wonder why emerging generations so often see us as fundamentalist, backward, oppressive, narrow-minded, cultic fanatics from another era. Regardless of our viewpoint, are we ready to talk intelligently about these Bible verses?

I know I wasn't. I was serving on the staff of a conservative Bible church which held a complementarian view in a pretty healthy and balanced manner. They allowed females to teach classes "under the authority" of the male elders, and females held high leadership roles. I used to teach part of the membership class and would always have a Q and A time. Not once in the dozen or more times I helped teach the class did anyone ask about the issue of women in the church. For the most part, those who attended the membership class were baby boomers or older and had transferred from other conservative churches, and probably they assumed that only men were the pastors and elders, since that is what they grew up being taught in their previous churches. They probably never really questioned it since that is what they were used to.

But then I started up a young-adult ministry that God used to bring many young adults into the life of the church. Many were in the eighteen- to thirty-year-old range and either had no church background or had dropped out of the church and were now returning. We decided to hold a separate membership class for them. Though I was to teach the same thing I did in the membership class for the older segment of the church, I wasn't prepared at all for the challenges I would face.

When we got to the Q and A time with the young adults, one of the first questions almost every single time was, Why aren't there female pastors or elders? It surprised me, but as I continued in ministry with emerging generations, I discovered this is a huge issue for them. At first, in response to their question, I would open to the place in the membership manual that listed our position and read it out loud. But reading it to them was incredibly awkward. The wording in the statement assumed you already believed that viewpoint. The wording didn't take into consideration someone to whom this was all new, nor did it have the scriptural verses written out. It just gave the book, chapter, and verse in parentheses after each statement. So it came across pretty much like, "This is the way it is. Take it or leave it, and don't question it."

When someone asked what these verses say, I cringed inwardly, knowing what I was about to read to this group. We opened up the Bible and read the verses out loud. Can you imagine what it was like sitting in a room with a dozen or so young adults, half of them female, and reading out loud entirely out of context: "It is disgraceful for a woman to speak in the church" and "A woman must be silent" and the other verses that were listed? It was pretty horrible, and I was actually quite embarrassed, not by the Scriptures themselves but by the fact that I couldn't explain them. Remember, this group wasn't trying to challenge me on this issue; they wanted to join the church! They trusted me as the pastor they had become familiar with and were there to place their membership in the church. They were just sincerely asking questions because the issue was important to them. I gave them the best explanation I could, but I really was not ready at the time. I had to apologize to them for not being able to go into it to the degree they needed.

This experience forced me to revisit theologically what I had been rather quickly taught in seminary. I also met a female pastor around this time who was an excellent teacher and who caused in me the desire to restudy this. The church I was in at that time was complimentarian, as were the people in my church circles, so I wasn't challenged to look at other views, since everyone believed the same. Also, as I moved to be serving and leading young adults, I could no longer just read the positional statement on women and see heads nodding in approval. These thinking, questioning, intelligent young adults were looking for more than the simple statement with a few short verses that, quite honestly, only raised more questions and concern. So I started over, approaching the issue like I was back in seminary, but this time looking at the history of the church and studying the different viewpoints. I was actually quite surprised to see really good arguments on either side of this issue. I had never encountered the arguments about women from the other point of view. In my formative years of studying theology, I was taught really only one viewpoint. So it was invigorating and challenging to study the different perspectives in-depth.

But from all of this, I learned a hard lesson. I could no longer avoid really studying this issue in-depth. I needed to be able to look at this subject from a different perspective. With emerging generations, we need to be much more understanding of the Scriptures and the context in which they were written. We cannot get away with avoiding the hard questions about this issue. We need to be much more open and honest and help people make some sense of the crazy sounding things the apostle Paul said about women. (You may be offended that I say "crazy sounding," but on the face of it, reading that women can't teach, must be silent, and are saved through childbearing sounds crazy to people today.)

So let me raise this question: Are you as a church leader really prepared to give in-depth answers to people's questions about women in the church? And if so, what is your attitude as you explain your position? Do you recognize that this is not a cut-and-dried, black-and-white issue you can address with canned answers? These tough passages should make our hearts a bit more humble and sympathetic. I believe that people will respect our stance, whatever it is, as long as we explain it with humility and respect for those who differ from us. Whatever our view, it should be plain that we honor females and empower them to serve and be in leadership to the highest capacity we believe Scripture allows, so that our churches reflect a healthy balance of male and female characteristics and don't erect artificial barriers that repel emerging generations.

We need to teach the people of our churches our position

Because many in our emerging culture don't go to a church, they don't really build friendships with pastors and church leaders. But they do meet other Christians. So not only is it important that church leaders be able to give clear explanations of our position; it's even more important that the average Christian be able to explain these passages too.

Recently I talked with someone who is part of a church who told me that he doesn't like women preaching or leading in the church. I asked him why, and he said (I'm not kidding) having women leaders makes men become more feminine. This is a college-educated person who works in the computer industry. I couldn't believe what I was hearing. I asked him if he knows anyone who has become feminine as a result of a female teaching. He said no, because he doesn't go to churches that allow females to preach. He went on to say that the Bible says that women should not teach men. I asked him where, specifically. He didn't know for sure, but he started quoting parts of the usual verses. I responded that if those passages are applicable to today's culture, then why doesn't his wife wear a head covering? If she should remain silent, then why does she talk in church? I asked him if his wife ever shared what she learned and spoke up in their home Bible study, and he said she does. I then asked why he is okay with a woman sharing from the Scriptures what she learned in a home Bible study to a mixed group but he's not okay with a woman speaking from the pulpit in the weekend church gathering. He said that's because home meetings really aren't church, so it's okay. I then told him that his home Bible study probably was a lot more like the early New Testament church, which met in homes, than what we do in most weekend worship services today. He said he hadn't thought about that. We talked about his concept of the pulpit as the official place of teaching, but I explained that there were no pulpits in the early church, since they met in homes.

Now, I understand that in post–New Testament times and throughout church history formal statements were made to define a "church meeting," and some people might not think that teaching or sharing in a home meeting is the same as a formal Sunday gathering, but that wasn't the issue. The issue was his dogmatic conclusion that women can't teach men the Bible in any scenario.

I have no doubt that this man has a good heart. We talked for a while, and I raised this question: Imagine giving a Bible and the same commentaries and word study tools to a Christian male and a Christian female. They are both prayerful and go off to study the same passage for eight hours. After diligent study, they arrive at the same conclusions of what the biblical text is saying. They each write out exactly the same outline and content for a sermon. Why can the male get up in front of a mixed audience and teach what he just studied, but the female, though she has come to the same conclusions and prepared the same content, cannot teach it to a mixed audience? Why must she teach only females? I shared with him that I would want to learn from anyone, male or female, who studies the Bible and gains insight. But he disagreed and restated that "the Bible says a woman should not teach and have authority over a man." He was unable to answer my question in any way other than to repeat that one Bible verse again and again, and he wasn't able to explain the other passages either.

It was an interesting and difficult discussion, and nothing I said changed his mind. At one point, he even said, "My mind is made up on this issue." It saddened me to hear that because it meant he wasn't willing to keep learning about this issue, yet from our discussions, I could tell he hadn't studied it in-depth. Nevertheless, he had come to a passionately held conclusion. After we talked, I kept thinking of all the people outside the church that he might share his viewpoint with and the impressions they must get. He is a good person who loves God, but in my discussion with him, he had an extremely strong opinion but wasn't prepared to defend it adequately.

On this issue, it is critical that we have a solid understanding of what we believe, whatever our view is. But it doesn't end with church leaders. We need to train people in our churches to understand the cultural context of the New Testament so they don't just spout Bible verses out of context and reinforce to emerging generations that the church is dominated by men and oppresses women. How well do you feel the members of your church understand your church's viewpoint? Would they embarrass you with the answers they'd give to questions about that view and by the way they come across to others? Would they perpetuate the perception that the church is dominated by males and oppresses females?

Before I continue, let me stress this to those who hold an egalitarian viewpoint as well. Are you ready to explain the key passages that say that a women should be silent and not have authority over a man? I recently asked a female elder in an egalitarian church how she would explain those passages. Her answer was, "I don't really know, but I do believe and feel strongly that females should be pastors and elders." That's just as bad as the other way! If you hold a viewpoint, you should be able to explain from the Scriptures why you hold it. No matter what view you have, it has to be more than just the feeling that things should be a certain way. We need to carefully study and explain our viewpoint from the Scriptures.

We need to stop thinking in stereotypes

I learned a hard lesson once. We were in a teaching series on relationships and marriage, and I scheduled a speaker who was known for his expertise on these subjects to speak at our worship gathering. I thought this speaker's wisdom would add a lot to the series. However, it all pretty much backfired on me. He taught from the Bible some really good things about relationships and marriage, but what got us into trouble were his attempts at humor using stereotypes, such as, "All women love shopping, so the men better guard the credit cards," and, "All the guys will be watching football on Sunday, so the wives will need to bring them their iced teas." He was joking and exaggerating, but he ended up insulting and hurting the women there. I was sitting in the back, painfully watching as some people got up and left. I spent the second half of our worship gathering out in the hallway trying to calm people down a bit and explaining to new people that this was a guest speaker. Again, what is interesting is that this humor, which is fairly commonly used by church leaders, goes over great with older crowds, who laugh and enjoy poking fun with stereotypes, but it backfires among emerging generations, who don't all appreciate it. It goes against the values of many in our emerging culture.

> WHAT IS INTERESTING IS THAT THIS HUMOR, WHICH IS FAIRLY COMMONLY USED BY CHURCH LEADERS, GOES OVER GREAT WITH OLDER CROWDS, WHO LAUGH AND ENJOY POKING FUN WITH STEREOTYPES, BUT IT BACKFIRES AMONG EMERGING GENERATIONS, WHO DON'T ALL APPRECIATE IT. IT GOES AGAINST THE VALUES OF MANY IN OUR EMERGING CULTURE.

I was once in a pastors' meeting in which we were discussing how staff decisions are made. I suggested to one pastor that he bring his administrative assistant into the decision-making process, and his response was, "Why would I do that? She's just a secretary." It felt to me that he was not only saying that her role as a secretary was fairly insignificant in terms of giving valid input but also that he was implying, "She's just a female, so she should just focus on secretarial things and leave the decisions to the men who lead the church." Even using the term secretary can be negative, since most secretarial roles go beyond just sitting behind a desk and typing. But beyond that is the ingrained stereotype that women in the church are not included in decision-making or providing input on the direction of a church. Not asking for female input means that we don't think their input is valuable, or we surely would be asking them. To me, it's a strange thing that we don't feel desperately in need of female as well as male input in our churches.

Recently I asked one of the female leaders in our church to give a devotional message in preparation for the communion time. During the worship gathering, I was hanging out in the back of the room and noticed a couple in their late thirties leaving, so I approached them and said, "Hi! Thanks for being here!" They stopped in their tracks, looked at me, and said intensely, "We are offended you have a female speaking. We thought this was an evangelical church and expected a feeding from the Word of God from a male pastor." I was caught off-guard by their somewhat hostile response to my friendly hello. I asked them sheepishly, "Are you from around here?" They said, "No. We are vacationing from back east. I'm a pastor and wanted to visit your church. But I am shocked that you allow a female to speak." I stood there, unable to believe what I was hearing and the attitude behind it, especially from a pastor. I looked at his wife, who silently nodded with a "tsk, tsk" expression on her face.

I know that these are extreme examples (I hope!), but nevertheless, these attitudes do exist and are picked up by those outside the church. It's sad that we, too, get stereotyped, but so often examples like these lead to the stereotype that the church is dominated by males and oppresses females.

We need to include females in visible roles

I feel silly saying this, knowing that so many reading this book have female pastors and elders in their churches or are female pastors themselves. But this is for those who don't have females serving in any major roles. There are a number of questions I would like you to consider. Even if we hold to the view that women should not be pastors or elders, is there any reason why we can't have females reading the Scriptures from up front? Is there any reason we can't have females giving announcements? Are there reasons we can't have females leading the church in prayer or reading responsive readings? You probably have females singing in the choir, singing solos, or singing as backup singers for the male-led worship band. But the reality is that when they are singing, they certainly are leading others and exhorting and challenging people with the lyrics they sing. Perhaps you could have them in other roles up front while not compromising your theological view.

If I were to visit your church, would I see female as well as male ushers? Would I sense that this church has a healthy balance of females and males in visible roles? If someone like Joni Eareckson Tada or Billy Graham's daughter, Anne Graham Lotz, were available, would you have them speak in your church? If so, why can't other females speak on occasion (besides just Mother's Day)? It seems that the primary place for females on stage in complementarian churches is usually as backup singers. It's also interesting to note that the females we put in these backup positions usually look like they've just stepped out of a glamour magazine, furthering the whole stereotype. It may be that we don't do this intentionally, but I have been in enough churches to notice a pattern, and though I'm not sure what it means, it's something we need to ponder.

Again, I apologize to the egalitarians for these questions; I know they are irrelevant to you. And again, if you are a complementarian, I'm not saying you need to change your view so that emerging generations will be part of your church. I just want you to examine whether there are ways you can avoid reinforcing the view that the church is dominated by males and oppresses females.

We need to include females in high levels of leadership and decision-making

If your church has only male elders and pastors, there's still the question of whether females have a voice in your church. I believe that emerging generations won't have as big of an issue with all male elders and pastors if we show that we also include females in high levels of leadership and in the decision-making process for the church. In fact, I know this is possible, since I know of complementarian churches with hundreds of younger people in them. And from what I know of them, they empower females and give them prominent roles in the church.

I know of a church that has all male elders yet also includes females in their meetings so they can provide balance in the decision-making process. I know of another church that has only male elders but has females teaching classes "under the authority" of the elders. I know of a church whose elders and pastors are all male but makes sure there is a female in their highest level of pastoral staff meetings. She isn't titled a pastor, but she is in the highest level meetings. There are all types of ways even a complementarian church can make sure there are females contributing to the church. Giving females a voice not only brings beauty and strength and health to your church but also sends major signals that your church is not just a boys' club.

I go into this more in the book *I Like Jesus but Not the Church*, but we can't just be saying there shouldn't be females in leadership because the twelve disciples were all males. The problem with using that argument is that you could also say they were all Jewish, so we shouldn't have non-Jews in leadership today. We also see that females were included in leadership roles. We have to be thinking through this issue deeper today, and no matter what viewpoint we hold, truly have thoughtful answers.

EMERGING GENERATIONS WANT MEN TO BE MEN AND WOMEN TO BE WOMEN

Well! I'm done with this chapter, and I hope my neck tension will now ease. I pray I achieved the delicate balance of speaking to both egalitarian and complementarian churches. It really isn't easy to do so, yet this is too important not to probe and challenge some practices in our churches.

As I wrap this chapter up, even though I may be exploring equality in some roles in the church, I can confidently say that people in emerging generations understand and appreciate that men and women are created differently. Over and over I have heard them acknowledge that God created men and women to be different and unique and that this is a beautiful thing. I talked just recently with a woman who shared she feels men should be the balance to women because of the way we each are designed. I believe that people desire to see men and women complement one another and partner on the mission of serving Jesus. I have had many conversations with females about this issue, and in my experience, I have yet to hear any female making this a feminist issue. Rather, it's about seeing females respected and empowered and put in leadership positions where they have a voice in the direction of the church. It's about not thwarting or stifling the incredible gifts that God gave both males and females. We can move from the perception that the church oppresses females to a better perception:

The church is dominated by males and oppresses females

→

The church holds women in the highest respect and includes them in the leadership of the church

No matter what theological position you hold to, our church communities must have a healthy balance of men and women serving Jesus, using their gifts, and having a voice in the church. The lack of this balance is not healthy and is noticed by those who like Jesus but not the church. Our attitudes and the attitudes of those in our churches ring loud in our communities. I hope and pray that we take this seriously, for the sake of having healthy churches and of making Jesus known in our emerging culture, and for the sake of females, who are created in God's image and have so incredibly much to offer the church.

LOOKING AT YOUR CHURCH THROUGH THE EYES OF EMERGING GENERATIONS

1. Read the following passages aloud and then discuss how you would explain them. As you read, imagine you're reading them to a twenty-five-year-old female. Imagine looking her in the eye as you read them.

   • 1 Timothy 2:1–15
   • 1 Corinthians 14:34–35

   Whether you are a complementarian or an egalitarian, are you as a church leader *really* prepared to adequately explain such passages? (Also, see the books recommended in appendix 3.)

2. How well is your church trained to explain these passages and your church's position on this issue? Are you confident that those in your church would represent your viewpoint with grace, compassion, and intelligence?

3. How many females would visitors to your church see on the platform during a worship gathering (besides backup singers)? How many ushers, greeters, and those serving in the adult ministries are females?

4. How many females would visitors see listed in your bulletin in major leadership roles? How would visitors know that your church respects females and gives them a voice in the life of your church?

5. Give examples of ways that females participate in major decisions in your church.

6. How many female teachers do you have? How many times (other than Mother's Day) do you have a female speak at your church?

7. If you are complementarian, are you ready to explain why you allow females to teach both male and female children, but not both male and female adults?

THE CHURCH IS HOMOPHOBIC

Why don't Christians try to make me feel included?
Why do you treat me like an outcast and not care
about my feelings or want to relate to me in any way?
You don't need to understand why I'm homosexual—
but to understand me as a person and a fellow human
being. Isn't that what Jesus would do? My homosexuality
should have no more relevance on how you interact with
me than hair color has on how you would interact with
someone who is blonde or brunette.

—PENNY

Without a doubt, people in our culture today perceive the evangelical church as homophobic and sexually repressive. I will focus on the homosexual issue, since that came up more in my conversations with the people I interviewed for this book. You have to understand that this criticism comes not only from the gay community. I have talked with both straight and gay people for whom this is a huge negative perception of Christians and the church. Many feel not only that the church is homophobic but that Christians often see homosexuals as enemies. This should be of equal concern to those of us who are respectful of Jesus and don't want to be incorrectly stereotyped as people who are homophobic and angry at the gay community.

Grappling with this is important because homosexuality is increasingly becoming a normal part of our emerging culture. With the increasing openness people have about their sexuality, almost everyone today has a gay friend, family member, workmate, or acquaintance. It's not uncommon to see gay dating featured regularly on television dating shows. Most television sitcoms have a gay character, and famous musicians, actors, and actresses who are homosexuals are much more open about their orientation. I recently visited a high-school classroom that had multiple signs proclaiming it as a "Homophobia-Free Zone." We need to understand, if we haven't yet, to what degree our emerging culture is aware of homosexuality and has come to accept it. I also hope we will understand how important it is for church leaders to be thinking clearly about this issue and responding with extreme grace and compassion and wisdom.

A DIFFICULT THING TO TALK ABOUT AND FULLY UNDERSTAND

Because this is such a huge issue in our culture, and because all of the tension and discussion on this issue is over what the Bible says about it, we can no longer just regurgitate what we have been taught about homosexuality. I think in the past, the teaching on homosexuality in many churches has been somewhat shallow, quoting a few verses and no questions or discussion allowed. We cannot do that any longer, out of respect for those we teach. We must approach the Bible with humility, prayer, and sensitivity, taking into consideration the original meaning of Greek and Hebrew words and looking into the historical contexts in which passages were written. When we do, we might be surprised to find that we can no longer with integrity merely quote a few isolated verses and say "case closed" with the sometimes heartless and naive confidence we used to.

I will talk later in this chapter about the various Scriptures used to form conclusions about homosexuality, but first I want to clarify where I stand. I need to do that up front so you know where I'm coming from. I have read just about every single book there is out there on this topic, written from *both* the conservative and pro-gay theological perspectives, and I have read the various studies and opinions on each of the Scriptures that mention homosexuality or that have been seen as addressing homosexuality. I have wrestled with the Scriptures and difficult viewpoints. I studied this issue not being afraid to reexamine all I had ever been taught before and to approach it with an open mind and heart. However, after much prayer and study of the sexual ethics and themes presented overall in Scripture, I have found that I just can't dismiss that in the Bible homosexual practice is considered a sin. Note that I am saying homosexual practice, not homosexual orientation, which I will address later. Likely some readers of this book will disagree with me on this. There are probably homosexual Christians reading this book who will disagree with me too. I recognize that by stating my position, I seem to be drawing ugly lines in the Christian world when I wish there didn't have to be an "us versus them" over this issue. But I hope you sense my heart in this chapter, and I hope that I demonstrate compassion and understanding to those who hold a different viewpoint than I do. If you knew me, you would know that I'm only trying my best to base my position on the Scriptures. It's from my best understanding of the Scriptures that I take the position that I do. So I don't take this issue lightly or without compassion for those who may be hurt by hearing my position.

Quite honestly, and some people might get mad at me for saying this, I sometimes wish this weren't a sin issue, because I have met gay people who are the most kind, loving, solid, and supportive people I have ever met. As I talk to them and hear their stories and get to know them, I come to understand that their sexual orientation isn't something they can just turn off. Homosexual attraction is not something people simply choose to have, as is quite often erroneously taught from many pulpits. That's what makes facing this issue all the harder.

But even so, what I hope to get across in this chapter is that it matters how we treat *fellow* sinners. We all are sinners (Rom. 3:23), but the church has subtly, and sometimes not too subtly, treated some sins differently from others. I will try to show why this is an especially big issue for people, both straight and gay, in emerging generations. How the church handles this issue is critical not only for those who like Jesus but not the church but also for the future of the church.

MEETING TWO FRIENDS WHO HAVE BEEN WOUNDED BY THE CHURCH

In this chapter you will hear from both Penny and Karen. Penny is a lesbian, and Karen was involved in lesbian relationships for several years but is now celibate and actively involved in the church. Let me introduce you to Penny first.

Unloving words from churchgoing Christians

I connected instantly with Penny, possibly because we share an appreciation for the singer Morrissey and his former band, the Smiths. But

Penny also makes people feel at ease and has a wonderful quirky sense of humor. She works at a local newspaper as an advertising director. We would meet weekly to do the formal interviews for this book, though most times we would end up talking about other things for two hours and then have to rush to talk about what she would be sharing in this book. I have grown to respect her tremendously. One time she came to our house for dinner right after she got back from a vacation where she spent a night in Quebec in a hotel made of ice, and then went dogsledding. She is an extremely fun person to spend time with.

Penny was born and raised in England, where she went to an Anglican church during her childhood. She says it was a neutral experience, and she stopped going when she was about thirteen years old. She has always respected and admired the wisdom of Jesus. I shared her comments about Jesus in chapter 4, but it's worth hearing them again here:

> I hold Jesus to be a wise man. Jesus was inspirational and pure. He was a wonderful man with great lessons to teach about love, acceptance, and peace.
>
> Jesus was someone who lived out his message and wasn't a hypocrite like many modern religious leaders. Jesus stood out among the others of his time.
>
> I believe 100 percent that Jesus walked the earth, and that because of his teaching, he sent a lot of people's gray matter spinning.
>
> PENNY

As I spoke with her on many occasions, it was obvious that she is open to Jesus and his teachings, respecting him as an honorable and wise historical figure. She shared passionately how she feels he is unique, full of wisdom, compassion, and love. She showed no hesitation whatsoever talking about Jesus in our conversations.

As Penny reached her later teenage years, she began exploring her homosexuality. She wasn't ready to come out in the open about it, but she was recognizing that this is who she is. As she raised questions and searched for answers, her orientation became the reason she didn't go back to the church she grew up in.

When I first started coming out of the closet, I knew that the church wouldn't approve. It was very, very clear that the church was against homosexuality. How could you not know that? It seems that homosexuality is one of the main things churches consistently and publicly condemn. So picture being gay and wanting to seek counsel or spiritual advice. Why would I go to a church? They already have thrown heaps of guilt on me and condemned me before I've even stepped my foot in the door. PENNY

During this time in her life, Penny wanted to find some "inspirational words of wisdom," as she put it, to the questions she was having about life. But she knew enough of what Christians and the church think of gays that there was no reason to go to a church for spiritual advice. She felt she would be instantly condemned. So instead of turning to the Christian church, she ended up exploring some Eastern religions, though not in great depth.

When Penny was twenty-two, she came to the United States to work on a ranch for a summer. The ranch was run by Christians and had many Christians on the summer staff. While Penny worked there, she didn't tell anyone that she was homosexual. Ironically, it was here, among Christians, where she first began to feel wounded by people about homosexuality. The staff would tell jokes about gay people and express what they thought of them. At the end of her time on the ranch, Penny decided to take a trip to San Francisco. One professing Christian commented, "So you're going to the Gay Bay where the faggots all go to rot." Remember, no one was aware that she was gay, so she heard how these Christians really spoke during their day-to-day lives and what they really thought of homosexuals. She said she had never heard such venomous words and experienced such a sense of persecution for being a homosexual as she did among this group of churchgoing Christians.

Penny ended up moving to Santa Cruz, where she now lives and where she once again encountered Christians. She volunteered at the gay center in town, helping troubled teens on a phone hotline. On more than one occasion, she would come out to her car in the parking lot of the gay center and find Christian tracts on the windshield. Some of them had sayings on them such as, "Homosexuality Is the Social Cancer of Today—Repent or Go to Hell." She would read them and see bits of Bible verses quoted, condemning her. She remembered thinking that here she was volunteering her time to help out troubled teenagers, and she comes out only to be condemned by tracts from Christians. They didn't even have the courage to talk to her; they just secretly left tracts on her car.

> When I was volunteering at the gay center, I would be on the phone talking to teenagers in trouble and feeling I was making a positive difference in the world. But then I'd go out to my car and find tracts which would utterly condemn me left by Christians on my car windshield. I'd look at these heartless words with little pieces of Bible verses quoted out of context and wonder, Why do they hate me so much? Why don't they even have the decency to come in and talk to me rather than leave anger and hate on my windshield and run?
>
> PENNY

I have learned from our times together that Penny is really mature and puts things in perspective. She is savvy enough to know that her experiences with Christians are not the way of Jesus:

> I know enough of Jesus to make a clear separation from the hateful, spiteful, unjust things Christians have said or done to me because I am homosexual. I know this hatred is not a Jesus thing; it is a "man" thing.
>
> PENNY

It was quite difficult for me to hear her stories. I empathized with her tremendously. I cannot imagine what it must be like being wounded this way by my supposed brothers and sisters in Christ. I felt angry, as well as embarrassed, as she told me her experiences. Although this is one person's story, incidents like these are a lot more common than we think.

Growing up gay in the church

Karen is a thirty-one-year-old who grew up in a Baptist church in which she was actively involved along with her family. She was even a student leader in her youth group. During her teenage years, she began to struggle with same-sex attractions, but she did not feel free to talk to someone in her church about her feelings. In fact, her church environment made it all the more difficult for her:

> *Growing up in a fundamentalist church, I was taught that gay people are immoral unbelievers with a sinister agenda. I too picked up on the rhetoric and condemned this faceless group of homosexuals without any true understanding of what the issues were. It took a long time for me to come out of denial regarding my same-sex attractions because I could not relate myself to the gay caricature that the church had created. I was the "good Christian girl" who was heavily involved in church youth leadership, wanted to be a missionary, and attended Bible college. How could I be gay? I couldn't relate the sexual attractions I was experiencing with the church's lurid picture of homosexuals.* KAREN

I'm not sure if we in church leadership realize, in spite of our good intentions, how we portray the gay community and homosexuality to our churches. If someone in our church is struggling with same-sex attraction, what do we make it like for them? What comments and attitudes do we express in sermons? What do the members of our churches say in their conversations about homosexuals? Do we create an environment that makes those who are struggling with their sexual orientation feel comfortable talking about what they are going through? Let's hear from Karen what it was like for her:

> *If the church had simply viewed homosexuality as one of the many natural sins that some people are drawn to as a result of living in a fallen world and talked openly about various sexual temptations, I would have been able to process it like any other temptation that all Christians face. But by stigmatizing homosexuality, the church has contributed to the problem and this continues to persist in the jokes and negative comments that Christians make about gay people. Just recently I heard a pastor make a subtle joke about homosexuality, not realizing my background. Again, he assumed that I or anyone else in the church (certainly not a good church leader type like myself) could have same-sex attractions.* KAREN

Karen shares how even little jokes and comments show our biases and prejudices. The problem is not only that we have judgmental attitudes and prejudices but also that those attitudes and prejudices influence our churches. We as church leaders set the example and create the culture for our churches. The people in our churches then express the same attitudes toward homosexuals in their neighborhoods, workplaces, and schools. No wonder there aren't too many homosexuals who feel free to talk to church leaders about their feelings and struggles. Imagine how incredibly difficult it would be for a person with same-sex attractions to feel that it's safe to be open with someone if the church makes jokes about them, condemns them, and even, as Karen heard, claims that they have a sinister agenda. No wonder so many people in emerging generations see the church as homophobic and unloving.

Two different newspapers in our community ran cartoons portraying the impression that people have of the church. One shows Jesus standing outside a church while the people file out after a service. Jesus says to a couple walking past him, "Love thy neighbor." The man says, "Hippie freak," and the woman says, "That sounds like something a queer would

Art by Steven DeCinzo—Used with permission

say." The church sign gives the title of the sermon as "Power of Love," and in smaller print says, "All welcome … except gays!" The cartoon makes the statement that the church is hypocritical because we say we are all about love, yet we limit our love only to straight people. It's interesting how the artist's depiction of Jesus in this cartoon echoes the title of this book. Jesus is the noticeably good guy standing outside the church speaking about love, but the people inside the church reject him, and we see a tear in his eye.

The other newspaper ran a cartoon alongside an editorial about how they perceive churches' view of homosexuals. The cartoon shows a man, which the editorial identifies as a pastor, running away, looking in horror over his shoulder into the sky. On four clouds, riding four horses, are "The Four Queers of the Apocalypse." This cartoon illustrates people's impression that church leaders are homophobic, running in terror as the homosexual population ushers in the end of the world.

Illustration by Charles Bernatowicz. Used with permission
of *Good Times* newspaper (www.gdtimes.com).

These cartoons ran in weekly entertainment newspapers that thousands of college students and people in our community read, once again reinforcing to both straight and gay people outside the church the idea that all Christians fear homosexuals and abandon them. Over and over people see images like these not just in newspaper cartoons but in real life. Seeing these cartoon depictions makes me want to get angry at the way we in the church are portrayed. Most churches are nothing like the way these cartoons portray us. But looking at it from an outside perspective, I can understand why we are seen this way.

I recently watched an interview of a well-known Christian leader on CNN, and frankly I was embarrassed by how he responded when the issue of homosexuality came up. He seemed oblivious to the fact that he was speaking to a national audience and not a church. Some of his statements probably pleased conservative Christians, but he wasn't speaking to a church group. He was speaking to a national audience and didn't come across as compassionate and understanding. He spoke about homosexuals in a technical way, as though they were inanimate objects, not people. I wonder if the interview did more harm than good, keeping people from wanting to know more about Jesus and Christianity. He seemed to merely reinforce the stereotype that Christians lack compassion and are culturally naive and theologically simplistic.

MY PERSONAL JOURNEY

Perhaps I'm more sensitive to this because I grew up outside the church. In high school, I was a drummer in a band in which the keyboardist was gay. We didn't talk about it much, but he shared with me that he was gay, and I didn't know quite what to think of it. I was a typical teenager and just assumed that some people were and some people weren't. In my junior and senior years, I worked in a furniture store, and my boss was gay. He was one of the nicest guys I had ever known. His boyfriend would sometimes come into the office. I'd visit him at his apartment in New York City. I didn't think about it; he was just my boss and he was gay. Remember, I had no biblical guidelines at this time to make me think any differently.

When I was a student at Colorado State University and really into music, my girlfriend and I would sometimes go to a gay bar in Boulder to hang out and shoot pool. We liked it there because they played the most progressive music from England and Europe. I didn't think anything of it since my girlfriend and friends were comfortable hanging out there.

When I lived in England for a year, I had several roommates, one of whom was bisexual. We became good friends and hung out and laughed a lot together. We talked about God and spiritual things too. That was during the time I was reading through the Bible, thinking about the lordship of Jesus and what it means to follow him, and beginning to make some significant changes in my life. I had many conversations with her about Jesus, Christianity, and even about homosexuality. I encountered verses in the Bible that seemed to indicate that sex outside of marriage and homosexual practice are sins. This was all entirely new to me. I didn't know quite what to think of it, but I remember wanting to study it more. When I left England, my friend even bought me a book on the history of Christianity as a goodbye present.

THEN I ENTERED THE CHRISTIAN SUBCULTURE

Coming from that background, I entered evangelical subculture and was pretty amazed at most Christians' lack of understanding of homosexuality. One of the first things I noticed was that the church consistently made a big deal about homosexuality and sex outside of marriage. I listened to how sermons depicted homosexuals and how Christians talked about them, and it seemed like they were talking about people I had never met. One time I went to a Christian camp and they showed a video clip of the gay parade in San Francisco. It showed people in drag and in bondage leather walking around and making out in front of the camera. The speaker then said something like, "This is what homosexuals are like!" He tried to rally the youth at this camp to see how terrible homosexuals are. I remember thinking, I have known several gay people, and none of them dressed like that, acted like that, or marched in a gay parade. It seemed to me the speaker characterized a group of people in an extreme way in order to manipulate impressionable Christian teenagers. I was pretty shocked at the stance most churches took toward all homosexuals, looking at them as their enemies.

Granted, a small percentage of homosexuals does fit in that extreme category. But so do some Christians fit in an extreme category, such as the fringe group that carries "God Hates Fags!" signs in public places. In the same way that people in emerging generations see extreme Christian groups and think that's what all Christians are like, so have some Christians drawn conclusions about gays that are more caricature than reality. From what I have experienced, most gays are regular folks, living normal lives just like straight folks, and aren't bent on converting children or anyone else to their sexual orientation. Yes, vocal gay activists get the press and are probably the ones you see on the street. But we can't let them shape our impression of gays as a whole. We don't like it when Christians are stereotyped by extremists, and we shouldn't stereotype others because of extremists we see. Imagine if all Christians were stereotyped by the extreme fringe Christian groups who hold up signs saying "God Hates America" and "God Hates Your Tears" at funerals for American soldiers killed in Iraq. They get the media attention by their actions, but by no means do they represent the majority of Christians. We shouldn't be stereotyping homosexuals in this manner either. I think Penny put it well:

> I am not a gay activist. None of my friends are gay activists. I am just Penny. I don't want people to regard me just by my sexuality. I want them to consider what kind of person I am. Am I loving? Am I caring? Why do Christians think that all gay people are like the ones who are dressed half-naked in leather out marching in the gay parade? That is so far from the truth. It would be like me thinking that all Christians are like Jerry Falwell telling people to stay away from Teletubby dolls or that all Christians bomb abortion clinics.
>
> PENNY

Remember what Karen said it was like for her, struggling as a teenager with her sexuality but feeling uncomfortable about confiding in people in her church? How many in our youth ministries right now are like Karen, struggling with same-sex attractions but unable to talk with the pastor or youth pastor because they heard them say how horrible all gay people are? What torment we must put people through, people who are trying to follow Jesus and need someone to talk to. We basically haven't left them much choice other than to go to a gay church, like the Metropolitan Church or some other church that endorses gay marriages and ordains gay pastors. But that's not what Penny would want to do:

> If I were to go to a church, I wouldn't want to be part of a gay church. Because that is not my primary identity. I don't want to be ghettoized. It is very sad, Dan, feeling that even if I wanted to go, I don't feel the church would welcome me, so I don't go.

Some readers may say, "Well, sinners don't want to admit their sin and that's why they don't go to church." That's true to an extent. But again I want us to put ourselves in other people's shoes. I was once getting my hair cut by someone who was filling in for my regular stylist. When this girl, around twenty-five years old, asked me what I do, I told her I'm a pastor and asked if she has ever gone to church. Without hesitation, she said, "Oh no. I am gay. You wouldn't want me there." How horrible that we have painted the church in such a way that we get that as a response from someone on the outside looking in.

A QUESTION TO SEE HOW YOU REACT

Imagine an unmarried couple who are living together and are sexually active. They enter your church and tell you they aren't Christians yet, but are interested in God and are checking out your church. They begin attending your worship gatherings, and you are happy to see them there, hoping they will come to trust in Jesus. You know they are living together, and you see them respectfully showing their affection by holding hands in church and putting their arms around one another.

But what if a gay couple did the same thing?

How would you answer the following questions?

- How are these two couples different in Jesus' eyes?
- Theologically, what is the difference between the straight couple and the homosexual couple?
- How would your reactions differ?
- How would your church react?

WHAT CAN WE LEARN FROM THIS MISPERCEPTION?

I trust that most of us care how the church represents Jesus to the homosexual community and to our culture at large. I'd like to suggest some ways that we can change the stereotype that the church is homophobic and sexuality repressive.

We must understand how emerging generations view sexuality

On the subject of sexuality, there's generally a disconnection between many church leaders, in particular older ones, and our emerging culture. I say that with respect and I don't mean to make anyone feel bad, since many older leaders are ministering to people in older age groups. But many have not stayed current with the changing values and worldviews of those growing up in our culture today, and these leaders are still expecting people to think the same way they do. Things have changed, and we need to think from the perspective of emerging generations if we want to understand them and know how to communicate with them.

Many pastors, especially younger ones, understand this and are preaching sermon series on human sexuality that would have been unheard of twenty years ago. Many churches now are unafraid of being bold and speaking of sexuality in a holistic way as something beautiful and sacred that God created. As the church lovingly teaches about sexuality and marriage from a biblical perspective, many people have never heard the biblical view before. Many have only heard, "Don't have sex before marriage," or, "Jesus is in the back seat of your car watching you." When we make such black and white statements without also presenting a full exploration of Scripture, people get the impression that the church is only negative about sexuality. But a wave of change is beginning as people make changes in their lives because they see that God's desire for them is sex within the covenant of marriage. For example, I just had a check-in conversation with a young unmarried couple who was sexually active. We talked through human sexuality and the covenant of marriage, and did not merely focus on "don't have sex before marriage." Though we came to the conclusion that they shouldn't have sex before marriage, we focused instead on the beauty of sex within a covenant relationship. They are struggling but are maintaining purity knowing that God has something better for them in their upcoming marriage, which they now see as a beautiful covenant between each other and God.

Today, the conversation is going way beyond just heterosexual sex and marriage. As homosexuality is being accepted as normal in our culture, I think many Christian leaders aren't in tune with that, so we either ignore it or just slam it down without any heart or thought. And people notice this. Not just homosexuals but heterosexuals also have negative perceptions about the church's treatment of gays. Gary, a heterosexual, says:

> I don't see anything corruptive or destructive about homosexuality. Jesus was about love, not hate. So homosexuality shouldn't be something the church hates. It shouldn't be a religious issue. With all the things wrong in this world, I don't understand why the church makes such a big deal about homosexuality.
>
> GARY

This is the viewpoint of many in emerging generations, who perceive that we fear and hate all homosexuals. Out of all the other things in the world we could focus on—poverty, AIDS, greed, abuse—we make a bigger deal about homosexuality.

We must be careful how we teach and preach about sexuality

Scripture is living and active and can change lives as the Spirit of God uses preaching and teaching (Heb. 4:12). When we are faced with cultural change, we need to be students of the Scriptures and not depend on our opinions to seek out truth. In a culture that teaches about sexuality through media, movies, music, and poor parental example, we need to take all the more seriously the teaching and preaching of the Scriptures on human sexuality.

What I mean by human sexuality is holistic sexuality, not just focusing on homosexuality and telling people they shouldn't have sex before marriage. More than ever, we need to teach the biblical meaning of marriage as a covenant before God. But we must not do so lightly and without prayer and study. No longer can leaders in the church merely quote a few verses without context, say, "This is what the Bible says," and then end it there. We need to respect those we speak to and do much more careful study than just simply pulling single verses out to make a case. Also, unlike previous generations, emerging generations don't immediately trust or respect what people say, especially church leaders. And because people have access to so many sources of information today, we can't assume that people are unaware of opposing positions on biblical texts.

Tough questions via email

After I spoke once about human sexuality, I got a series of emails from a guy who said he was at the worship gathering and had follow-up questions. He asked questions about heterosexuality, and then asked some questions about homosexuality. He said something like, "If the church teaches from Leviticus 18:22 that people of the same sex should not be together sexually, what about Leviticus 18:19? Can a husband really not have sex with his wife during her menstrual period? What about Leviticus 19:27, which says, 'Do not cut the hair at the sides of your head or clip off the edges of your beard'?" He wrote that I and the other leaders in our church seem to cut the hair at the sides of our heads and don't have beards. Are we then committing as serious a sin as someone who is physical with someone of the same sex? He asked me, "What about in Leviticus 20:13, where it says, 'If a man lies with a man as one lies with a woman, both of them have done what is detestable. They must be put to death; their blood will be on their own heads.' Are we really supposed to kill them?"

We emailed back and forth, and finally I asked him to meet me the following week at the front of the church after I spoke. I waited after the service and this junior high boy approached me. The guy who was emailing me was thirteen years old! He would come to church with his parents, and then take home the notes he took during the sermon and look up the verses. He had found a web page that pointed out problematic verses from the Old Testament and he was sending them to me. He was sincere and wasn't trying to trick me, but I remember thinking that the days are over when pastors can just get up to preach and assume they won't be challenged by people who want to dig deeper. A thirteen-year-old boy was asking me questions about Levitical law and homosexuality. Sure, he wasn't the average thirteen-year-old, but any adult serious about looking into the Bible can find the same information. Are we ready to address these questions?

How would you answer them? Do we address these types of questions in our sermons, or do we just quote the few verses that seem to back up whatever case we are trying to make and leave it at that? We need to have more respect for people in our churches and in our emerging culture.

I was visiting the campus at the university in Santa Cruz and spotted an ad in the campus newspaper for a class titled "How to Refute Fundamentalists about Homosexuality." The description said this class would show how fundamentalist Christians misinterpret Bible passages and how to refute anyone who says otherwise. Do you see why we must be serious students of Scripture no matter what position we hold on this? As we assert what the Bible says about sexuality, we had better be ready to discuss intelligently and lovingly why we come to the conclusions we do.

Knowing key theological arguments is not optional

I talked to a non-Christian twenty-something who said she dismissed Christians because she, as a non-Christian, knew more about the Bible than a Christian friend of hers did. A college English literature class had taught her that the words many Bible versions translate as "homosexual" or something similar really shouldn't be translated that way. She pointed out that the Greek words *malakos* and *arsenokoitai* used in 1 Corinthians 6:9 literally mean "soft" and the specific meaning of *arsenokoitai* is in question. She had learned that this passage is most likely a reference to male prostitution, not just homosexual practice. Her Christian friend had no idea about that, and she was disappointed in her friend's faith because of that and because she wasn't aware of other critical issues of the day. She felt that her friend's faith was elementary and blamed the church for not teaching her these things.

Maybe these examples are exceptions rather than the norm, but even if that's the case, soon they will be the norm. Pro-gay theological arguments are becoming more and more well-known to the average person. If you hold to a different position, are you ready to answer these arguments? Are you teaching your church about these issues? We need to do our homework so we aren't just putting out shallow answers on the positions we take. We do more harm than good if all we can do is quote isolated verses and then say that homosexuality is a sin, and we will lose our credibility if we aren't prepared to address challenges such as the following:

- *The sin of Sodom.* We generally have taught that the primary sin of Sodom was homosexuality, yet neither Jesus nor any of the five prophets who mention Sodom talk about sexual sin as the sin that led to Sodom's destruction. Ezekiel 16:48–49 says that the sin of Sodom was its lack of hospitality and not helping the poor. Another argument is that the sin of Sodom was gang rape, not homosexual sex. We also have to look at the similar account in Judges 19–21 to determine which sin was really at issue there and to see whether in light of that account we can justifiably say that homosexual sin was the sin of Sodom.
- *Leviticus passages.* Leviticus 18:22 and 20:13 are verses quoted all the time about homosexuality that are part of the holiness code, which lists forbidden behaviors. When other parts of the code talk about haircuts, tattoos, working on the Sabbath, wearing garments of mixed fabrics, and even touching the skin of a pig, we would agree that the code was written for a specific time, place, and people. But if we say we aren't bound today by the code on such items as these, how do we explain our being bound by these verses about homosexuality, which were written in the same context?
- *Romans 1:26–27.* A growing response to this passage says Paul was writing about people who worshiped fertility deities, which involved homosexual sex, orgies, and sex with temple prostitutes. Therefore he is condemning straight people who "unnaturally" have homosexual sex, not those who are "naturally" homosexual. How would you address this?
- *1 Corinthians 6:9.* Some would argue that we inaccurately translate certain words in this passage. Instead of referring to homosexual sex in general, this verse refers specifically to male prostitution. According to this argument, since the Greek word *malakois* means "soft or weak," it is referring to effeminate and young male prostitutes. The second word in question is *arsenokoitai.* The meaning of this word is not certain, but most scholars believe it is referring to the male who takes the active genital role in male-to-male intercourse. So piecing this together, this view understands this passage to be talking about those who pay for sex with young male prostitutes, not to all homosexual sex or relationships.

- *1 Timothy 1:10.* The Greek word *arsenokoitai* is used here also. Again, its actual meaning is unclear. But it is argued that in this context, as in 1 Corinthians 6:9, it is referring not to someone who is simply homosexual or about all homosexual sex but to those who hire young male prostitutes. How do you answer these claims?

I bring these challenges up because they are becoming more common and it's fair to say that many pastors are not prepared to address them. And if pastors aren't able to address them, then the people in their churches certainly aren't either. Yet anyone, whether a pastor or a person in the pews, who uses these verses to say homosexuality is sin needs to be prepared to explain why and to answer questions about them.

At the same time, those who hold the pro-gay theological position should also study the Scriptures on these issues. I just read an article called "Does God Love Gays?" It made great points about God and love, and how God loves all people. But it also said that God approves homosexual sex. The article rightfully challenged conservative evangelicals to make sure homosexuals understand that God loves them, but it didn't use even a single verse from the Bible to support its position on homosexuality.

Human sexuality is such a complex and emotional subject. We have to be thinking through how to respond to all types of situations. For example, people are more aware of the rare cases in which people are born with both male and female sex organs. We need to be able to understand these are issues people are aware of and be able to look at situations like this in light of Scripture. (In appendix 3, I include a list of recommended resources for further study.) But our teaching about homosexuality must go beyond just theological understanding.

Make sure you understand who you are talking about

I once listened to a sermon that a preacher gave about homosexuality. It was composed of several points, each stating specific reasons why homosexuality is a sin and is wrong. The preacher quoted the usual verses, then gave a whole bunch of scientific data on whether homosexuality is genetic and on the dangers of gay sex. You could tell by their "amens" and their "attaboy, preach it" attitude that the whole church approved of his one-sided argument. There wasn't a single story of any personal relationship or friendship that the pastor had with anyone gay. His arguments from the Scriptures also made no mention of alternative interpretations and pretty much skipped the difficult issues regarding these passages (like the ones I list on the previous page).

Two things really saddened me that day. I was saddened by the way the sermon was preached, almost as if the pastor was preaching about an inanimate object called a homosexual. There didn't seem to be any heart or emotion or understanding expressed. My guess is that's because the pastor couldn't tell even one story of actually having any homosexual friends himself, so he viewed them and spoke of them more like someone would talk about an object. There was no consideration of the lives and stories of homosexuals. I was also saddened by the people's response. I could tell by their applause and all the nodding heads that the pastor was just preaching to the choir. As all these people go out into their world having heard this sermon, how will they react to homosexuals?

As church leaders, we may have given sermons on homosexuality. We may have read theological books on homosexuality. But have we ever talked to someone who is gay, to really try to understand how the church and Christians come across to them? If we did so, we'd learn why we tend to come across to them as being hateful and judgmental.

Whenever I speak on homosexuality in a sermon, I usually try not to do it in a hot-topics type of series. Instead, I include it when I address human sexuality. I paint a bigger picture, always going back to the garden of Eden to talk about what it means to be in a fallen world and about how sin impacts sexuality and marriage. Instead of my just teaching, I usually try to bring in those who have struggled with homosexual attraction and let them share their lives and hearts. Karen, whom I interviewed for this book, will be sharing at our church soon, and after the worship gathering, we are going to have a Q and A with her and a male who struggles with same-sex attraction. So instead of just teaching facts and Bible verses, we will also hear gay people's struggles and how the church makes them feel. When dealing with a subject as sensitive as this, it makes a big difference to have someone who has experienced what we're talking about to help teach from experience how God has made a difference in their lives.

We must understand that homosexuals are in our churches

I was in a meeting with a dear elderly gentleman who was a leader in his church. Somehow the topic of homosexuality came up. When I said something about homosexual Christians, he stopped me and said, "Dan, correct me if I'm wrong, but did you just say homosexual Christians? There can't be Christians who are homosexuals." What this dear but wrong man was thinking was that when people come to see that homosexuality is a sin, they will decide not to be homosexual anymore. He quoted 1 Corinthians 6:9–11, which says, "Do you not know that the wicked will not inherit the kingdom of God? Do not be deceived: Neither the sexually immoral nor idolaters nor adulterers nor male prostitutes nor homosexual offenders nor thieves nor the greedy nor drunkards nor slanderers nor swindlers will inherit the kingdom of God. And that is what some of you were." Part of his understanding is right. God doesn't see us as anything but forgiven sinners, pure as snow. This gentleman, though, meant more, that people can stop being homosexual at once. But homosexuality is not like that at all. It isn't something people choose and can turn on and off. Granted, there are wonderful stories of people who over time and with counseling have found their sexual attraction changed to opposite-sex attraction. But it doesn't come easy for most.

This older man wasn't aware of the many Christians who conclude that they are homosexual but choose to be celibate. He wasn't aware that someone can be a Christian and still have a homosexual orientation. He also wasn't aware of the growing number of pro-gay churches and pro-gay theological arguments. He didn't know that telling someone to change their sexual attraction isn't the same as telling someone to stop having sex with their boyfriend or to stop getting drunk. If you're straight, imagine someone telling you, "You now need to be sexually attracted to the same sex." How would you feel? I suspect many leaders don't understand homosexuality, or surely some of the sermons I've heard wouldn't have been given the way they were.

More common than instant change is the experience of the person I talked with who decided after years of counseling that he is not going to change and will always be attracted to the same sex. He decided that he was homosexually oriented and that he wasn't going to fight it anymore. But because of his love for Jesus and his understanding of the Scriptures, he felt that practicing homosexuality would be sin, so he decided to be celibate and not engage in any relationships.

I spoke with Chad, a twenty-six-year-old who struggled with same-sex attraction, and he explains another level of struggle homosexuals face:

Gays who give up their homosexuality are giving up not only an entire sexual attraction but an entire support system as well. "Gay" most likely has become an identity for most of them and permeates every part of their life. Most church leaders do not understand how much someone leaves behind when they make the decision to walk away from homosexuality, and most in the church are not ready to help rebuild a support and relational structure. The church does not realize how desperately they need emotional support. I know plenty of examples of gays who were trying to change and joined a church but could not find the support they needed. CHAD

GOOD THINGS ARE HAPPENING IN OUR CHURCHES

Though this chapter may paint a negative picture, some good things are happening in many of our churches. Churches are starting ministries to homosexuals, quite often led by those who struggle with their sexual identity. Karen is one of them. She is a Christian and is now helping churches understand what it's like to grow up in a church being gay. She is celibate and is letting God use her story to help others. So before closing this chapter, instead of my suggesting how to respond, let's listen to someone who knows firsthand what it's like being gay and who has some advice for the church. Here's some input to leaders from Karen in her own words.

"One of the primary mistakes the church has made, and still makes, is presuming that gay people are outside the church. This had a significant impact on the way I ultimately dealt with homosexuality. The church has been a large contributor to the phenomenon of the gay identity. By labeling gay people as a group outside the church, they promote the concept of a quasiethnic identity.

"Church leadership plays a vital role in determining whether a transparent culture develops in their church. It has to be championed by the senior or lead pastors in the church, who have the power to influence the congregation. Church leaders can take steps to enhance authentic community by:

- "Discussing sexual issues, including homosexuality, in an open and grace-oriented way that does not stigmatize or single out certain sexual problems. This will minimize the tendency for people to keep things secret due to fear of being rejected or believing their sin is particularly bad. We should talk about homosexuality as comfortably as we do gossip or jealousy.

- "Creating 'Transparent Fellowship Groups'; that is, small group Bible studies that incorporate not only study but also authentic fellowship. This is what church leaders usually want anyway, but it never happens. This is due, in part, to poor group facilitation and the short duration of most groups (i.e., the six-week study). A leader of a group will determine how transparent a group becomes. Churches need to train Bible study leaders in Bible interpretation, prayer, and facilitation. Specifically, leaders need to be prepared to be transparent themselves and need to be trained to guide the group toward deeper intimacy. Unfortunately, many churches lack formal training for group leaders.

- "Becoming better equipped to address the issues that arise, instead of automatically referring people with problems to a psychologist or ex-gay ministry. It is easy to refer out when pastoral staff is overworked, but systems need to be created so that peer counselors, men's and women's ministry leaders, youth workers, and others are educated on specific issues such as homosexuality. This means creating an expectation within the body that church is not only a place to sit in the pew and be encouraged but also a place to be trained up to truly love others and walk with them in their struggles. The number-one thing that those who struggle with homosexuality need is healthy, intimate, same-sex friendships with 'straight' church members; this cannot be addressed by always resorting to referring someone to a psychologist or an ex-gay support group. Those are good, but the church needs to see homosexuals as they would anyone else, not just isolate them. Men's and women's ministries could make a powerful contribution in this area if they were better equipped.

- "Rediscovering corporate prayer. Unlike the early church, the American church has relegated prayer to the private life. As a result, we miss out on the richness of corporate prayer that fosters intimacy with one another and God. In particular, the leaders of the Jewish people in the Old Testament often prayed public prayers of corporate confession. When all of the people are on their knees together acknowledging their inadequacy and failings before God, it reinforces that we are all in the same boat and are all in need of God's grace. This undermines the sense of superiority and judgment that develops when some believe they are less sinful than others.

- "Not being afraid to teach about human sexuality without apology. Church leaders need to find a balance between grace and truth. Fortunately, some churches are beginning to discard the legalistic tendencies of the past that create a culture of criticism and condemnation. However, some churches risk going in the opposite direction, focusing exclusively on grace without upholding truth. Many churches seem to be like deer caught in headlights—frozen and uncertain about what move to make. They don't want to be condemning, as in the past, but they are not sure how to address the issue without hurting people. Not doing anything at all, however, only serves to create new problems that are equally harmful.

  "The church must be full of love and grace, but it also must be a place that upholds truth. Too often church leaders seem apologetic for having to tell a person that homosexuality is wrong. The church cannot value the approval of society more than the approval of God. In Scripture, true righteousness (not legalism) is associated with well-being, joy, glory, life, and all that is good. It is described as putting on a clean, refreshing garment. When the church does not uphold the truth about righteousness, it robs people of the peace that comes only from following the ways of God. The truth does set people free, and we must use it not to beat people down but to open the gates and release the prisoners. It is hard enough for me to be faithful in following God on the issue of homosexuality without having to watch church leaders shrink back and Christian friends waffle on truth. Stand up for your brothers and sisters who struggle, and don't be ashamed of the ways of God. If we truly believe and trust that God's ways are best and are lifegiving, then we are selfish and cruel not to stand firm."

HOW THIS PLAYED OUT IN OUR CHURCH

A twenty-one-year-old girl who was still in college began coming to our worship gatherings. She was a creative musician studying fine art. She approached me with some questions, and it turned out she was gay. In fact, she was in a relationship with another girl at the time. But we embraced her into our church community, discussed Scripture with her, and let her serve in several ways, since she wanted to contribute to the church. She got involved in one of our midweek home communities. She also started serving on a ministry team, helping to set up the art that we used in our worship gatherings, and handed out bulletins.

But when she approached me about another position of ministry that involved being in more of a teaching role, I was in a rough spot. I needed to make her understand that letting her take on this role would be in contradiction to what we teach on homosexuality. I met with her after the worship gathering one night, and we talked for about three hours. It was a horrible situation for both of us. With anguish and tears, I explained that I couldn't let her serve in that position. I felt like I was yanking my heart out, and yanking her heart out, and slamming them both on the ground. But I had to remain true to what I felt the Scriptures say, since putting her in this role would have endorsed her practicing gay lifestyle. We prayed together, and then she left in tears. It was horrible. Absolutely horrible.

The next day, I emailed her to see how she was doing. I didn't hear back for a day, and then I received this email:

> Anyway, thanks for the response. Don't get me wrong, I'm not about to leave the church. No way. It has brought me closer to God than anywhere else. There is peace there that I can't find anywhere else. Yeah, this turmoil I feel at times makes me want to stop believing so I can just have my mind back at least.
>
> Anyway, I came in the computer lab to type a paper that is due in an hour (how classic). I was supposed to be writing it last night, but instead I sat down to write—just journal writing, and I ended up picking up my guitar and writing a song.
>
> Basically it's about this whole issue of being gay, directed toward you. A lot of the lyrics turned out pretty angry. But then when I was trying to come up with music for the lyrics, the music didn't match the lyrics. The music that was coming out was not angry, but more peaceful and about

the compassion you have shown me. So I ended up not going with the original lyrics and took out the angry parts.

Basically the song just talks about how I felt when we chatted at church, how hurt I am, questions about how the church can call being gay wrong. I find it ironic that my anger sometimes is aimed at you when you are the only one in the world willing to be kind to me, even though you disagree. I can tell that you really have the love of God in your heart. I want to apologize for feeling angry sometimes. Really, I am not mad at you.

Even though she was angry, she knew I cared. She knew I was not just pointing a finger at her to shame her or judge her. She knew I was holding to what I believed but doing so in a way that showed love, understanding, and grace. She stayed part of our church until she moved out of town after her graduation. As I type this, I'm wondering what happened to her. In fact, I took a break from writing this chapter and sent an email to the last address I had from her. So maybe I will find out how she's doing now.

I'm telling this story not to pat myself on the back but to try to express how we can break the stereotype that the church is homophobic and sexually uptight. I firmly believe that it isn't just what we teach about human sexuality but how we teach it that is important. I am convinced, like Karen stated earlier, that no matter what the issue is, even if it goes against the grain of culture, how we say what we believe is critical. Most of emerging generations' misunderstandings derive not from the church's beliefs but from the way we go about holding and teaching our beliefs. An insightful book about homosexuality is called *Welcoming but Not Affirming* by the late theologian Stanley Grenz. I believe it is possible to do what the title of the book is suggesting. We can hold to a doctrinal position about homosexuality while moving from being known as a community that fears and even looks down on homosexuals to being known as a community that welcomes and loves them, yet doesn't affirm anything that the Scriptures don't:

The church is homophobic → The church is a loving and welcoming community

LOOKING AT YOUR CHURCH
THROUGH THE EYES OF
EMERGING GENERATIONS

1. What are your feelings about and attitude toward homosexuals? What types of comments are made about them in your worship gatherings? What do you say in the privacy of your home? Do you know any homosexuals who have shared their lives and feelings with you?

2. On a scale of one to ten, how prepared are you to explain the tough passages in the Bible about human sexuality and homosexuality? How would you handle the questions and passages I listed in this chapter? What can you do to be more prepared? Go back and look at the specific passages and pro-gay theology arguments I listed. How do you respond to each one?

3. What do the members of your church think about homosexuals? Would they be able to explain from the Bible what your church's position is? If a homosexual lived next to someone from your church, what do you think they would say about the person from your church and their attitude and actions toward homosexuals?

4. Do your church's teaching and preaching include messages about human sexuality? How often? What changes should be made in this area?

5. Right now, where would a homosexual or someone struggling with same-sex attraction go in your church to seek advice or to talk? Do you feel you have created a culture of trust that would make someone feel it's safe to talk to you or others in your church? If they did approach you, what would you say?

THE CHURCH ARROGANTLY CLAIMS ALL OTHER RELIGIONS ARE WRONG

9

> When I was a teenager, my dad gave me several books to read—the Bible, the Koran, the I Ching, some Buddhist writings—so I could be open-minded and discover a spiritual path for myself and understand God more fully. Christians don't seem to appreciate the beauty in other faiths. They seem so closed-minded and even look at other religions as enemies.
>
> **—DUGGAN**

Duggan is a young full-blooded Irish man with a smile and personality that make you feel like you are his best friend the first time you meet him. We have been getting to know one another over the course of the past year through conversations at the coffeehouse where he is the manager. Duggan introduced me to Creamy Carrot, a carrot drink that I've consumed at least twenty times this past year. Quite often within a few minutes of my entering his coffeehouse, a Creamy Carrot appears on my table. Duggan knows I crave the Creamy Carrot. In fact, I think of the Creamy Carrot quite often in midafternoon, especially when a little sleepiness kicks in and I want a pick-me-up.

I find that music is a natural entry point into conversations with new people, so it's not surprising that when Duggan and I met, we talked about music. The CD he was playing on the stereo of his coffeehouse was by the Pogues, a band from England that mixes traditional Irish music with punk music. When I was playing in a band in England, I hung out a couple of times with Shane MacGowan, the lead singer of the Pogues. Shane is an unusual and flamboyant character, and I had some interesting stories about my times with him that Duggan found amusing. So after going to the coffeehouse regularly and having several casual conversations with

Duggan about music, I eventually started talking about faith. As I learned about Duggan's background, I concluded he's a good voice to listen to if you want to understand the hearts and minds of many growing up in our emerging culture. He provides some really good insight.

A PLURALISTIC ACCEPTANCE OF ALL FAITHS

In Duggan's home, religion wasn't really talked about much. He went to a Catholic church sometimes as a child, since his family was Irish. But when he reached his teenage years, his father wanted him to be open-minded about spiritual things, so he gave him a Bible, a Koran, some Confucian writings, some Buddhist writings, and other writings. Duggan actually read through all of what his father gave him and even as a teenager enjoyed the diversity of religious faiths. He was more intrigued by Buddhist writings than the others:

> After reading the various religious writings that my dad gave me, I was drawn to more of a Tibetan Buddhist spirituality. The mysticism is very attractive and it is steeped in history and tradition that predates Catholicism and Christianity, which I also found fascinating. I didn't realize that most world religions have beginnings that predate the church.

Now as an adult, Duggan continues to appreciate that his father did not limit his exposure to only one approach to spirituality. I hear quite often today that parents want their children to have spiritual beliefs but encourage them to discover them on their own and want them to consider a diversity of choices. Duggan grew to appreciate beauty in all religions and to see truth in all of them. He doesn't practice any one faith exclusively but sees himself as a spiritual person with Buddhist leanings. He doesn't understand why most Christians can't see the beauty in other faiths. It disturbs him to encounter Christians who slam other faiths by saying that theirs is the only right one and that all the others are wrong.

> All I hear from Christians is that all other world religions are wrong and going to hell. I have tried to have an intelligent conversation with them about this and discuss the beauty in other expressions of spirituality, but they go into this religious rhetoric and avoid the hard questions. It seems

> *they have programmed dogmatic answers that someone has told them, and they can't even hold any type of normal back and forth conversation about any other spiritual beliefs but theirs.*

In the many conversations we've had, Duggan consistently expressed that it isn't that Christians are exclusive that disturbs him; it's the attitude Christians have about other spiritual beliefs—the way they talk about them, their inability to see any value in other faiths, and their dismissal of other religions, saying that the people who practice them are all going to hell. He also shared several times that what bothers him is Christians' naive view of other world religions. He feels that Christians who don't know anything about other faiths yet say that all other faiths are wrong show a tremendous lack of respect. This attitude repels him and keeps him from wanting to be a Christian. As an example, he shared an encounter he had with two students from a prominent evangelical campus ministry:

> *I once tried talking to two Christians about Buddha and the Dao. They looked at me like they were going to freak out and didn't know what to say. They could only talk to me about their beliefs and wouldn't even talk to me about any other beliefs. It makes me think that Christians are like horses with blinders—they have an isolated and inflexible view. They are so fixated only on what they believe, they aren't able to take in their surroundings and see other elements in the world around them. Christians need to take off the blinders so they can see the world around them and maybe we could then have more intelligent conversations.*

What Duggan's saying is that Christians come across as naive and arrogant when they can't even carry on a conversation about the religions they reject. We need to understand that people in emerging generations, like Duggan, place a high value on respecting and seeing beauty in all faiths and expressions of spirituality. If we don't recognize this and aren't sensitive in how we talk about other faiths, we come across as unintelligent, primitive, closed-minded, and uncaring of people who hold different views.

Penny, whom you met in the previous chapter, said this about the attitudes of Christians toward world faiths:

> *Why do Christians act so horribly self-righteous when they tell us that they are the only true religion and everyone else who holds to other faiths is wrong? They have this "my god is the biggest god on the block and can beat up your god" attitude. I don't see this attitude in what I know of Jesus.*
>
> — PENNY

Christians rightly believe there is one true God (Deut. 6:4) and that apart from him there is no other God (Isa. 45:5). But we shouldn't act like bullies when we assert that we believe in the one true God, nor should we paint God as a bully. Penny agrees with Duggan that what disturbs her isn't our holding to a specific belief but our attitudes and the way we talk about those who hold other beliefs. Our speech, attitudes, and lack of knowledge discredit us with people in emerging generations and prevent their being open to further conversation with us, often even causing them to look in other places for spiritual meaning. Of her time of searching, Penny said:

> *Eastern religions were more attractive to me, because they focused more on being kind to others, loving other people of other spiritual beliefs even if they are different from you, treading lightly, and being humble. I think that was similar to the message of Jesus, ironically, but that's the opposite of what I experienced from church and Christians.*
>
> — PENNY

We need to be wise missionaries, taking into consideration the culture people of emerging generations are being raised in and how they think. If we do, more people will listen to what the Bible teaches about Christianity and other religions and the Spirit of God will be given much more opportunity to work in people's lives.

In my conversations with people outside the faith, I have been able to strongly and clearly explain to them the exclusive claims of Jesus and my belief that salvation comes through Jesus alone. I don't have to hide anything or water anything down because my approach makes all the difference. Because I have established relationships with them, listened to their spiritual perspectives, and built trust with them, I have been able to share Jesus' words that he is the way, the truth, and the life and that no one comes to the Father but through him (John 14:6). I have found that people are actually curious about Jesus' statement, and I've had positive dialogue with them about it. I've even found that people are willing to open the Bible and have positive conversations about strongly exclusive passages such as Acts 4:12, where it says of Jesus that "salvation is found in no one else, for there is no other name under heaven given to men by which we must be saved." But before we can have such conversations with people, we have to build relationships with them and understand other faiths well enough that we can talk about them intelligently. There seem to be plenty of Christians who will hand out a tract or hold a street sign saying "Jesus is the only way," but not many who build friendships and trust with people to dialogue about what that means. Most Christians can quote Acts 4:12 or John 14:6, but have we earned the trust of people outside the church that allows us to intelligently dialog about what they mean?

WHAT WE NEED TO UNDERSTAND ABOUT EMERGING GENERATIONS

I once talked to a Christian leader about how emerging generations feel about the church's view of world religions, and he commented, "You're wasting your time talking with people outside the church and even listening to their opinions. Jesus is the one way and the one truth. They either accept him or they don't. They're sinners with hardened hearts, so of course they won't like us. Their opinion of the church doesn't matter."

But their opinion does matter. And I believe it matters to Jesus, who went out and talked with people outside of religious circles and had compassion on them. He stopped and asked questions of the Samaritan woman (John 4) and didn't just jump in and say, "Samaritans are all wrong." He told the parable of a prodigal son to show the love of the father for the son, despite his son's actions. Jesus wept when looking down upon Jerusalem, knowing the people there would reject him. Furthermore, when you read the stories of effective missionaries throughout church history, you discover that they lived among the people, built relationships with them, and understood their thinking and beliefs.

So to be effective missionaries in our emerging culture, what do we need to understand about where people are coming from?

We need to view our world as a post-Christian culture
In Buddha-Allah-Goddess-Kabbalah-Tarot-God we trust

In past generations in America, if you went to the grocery store, you might bump into your neighbor, who was a member of the First Baptist Church. At the bank, the teller was a member of the Presbyterian Church, and the manager was a prominent member and an elder in the Evangelical Free Church. The school teacher was a member of the Methodist Church, and the policeman who stood at the corner and waved as people drove by was a member of the Catholic Church. Most people, even if they weren't faithful worshipers, would associate themselves with some expression of Christianity, usually depending on their families' denominational background.

Today things are quite different. We are living in a pluralistic culture. The grocery store is owned by a friendly family of Korean immigrants who are Buddhist. Your neighbors are Mormons. The bank manager is Hindu, and the teller is a twenty-something who dabbles in Tarot card readings and in earth- and nature-focused spiritual practices. On her car in the bank parking lot is a "In Goddess we trust" bumper sticker. Your junior higher's teacher is into meditation and appreciates all world faiths, believing that they all lead to God, and a classmate wears a red string around her left wrist as a fun way of copying a celebrity she admires who also wears this Kabbalastic symbol of protection. The policeman on the corner was raised Catholic but hasn't been to church since he was thirteen.

I was watching an episode of a popular television sitcom in which a family was discussing which religion to dedicate a newborn baby in. The father wanted the baby baptized. But the mother wanted to have some sort of Hindu ceremony performed. And the grandparents wanted the baby to be circumcised by a Jewish rabbi. Before you knew it, the whole family was arguing. In the end, they compromised and said, "Each of us will bring our own religious leader and we will do all of them." This approach represents where we are today. In my experience talking to people of other faiths, most aren't hard-core committed to any one world faith. Instead they generally have an appreciation for all faiths and hold to a mixed personal belief system. So I don't think emerging generations are all becoming hard-core Buddhists or Wiccans. But they are aware of global faiths and most place a strong value on the belief that everyone should believe what they want to and that no single religion should claim exclusivity over others.

But I don't see this lack of commitment to any one faith as being much different from past generations, when many people said that they were Methodist or Catholic or some other denomination of Christian but attended services only at holidays and their faith didn't affect their daily lives. Still, they considered themselves to be Christians, and being Christian was viewed as a positive thing. It was easier to talk about Jesus' being the only way

> IT'S STRANGE BUT TRUE THAT IF WE WERE TO SAY, "I AM THINKING OF BECOMING BUDDHIST," THE RESPONSE TODAY WOULD PROBABLY BE, "OH! VERY COOL!" BUT IF WE WERE TO SAY, "I AM THINKING OF BECOMING CHRISTIAN," THE RESPONSE WOULD BE, "OH NO! PLEASE DON'T BECOME ONE OF THEM!"

because most people already had a basic understanding of Christianity and weren't as aware of other spiritual views. Christianity was the popular choice. But today being a Christian isn't seen as a positive thing. It's strange but true that if we were to say, "I am thinking of becoming Buddhist," the response today would probably be, "Oh! Very cool!" but if we were to say, "I am thinking of becoming Christian," the response would be, "Oh no! Please don't become one of them!"

Interfaith chapel in the heart of the Bible Belt

I visited a Bible Belt state to speak at a conference on the topic of America's not being a Judeo-Christian nation anymore. Several pastors disagreed with me, saying that in their towns there are churches on every block and nothing is changing. In response, I asked them to tell me the name of the chapel in their airport, which I had just passed on my way to the conference. Out of the several hundred there, no one could. I informed them that in their own city, the airport chapel was now called an "interfaith chapel" and that the entryway of the chapel was lined with religious symbols of all the world faiths. In *The Emerging Church*, I quoted from the book *A New Religious America: How A "Christian Country" Has Become the World's Most Religiously Diverse Nation* by Diana Eck, a Harvard professor who says that America is now the world's most religiously diverse nation. She also makes the point that most Christian leaders aren't aware of this change going on. I suspect that some Christian leaders are so consumed with their church activities and meetings that they don't realize the extent to which culture is changing around them — even in the Bible Belt.

That we are living in a culture with a pluralistic understanding of spirituality is illustrated by the rising popularity of the Coexist shirts and stickers, which use the Islamic crescent moon, the Jewish Star of David, and the Christian cross to spell out the word coexist. I'm not saying this logo is bad. Of course we should coexist with and respect people of other faiths; you don't have to hold a universalist viewpoint to say so. But the popularity of the logo illustrates that people pay a lot of attention to how we treat other faiths. Another example is a new board game called Enlighten, which teaches about world faiths. (I actually want to get the game, since it could be a fun way to become aware of the basic beliefs of world faiths.) I read about the game recently in a newspaper article, which viewed Christianity simply as one of the many religions, not *the* religion. Christianity is not the only choice anymore in our culture. We are but one of many in our culture today.

I'm not saying that we need to keep quiet about the exclusive claims of Jesus. Quite the opposite, actually. But in some cases our hearts and attitudes need to change in how we talk to people about the claims of Jesus. When Paul spoke in Acts 17:1–4 to the religious Jews and God-fearing

Used with permission of www.enlightengamesinc.com

Greeks, he was able to reason with them from the Scriptures, since they already believed in them. But when Paul spoke to the people of Athens at the Areopagus, his approach was different (Acts 17:16–34). They didn't have the understanding that the religious Jews and God-fearing Greeks in the synagogue had. He still ended up preaching about Jesus and the resurrection, but his starting point and approach were different.

I think the problem today is that many of us expect the people of Mars Hill to have the same knowledge as the people in the synagogue. Paul recognized that different worldviews require different approaches. The same is true today. So let's look at some suggestions for how we can communicate to emerging generations about the one true God more like cross-cultural missionaries would.

WHAT CAN WE LEARN FROM THIS MISPERCEPTION?

We need a basic understanding of world faiths

We don't have to become experts in world faiths, but we certainly can acquire at least a basic level of understanding about them so that when we teach in our churches and when we meet people of other faiths, we can talk intelligently about other religions.

Molly, a twenty-four-year-old woman, is now part of our church after having plenty of experience with other faiths. She grew up outside of church but says she always sensed there was a God. She had a Jewish boyfriend once, so she went to a Jewish camp and learned various Jewish traditions. She says she was drawn to the rituals, the food, and the celebration of the various holidays in the Jewish calendar. In college she was attracted to Hinduism and practiced it for three years. She was drawn by how Hinduism uses the body as part of the worship experience. Hinduism also includes food, dance, and ritual, which she felt were big parts of her spiritual expression. She prayed to various Hindu goddesses and gods, depending on what her needs were. She went on Hindu retreats and was very involved.

But then she moved into a house where some people from our church lived. She didn't know any of them beforehand; she just answered an ad for a roommate. But she formed ordinary friendships with these Christians, who weren't judgmental of her Hindu beliefs. They loved her and hung out with her, and eventually, as she came to trust them, she started coming to our worship gatherings. As she began to see the faith of her Christian roommates, she realized that some of her perceptions of Christians and the church were wrong. She says:

> *My original perception of Christians was that they were all negative and focused on how sinful the world is. I felt that they were obsessed with what people do wrong and like pointing that out constantly, and that the men ruled everything in the church and women cannot have a place in decision-making. For me as a Hindu, I felt that Christians would only want to strip every bit of different culture and color from me and turn me into something bland and black-and-white like they are. I felt that they were obsessed with Jesus dying on the cross, since all you hear from them when they speak, again and again and again, is that Jesus suffered. Of course it was a horrible thing and a great thing what he did, but isn't there more to living this life than to constantly be talking about death and suffering? They seem to hate this life and can't wait until the next one when all the bad people here will be in hell and be gone. But then I began hearing and reading more about who Jesus is and meeting some Christians who weren't like that. It made me think that maybe Christianity isn't what I thought it was.* MOLLY

Too many Christians will only stick with other Christians in the bubble and not socialize or befriend non-Christians to this degree. It took Christians opening their home and their lives to a Hindu to build trust with Molly. If these girls hadn't done that, Molly might not have met normal Christians and gained a different perspective on them.

I ended up meeting with Molly about her growing interest in the claims of Christianity. When the topic of world religions came up, I found that she knew quite a bit about the development and various branches of Hinduism. At one point, she asserted that Hinduism predates Christianity. In response, instead of focusing on how Christianity and Hinduism differ and trying to prove Hinduism wrong, I asked her a lot of questions. What about Hinduism was attractive to her? What was her worship like? I wanted to understand more about her beliefs rather than just spout out my beliefs.

Eventually she asked how Christianity fits in with the various world religions. So I pulled out a piece of paper and began sketching. I shared that I don't see Christianity as a modern religion at all, and that it actually predates Hinduism. This caught her by surprise and piqued her interest. I told her that I was going to tell her the grand story of the Bible, starting with the story of creation. I told her that God created everything and was in a wonderful relationship with Adam and Eve in the garden, but they chose to go against him and sin entered the world. I shared how humans began searching for other gods, because they weren't satisfied with the one God who created everything. I even talked about the Tower of Babel and how human beings spread across the globe. Because I had a basic knowledge of the development of world religions, I was able to place them on a timeline, which I drew for her in a rough diagram (see figure below).

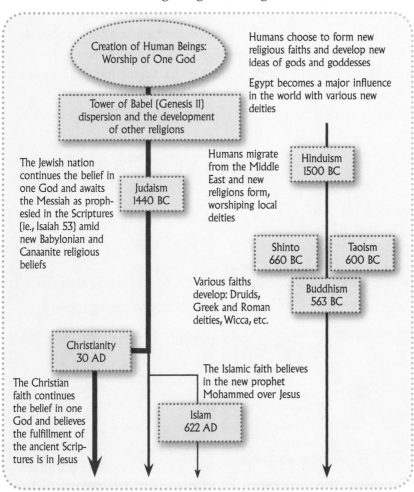

I admit this is a very elementary explanation of the origins of world faiths. Charting the complex development of world faiths in a simple diagram doesn't do them justice. But it's good for when I'm having conversations with people. I don't get into the various Tower of Babel viewpoints; I simply try to paint a picture of how history started with belief in one God and then through time other faiths developed and spread across the globe. Many times I draw a world map as I explain this, using the basic migration patterns that people are taught in elementary school to show when and where the various world religions developed (see figure below and on next page). Most people have never put the development of various world faiths in chronological perspective or seen how Christianity actually stems from the creation story and Judaism. I share a little about the prophecies about Jesus in the Hebrew Bible and how the roots of prophecy about Jesus are even found in the early chapters in Genesis. Telling the whole story of the need for a savior from the beginning and diagramming when and how other faiths sprang up puts Christianity in perspective for people, and then I can share why Jesus said, "I am the way, the truth and the life." Instead of

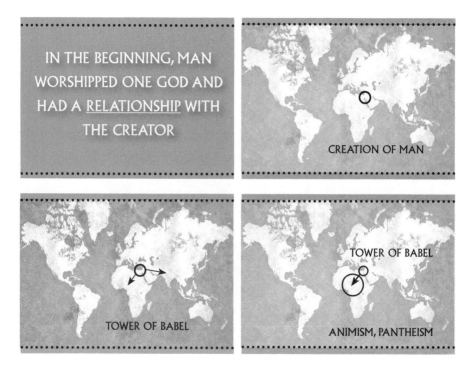

IN THE BEGINNING, MAN WORSHIPPED ONE GOD AND HAD A RELATIONSHIP WITH THE CREATOR

CREATION OF MAN

TOWER OF BABEL

TOWER OF BABEL

ANIMISM, PANTHEISM

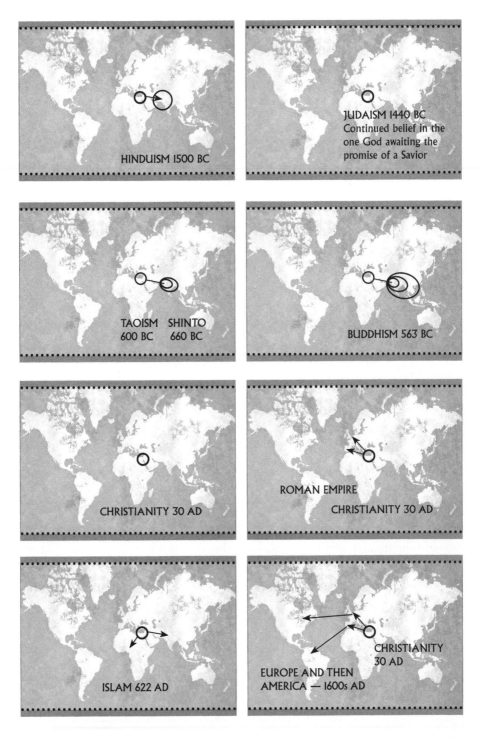

HINDUISM 1500 BC

JUDAISM 1440 BC
Continued belief in the
one God awaiting the
promise of a Savior

TAOISM   SHINTO
600 BC   660 BC

BUDDHISM 563 BC

CHRISTIANITY 30 AD

ROMAN EMPIRE

CHRISTIANITY 30 AD

ISLAM 622 AD

EUROPE AND THEN
AMERICA — 1600s AD

CHRISTIANITY
30 AD

hearing his statement in isolation, they can see how it points back to the beginning and fits in the whole story. It makes *all* the difference if instead of just quoting John 14:6 and presuming people will understand it we put John 14:6 into the grand story of God, creation, and the development of world faiths.

This is a pretty simplistic way of telling the story, so when someone raises a question about other faiths that I can't answer, I simply say, "I don't know, but let me do some research on it and let's talk about it another time." I'm not an expert in world faiths, but having a basic knowledge of them shows people that I respect and am interested in their beliefs enough to do some homework. It also gives me credibility with them and helps lessen the impression that Christians are dogmatic and closed-minded.

Molly eventually did become a Christian. She fell in love with Jesus, felt the presence of the Spirit in her life, and recognized that the Hindu gods and goddesses are not anything like the one true God of the Bible. She was baptized and is still part of our church, blogging about her love for Jesus and participating in a midweek community group that studies Scripture. This past Easter she even shared with the whole church a poem she wrote about her love for Jesus.

We need to train our churches to understand world faiths

Church leaders aren't the only ones who need to have a basic understanding of world religions. Those in our churches need this understanding as well. People in our churches will be meeting more people, becoming friends with them, and having conversations with them than we will. So we need to provide basic ongoing training in the origins and basic beliefs of Christianity and other world faiths. At our church, not only did we teach a class that covered world faiths but the teacher also did a study of what the specific local religious beliefs are, which include not only the major world faiths but also Wicca, Tarot, Rastafarian spirituality, and others. In the series we offered, this class had the largest attendance. I believe that among Christians who are out talking to people there is a high felt need to know more about other faiths so they can intelligently and lovingly talk to people about them.

Recently I spoke at an event in Dallas in a church that is known for seeing lots of young adults become part of the church. As I walked through the halls, I saw that they offer a regular class on world religions. Looking at the literature for the class, I could tell that they were sensitive in the way they spoke about other faiths. I wasn't surprised to see this in a church that is reaching emerging generations; they are simply being wise missional leaders. There are a number of books that are appropriate for a class like this, or for a book club or for whatever format you want to teach in. (See appendix 3 for recommended resources.) I know of one church that devoted five weeks in their main worship gathering to learning about world religions, even inviting individuals from various faiths to come in and be interviewed. Whatever method you use, the important thing is to train and prepare people to be culturally sensitive, compassionate, and understanding of the pluralistic and diverse culture we live in.

We need to be able to explain why not all paths lead to God

Madonna, in a magazine interview, made a comment that represents what so many today think: "I do believe that all paths lead to God. It's a shame that we end up having religious wars, because so many of the messages are the same."[14] Many people believe that all paths lead to God and that it's wrong for religions to fight and to say that they are the only true religion. Ironically, when you study other world faiths, you discover that Christianity is not the only religion which claims to be the one path to God. Most others teach that their beliefs are accurate and others' are wrong. But it seems that Christianity takes all the heat for saying

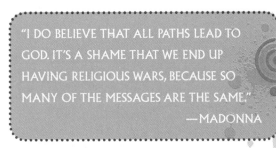

"I DO BELIEVE THAT ALL PATHS LEAD TO GOD. IT'S A SHAME THAT WE END UP HAVING RELIGIOUS WARS, BECAUSE SO MANY OF THE MESSAGES ARE THE SAME."
—MADONNA

this. The predominant impression is that we aren't open-minded, that we aren't loving, and that we strike out at other faiths, which, in the end, are all pretty much the same. When you study other faiths, you will also find that many of them believe in some form of hell. But again, most people seem to believe that Christianity is the only faith that holds there is a hell because we've put hell at the forefront of so much of our evangelism methods.

Earlier, Duggan commented on Christians who freeze like deer caught in headlights when asked to talk about other faiths. He also said this:

> If Christians want us not to think they are just brainwashed and that they basically have thrown out their capacity to think for themselves, then they should be able to articulate and dialogue with us about why they hold that Christianity is the one true religion. I don't want a lecture. I want to hang out and talk. Like we are talking now. Back and forth. And I want them to show me why they don't think that all faiths and all spiritual expressions are valid. Not just spout out a Bible verse but give me some reasons so I understand them and why they believe what they believe. I would respect them more if they did. But all I normally get is a quick Bible verse and a "Jesus is the only way" answer.

Duggan is a good example of how many people today are open to dialoging about what Christians believe and to hearing why they feel that not all paths lead to God. But dialog isn't monolog, focusing just on the Christian's perspective but not the other person's. Duggan suggests that we do our homework so we can have intelligent discussion and not just spout out Bible verses and not be able to talk further.

I am more of an introverted person, and it takes effort for me to be more extroverted and to meet people and to have conversations about sensitive topics like this. But if I can do it, I'm certain others can too. After I have built trust and friendship with someone, it is so much more natural to talk and to share what each other believes. When I ask what the other person believes and why, I simply listen. In Duggan's case, he shared that he feels all roads lead to God, and in the context of trust, I asked him if I could probe that bit. Because he trusts me, I could try to explain why I don't believe that would make sense. I usually grab a napkin or a piece of paper, which is what I did when talking with Duggan. I explain that people generally will say that all paths lead to God, and then I draw a mountain and write "God" at the top. Then I draw various paths making their way up the mountain and label them "Christianity," "Islam," "Hinduism," and so on.

Then I explain that because this is an important idea, we should really take a look at each of the paths to see what the various faiths believe. I explain that in many ways this metaphor of God living on a mountaintop breaks down because God isn't limited to a mountaintop; he is everywhere. But then I keep going, since it is a way to visually make some sense of this common way of thinking about God and other faiths. After I draw a mountain, I ask the person to list some of the fundamental beliefs of each faith concerning who God is, who Jesus is, what salvation requires, and what each believes about the afterlife, and I'll jot them down, adding to the list if the person doesn't know

DO ALL PATHS LEAD TO GOD?

HINDUISM   CHRISTIANITY   ISLAM
DO ALL PATHS LEAD TO GOD?

much about the different faiths. For the purpose of this book, I'll give a simplified version, but basically I explain that according to the Hindu path:

> God: there are many gods (thousands of them)
> Jesus: could be one of many gods but is not the only way
> Afterlife: reincarnation to pay off karmic debt, eventually becoming one with the impersonal Brahman

So the path of Hinduism leads to a mountaintop where there are thousands of gods.

Then I explain that according to the Islamic path:

> God: one God, Allah
> Jesus: a prophet but not the Son of God

Afterlife: paradise or hell; salvation is based on weighing the good and the bad done in life

So on this mountaintop there is one God, but Allah is different from the Hindu gods, and, as we will see, different from the Christian God. And then according to the Christian path:

God: one God (Father, Son, Holy Spirit)
Jesus: the Son of God, the way to salvation
Afterlife: heaven or hell, based not on anything we do but through what Jesus did

I explain that when you look at various world faiths at a base level, in most cases, you do see similarities. For example, most faiths teach that we should love one another and love our neighbors as ourselves. Because more and more people are familiar with Buddhism, I generally will point out that Buddha and Jesus both taught similar sayings. Jesus said, "Do to others as you would have them do to you" (Luke 6:31), and Buddha said, "Consider others as yourself" (Dhammapada 10:1). In my hand-drawn diagrams, I usually circle the commonalities among the beliefs I've listed at the bases of the mountains, and I draw some paths intersecting at the bases to show that there can be similarities at this level.

But then I explain that after you move past these base-level teachings, continuing up the paths of what each world faith believes, you arrive at

the top and find that each world faith takes you to an entirely different mountaintop (see figure). Because most people who claim that all roads lead to God or that all paths lead to the same mountaintop don't usually look too deeply into the beliefs of each religion, their conclusion is only superficial. If they looked into each one, they would see drastic and contradictory differences between them. I explain that they all lead to different mountaintops. I usually also explain that while often only Christianity gets a bad rap for exclusivity and its belief in hell, most other faiths also claim to be the only true way and there are various forms of hell in many other faiths as well. Most people I talk to don't know that.

So when we actually study world religions, we see that it's not the case that all roads lead to God, because you cannot have God saying he is one God, as in Islam and Christianity, but have thousands of gods in Hinduism. And you can't say that Jesus is the Son of God and the Savior, as Christianity teaches, but then have Islam say Jesus is just a prophet. These beliefs are different and even contradictory. Explaining this to people who have never really thought it through leads to the question, So which one is true? When it comes to the fundamental teachings of the various world faiths, either they are all wrong, or only one is right. They can't all be true.

In all of the times I have taken people through this process, I have never once had someone say, "This doesn't matter. Everything is relative and they can all be right." Usually it catches them off-guard because they never viewed it like this before. But time and time again, I don't get counter-arguments once it is explained like this. Despite what you may hear about our relativistic world and the impact of postmodernism, when you logically and gently lay the facts out for people, there's not too much arguing. People see the contradiction and aren't afraid to say that it seems like all paths can't lead to the same God. At this point, nothing has been proved, but the question is raised, Why do Christians believe they are the right path? This is where apologetics and logic come in. This is where we need to be ready to give an apologetic for why we believe the Bible is inspired and true. This is when we can speak of Jesus' resurrection and how he has changed our lives. Since they know us and trust us, our words have far more impact and meaning when we share. If we are praying for them, hopefully the Spirit of God will soften their hearts and draw them to put faith in Jesus.

We need to understand that not all religions are wholly wrong

Something I make clear when I share with others is that not everything in other faiths is wrong. There are truths in other faiths that parallel Christianity. If a faith says to treat your neighbor as yourself, or to be faithful to your spouse, or not to lie, then these are threads of truth in that faith that intertwine with Christianity. I'm not talking about syncretism here. But acknowledging that not everything about another faith is wrong changes our approach to communicating our beliefs and helps avoid giving the impression of arrogance when we explain why the Christian faith is the only way to God. People assume that Christians just slam other faiths and believe there is nothing good in them. To correct this, it helps to share how Christian spirituality is different from other faith's. But it's critical to always put yourself in the other person's place as you speak about these things.

In Acts 17, when Paul spoke to the Athenians, he changed his approach depending on his audience. Paul did not just slam them or point out that they were wrong; he used what truth was in the other faiths to weave his message to the Athenians and eventually was able to show how everything pointed to Jesus and even talk about judgment. But I love how he did it. He didn't just point to their idols and say, "You're all wrong." Instead, "Paul then stood up in the meeting of the Areopagus and said: 'People of Athens! I see that in every way you are very religious. For as I walked around and looked carefully at your objects of worship, I even found an altar with this inscription: TO AN UNKNOWN GOD. So you are ignorant of the very thing you worship—and this is what I am going to proclaim to you'" (Acts 17:22–23 TNIV). He commended them for being "religious." Paul seemed to be indicating that God was at work in their lives, causing them to seek some sort of higher being or beings. Paul even referred to the unknown god that they had dedicated an altar to, and used that as a springboard for telling them about the God that they could know. It seems God is at work in people of other faiths and can work in other faiths to draw people to the one true God when the message of Jesus is made clear to them. So we can look for where God is at work and use commonalities with other faiths as a starting point for discussion.

TALKING ABOUT THE RESURRECTION

In the time I talked with Duggan, after discussing the question, Do all paths lead to God? the conversation eventually turned to the resurrection. As we talked about differences between faiths, I mentioned that the resurrection sets Jesus apart from most other religious leaders. Duggan asked me for reasons why I believe in the resurrection, so I opened the Bible and showed him some of the places where Scripture talks about it. As we talked, I also ended up using classical apologetics. Some people think apologetics isn't useful today, but I think it still is, though only after trust has been built and we have been asked questions. We shouldn't use it as a weapon to shoot others down. In my experience, even those who grew up outside of the church in our emerging culture consider having reasonable answers a respectable thing. In fact, people want to know there's validity to what I believe, and apologetics has been helpful to me in showing that to them. I believe we need apologetics more than ever today, but we need to know what the current questions are. Sometimes in apologetics we develop detailed answers to questions people in emerging generations aren't asking. We need to know people in order to know how to be ready "to give an answer when asked" (1 Peter 3:15).

In our conversation about the resurrection, I walked Duggan through an apologetic on why I believe what I believe, but I didn't ask him to say the sinner's prayer or press him to believe. I simply prayed silently while we talked until our time ended. The conversation was friendly, not a lecture but a natural back-and-forth talk. I was able to articulate some basic beliefs of other faiths and even talk a little about Buddha, whom Duggan respects. We said goodbye and left it at that. A few days later when I went back to the coffeeshop, Duggan caught me off-guard. He said, "After we talked last week, I went to my parents' house and got a Bible from them over the weekend and read the parts about the resurrection. I thought about it, and now I believe Jesus did rise from the dead." I was pretty amazed at what he said. I was not expecting that! He said he never had a Christian take the time to talk about what he believed and why. He said he never thought about how all paths might not lead to God, since he had never looked at it like we did.

We talked more, and the story is not yet over. Though Duggan believes that Jesus rose from the dead, he still isn't interested in being part of a church or exploring how the resurrection changes our lives. But I'm hoping our conversation will continue. I'm trying to do my part, and I'm seeing God move in Duggan's life little by little. I just went to a Pogues concert in San Francisco with Duggan last week, and we talked some more. I will leave things up to God, and I will do my job to pray and simply be Duggan's friend. But I can tell you that Duggan no longer thinks that all Christians see other faiths as enemies, as he put it before. He now knows that not all Christians are closed-minded and that many do study other faiths. I pray regularly for Duggan and I'm hoping that the Spirit of God will continue to draw him to Jesus. I hope that this type of conversation will occur more and more in our churches. And I hope we will consider how to believe that Jesus is the only way and yet show the utmost respect for those who practice other faiths, changing the perception that we think that everything about all other religions is wrong and that we arrogantly slam other faiths:

The church arrogantly claims all other religions are wrong

The church is respectful of other people's beliefs and faiths

WORKING AT THE WITCHCRAFT STORE AND THEN WALKING OVER TO THE CHURCH

Let me close this chapter with another story of hope. I once sat in on a class in our church about various world faiths. When we got to the part about witchcraft and pagan religion, a twenty-four-year-old girl raised her hand. She shared that she had a Wiccan background and had become a Christian just a few months earlier. She encouraged the teachers of the class, saying that what they are teaching is important for people to understand. Of course, I was thrilled with what she said, so I talked with her afterward. It turned out that she had been heavily into witchcraft and magick. She had even joined a coven and had worked at a local witchcraft and magick store. She had been downtown around Easter when our church had an outdoor art event during which we had displayed the stations of the cross on the sidewalk and had pamphlets about our church available for people to pick up. She ended up visiting our website and read about our vision and who we are. She eventually started coming to our Sunday night worship gatherings right from her job at the witchcraft store. I find that so fascinating, getting off work at the witchcraft store, and then going to a church worship gathering! Through time, she ended up putting faith in Jesus and was baptized in our evening service.

Her story is complex, since many factors and people outside of our church led to her placing faith in Jesus. But her story shows that even though we live in a pluralistic culture, someone practicing witchcraft can find Jesus and put their faith in him. I am confident that when we provide logical answers to questions with compassion, understanding, love, and prayer, we will be surprised at how many end up putting their faith in Jesus, the Savior of the world.

LOOKING AT YOUR CHURCH THROUGH THE EYES OF EMERGING GENERATIONS

1. Assess to what extent you and the people in your church view your community as a post-Christian world with post-Christian pluralistic beliefs. Has a shift come to your community? Where do you see this change happening?

2. When's the last time your church taught people about other world religions? What was the approach used? Is it done with respect to the people of the other faiths?

3. How would the average person in your church explain why they believe Jesus is the only way to salvation? What specific ways or apologetics do you and your church use to explain to people why we believe that Jesus is the only way?

THE CHURCH IS FULL OF FUNDAMENTALISTS WHO TAKE THE WHOLE BIBLE LITERALLY

10

Christian fundamentalists seem to use the Bible like a weapon, quoting verses out of context like bullets to shoot anything or anyone they don't like.

— PENNY

Six words will send most people who like Jesus but not the church running away from the church even faster than they already are: "fundamentalists who take the Bible literally." Before we get started, let me say that I have fundamental beliefs and that I take the Bible literally. Quite honestly, it's hard for me to describe myself with those words. Applying them to yourself is almost like calling yourself a terrorist or a violent backwoods hillbilly like the ones who chased Burt Reynolds in the 1972 movie *Deliverance*. I usually cringe when I hear these words. Why? Because images come to mind that make me want to hide and not tell anyone I am a Christian.

"THOSE CRAZY AMERICAN FUNDAMENTALISTS"

It's important to address this topic because repeatedly people who like Jesus but are outside the church say that fundamentalists give Christianity a bad name. They are highly suspicious of anyone who uses the word *literal* to describe how they view the Bible. In media and in conversations, the words fundamentalist and literal are always negative terms. Chris Martin of the band Coldplay mentioned in an interview that he believes in God, but he was very quick to make sure he was not equated with "those crazy

American fundamentalists."[15] Do a Google search on the word fundamentalist and you will find a ton of websites that mock fundamentalists and warn people to stay away from them. Descriptions of Christian fundamentalists on various websites use words such as "restrictive," "destructive," "crippling chokehold," "narrow belief system," "dark-age dogma," "dangerous," "evil," "fanatic," "right-winged," "bigoted," "anti-intellectual." Not too favorable. But these stereotypes are often associated with all Christians today.

Listen to the reflections of a couple of the people I talked to while writing this book:

> Christians seem really silly with some of the fundamentalist views they have. They take apart the Bible and pull out the verses that they want to shame people with. They take Jesus' words and then embellish them and give meaning to them in order to control the people in the way they want to.
>
> MAYA

> I tell you what is scary ... it's the fundamentalist Christians who take the Bible literally and go on crusades and campaigns to verbally beat the hell out of those who disagree with their particular interpretation. I bet Jesus is pretty pissed at them when they go and smugly claim Jesus is on their side and behind all they say and do.
>
> GARY

When I asked Gary where he sees the type of fundamentalist Christian he describes, it turned out he doesn't personally know anyone like this. His impression comes from television and newspapers, from street preachers, and from people who equate Christianity with a political party. So the bad news is that the impression that Christians are fundamentalists like Gary and Maya described is clearly etched in many minds. But the good news is that most Christians are not like these fundamentalists. In fact, when you look at the original fundamentalism, it wasn't at all like what we think of today.

WHAT IS A FUNDAMENTALIST?

Christian fundamentalism began when Protestant church leaders in the nineteenth century reacted against the rise of what they felt were threats to the Christian faith, primarily the liberalizing trends of German biblical criticism and Darwinian theories of evolution. It's not known who first used the term fundamentalist in relation to Christian theology, but most agree that the word started being used when the General Assembly of the Presbyterian Church met in 1910 and listed the "five fundamentals" of the faith:

1. The verbal inspiration (and inerrancy) of Scripture
2. The divinity of Jesus Christ
3. The virgin birth of Christ
4. Substitutionary atonement by Jesus
5. The bodily resurrection and future return of Jesus

That same year, the first in a series of booklets called The Fundamentals[16] was published, and the term fundamentalist began to be used as a label for those who held to the key five fundamental beliefs. In 1920 the term fundamentalist was also used in the Baptist publication *Watchman-Examiner* for that very purpose. A quick look at the list of five fundamentals would lead many to say that most mainstream evangelical Christians hold to these five core doctrines. For example, most evangelicals believe in the inspiration of the Scriptures, though some evangelicals would hesitate to use the term inerrancy because of the variety of ways it's defined. I primarily use the word inspired to describe what I believe. When I say I believe in the inspiration of Scriptures, I am saying I believe in God's superintending of the human authors of the Bible by the Holy Spirit (2 Tim. 3:16), allowing them to use their individual personalities and writing styles to compose the Bible. So exactly what God wanted in the original manuscripts is what is included in them. I like the picture evoked when 2 Timothy 3:16 is translated to say that all Scripture is "God-breathed." The Holy Spirit of God guided the human writers so that what they wrote in the original manuscripts is what God wanted written. This major doctrine shapes how the believer sees and values the Bible's authority, so I can say I have a fundamental belief that the Scriptures are God-breathed, fully inspired, and an authority and a guide for us.

Sometimes I jokingly say that I'm a fundamentalist, but what I mean is that I believe that there are some core biblical doctrines we can fundamentally believe in. If you think about it, if you believe that there is only one God, then you have a fundamental belief. So most of us are fundamentalists to one degree or another. But most of us are not in agreement with or want to be associated with what fundamentalism has become known as.

BUT THEN THE FUNDAMENTALIST SUBCULTURE WAS CREATED

As I share about doctrines and fundamentals, I fully know that following Jesus is not about following a checklist of beliefs; it's about following him. I don't imagine Jesus holding a little pad and pencil, checking off boxes as he asks people, "Do you believe I was born of a virgin? Do you believe in the inspiration and inerrancy of Scripture?" and judging us based on how many items on the checklist we believe. Following him is about devoting our lives to him and modeling our lives after his teaching and seeing our lives transformed by the Spirit as a result. Following him is about being salt and light in our communities.

But it's true that following Jesus means we can say with confidence that we believe in certain fundamental things. Jesus was always saying that we need to believe in his name, and he often questioned his disciples, asking them, "Do you now believe?" (John 16:31). So Jesus does want us to believe in him and follow him. As I already mentioned, if you believe in the resurrection of Jesus, you have a fundamental belief. There is nothing wrong with having some fundamental beliefs. But that's not the negative perception we face today. The problem is with everything we've added to having some core fundamental beliefs.

Being a fundamentalist today means going far beyond just having a few core fundamental beliefs. The list of the five fundamentals doesn't include a view of women in ministry, or of the end times, or of the creation-evolution debate (though it was implied that their understanding of the Bible argued against evolution). They don't mention methods of baptism, or cultural matters such as dress codes, drinking alcohol, getting tattoos, style of worship, evangelistic methods, or political involvement. The original five fundamentals were more of a creed, something like the Nicene Creed or the Apostles' Creed. But fundamentalists began adding more and more things to that original list, formally and informally.

Through time the term fundamentalist ceased to be associated with only the five fundamental core beliefs and instead became associated with a much more extended list including a specific end-times view and a specific timetable for the creation story. Fundamentalists added dress codes, views on music, movies, and all types of things that are very subjective, not based on the Bible. So Christian fundamentalism became something far beyond just having some core beliefs. It became a whole subculture within Christianity that added on many peripheral doctrines as core beliefs.

So today when people who like Jesus but not the church hear the term fundamentalist, they don't think of people who only believe in the inspiration of Scripture, the divinity of Jesus, the virgin birth, substitutionary atonement, and the bodily resurrection and return of Jesus. They think of people who are always saying negative things about the world, are anti-gay, take the whole Bible literally, are card-carrying Republicans, are pro-Israel, read end-times novels, and endorse snake handling and fire-and-brimstone preaching. They think of King-James, finger-pointing, teetotaling, vengeful people who credit God for using natural disasters to punish people for sin, and who use Christian jargon and are arrogant and unloving toward anyone but themselves. I realize, of course, that this caricature doesn't fit all fundamentalists, but this is the way many outside the church view any kind of conservative Christian. It's why I never publicly use the word fundamentalist for myself, because the word has a different meaning today. But just because I don't call myself a fundamentalist doesn't mean I don't hold some fundamental beliefs or take the Bible literally. But let me explain that further too.

WHAT DOES IT MEAN TO TAKE THE BIBLE LITERALLY?

While researching for this book, I found an interesting photo on a website. It was of a nice black Bible with a huge red warning sticker on the cover: "WARNING: DO NOT TAKE THIS BOOK LITERALLY. IT IS A WORK OF FICTION." In smaller letters, it read: "EXPOSURE WARNING: Exposure to contents for extended periods of time or during formative years in children may cause delusions, hallucinations, decreased cognitive and objective reasoning abilities, and in extreme cases, pathological disorders, hatred, bigotry, violence including but not limited to fanaticism, murder and genocide." On a different website, I saw a similar label designed like a poison warning label with a skull and crossbones: "WARNING! Literal belief in this book may endanger your mental health and life." Yikes. This is what some people think the Bible does to those who read it. They see taking the whole Bible literally as a dangerous thing, and I agree. Because we aren't supposed to take it all literally.

When at the beginning of the chapter I said that I'm one of those Christians who takes the Bible literally, I meant that I take literally the passages that are meant to be taken literally. I believe, of course, that there are passages that are metaphorical, such as the parables or sections of poetry. So taking the Bible literally doesn't mean ignoring the literary genre or grammatical and historical contexts. Quite often when I'm talking with people who like Jesus but not the church, I find that they generally assume that most Christians take the whole Bible literally and don't discern that God chose to inspire the authors to write in various genres. There is a general assumption that most Christians are illiterate when it comes to understanding the origin of the Bible and how to use it. They feel that we use only literal passages to defend against attacks or to attack others with. For example, consider what Dustan, who grew up in a conservative evangelical church and left late in his teenage years, has to say:

> The Bible is a cool book, but it shouldn't be taken literally. I don't want to knock the Bible itself, but I think the problem is the church. The Bible has good stories in it that we can learn lessons from. But the church goes and takes it all literally, which is what causes all the trouble. I don't think most Christians have any idea about the origin of the Bible or how to really read it. So kind of by default they just read it literally and assume that is what it means. It's sad really. No offense, but that's my impression.

Let's give Dustan some credit here. He's admitting that there are good things in the Bible. But he points the finger at the church for not teaching about the origin of the Bible or how to separate what is literal in it from what is not. I checked out Dustan's blog the night I wrote this. He commented on a book he read that went into the origins of the Bible and of Christianity. With his permission, let me share some of what he wrote:

> I'm home from dinner at my girlfriend's house. Now I'm gonna try to finish a book I am reading. It's got a lot of facts about the beginnings of Christianity. It sheds light on many of the stories in the New Testament. Important,

mind-boggling facts about Jesus, John the Baptist, and Mary Magdalene. I'm not talking about conspiracy theories. It's factual information based on historical documents from around the time of Jesus. It makes me insane to think that most Christians don't even know this stuff ... things like the whole story of Jesus is derived from Egyptian theology where Osiris is birthed by a virgin, visited by magi, performs miracles, dies to save the world, and is resurrected after three days.... You realize that something you've been told your whole life is a great big lie. DUSTAN

Dustan, who was raised in a church, started exploring because of his interest in Jesus and spirituality, and found a book which gives the historical background of various pagan religions and describes other stories of virgin births, stories as old as ancient Egypt, and Roman and Greek myths that predate Jesus. The book concludes that the story of Jesus' birth and life was a myth like the others, and that Christians borrowed from these other virgin-birth stories to turn Jesus into something he wasn't. Dustan is sincere in his search, and I commend him. But the information available to him leads him to feel that his family and the church had let him down and that everything he had been taught was a lie. On his blog, a girl in her twenties left this comment:

yes indeed.... I am so glad that you have done your homework in this arena.... not many religious people bother to do so ... that is one of the things I find so wrong with many followers of organized religion ... they step into a whole way of life and belief system that they really know nothing about.... ugh....

Once again we are accused of not doing our homework. It's not the first time I've heard this accusation. The average person is becoming more aware of the historical background of other faiths and pagan religions, and of comparisions of Christianity to pagan virgin-birth stories. Think of the millions around the world who read *The DaVinci Code*, saw the movie, or both. Even though the movie makes the disclaimer that it is a work of fiction, it's done so well that it's raising many questions. Turn on any History Channel or PBS television program about Jesus, the early church, the apostle Paul, or the origin of the Bible and this is exactly what is being taught, a deconstruction of the Bible and Christianity. I actually love watching these shows, and I think they are forcing Christian leaders to be ready to answer many of the claims being made. We need to "do our homework," as Dustan's friend said. We are now having to address questions that we never had to address before. When we aren't ready to give answers, more and more people in our emerging culture are getting the impression that Christians aren't too smart, are ignorant of the origin of their faith, and accept without question whatever their pastor says and whatever they read in the Bible. Don't think that younger people in your church and community aren't being exposed to this. If you haven't yet been questioned by them, it's only a matter of time before you are.

WHY DID YOU LIE TO ME? YOU WERE MY YOUTH PASTOR AND I TRUSTED YOU!

Several years ago, when I was serving as a youth pastor, a high schooler named Bill became a Christian and joined the youth ministry. He was a sharp guy who took studying the Bible seriously. After he graduated from high school, he went to a state university to study business. During Thanksgiving break in his freshman year, he called and asked to meet with me. That didn't seem unusual, since many former high school students contact me to hang out when they come back for holiday breaks. But this was different. I could tell something was wrong when Bill walked into my office. At first I thought maybe someone had died or that he had some other terrible news. He sat down and plopped a green spiral notebook on my desk. He opened it up and said in a calm but hurting voice, "Why did you lie to me?"

I was stunned. That was the last thing I expected to hear. I asked him what he meant, and he told me that he had an English literature class which looked into various writings, and the professor taught about the Bible. He began reading notes about the JEDP theory of the formation of the Hebrew Bible. The JEDP, or documentary hypothesis, theory states that the first five books of the Bible (the Pentateuch) were written not by Moses, who died around 1451 BC, but by different authors who lived long after Moses. The theory is based on the fact that different portions of the Pentateuch use different names for God and have detectable differences in linguistic style. The letters of the JEDP theory stand for the four supposed authors: one who uses Jehovah or Yahweh for God's name, another who uses Elohim for God's name, the author of Deuteronomy, and the likely priestly author of Leviticus. The JEDP theory goes on to say that not only was Moses not the author but also that the Pentateuch was most likely written far later and compiled in the fourth century BC, possibly by Ezra. So it questions not only Mosaic authorship but also the dating of the first five books, putting many other things into question.

Bill also pointed out a list of alleged contradictions in the creation account, then turned to another page and began talking about the alleged contradictions in the resurrection story. From there he pointed out verses which on their own sound crazy; passages such as when God said, "Now kill all the boys. And kill every woman who has slept with a man, but save for yourselves every girl who has never slept with a man" (Num. 31:17–18). Then he stopped, closed the notebook, and said "I trusted you. You were my youth pastor. Why did you keep all this a secret?" I talked with Bill a long time, and he shared that his professor had challenged any Christian students to ask their pastors about this, so Bill did. He told me that the professor said that most Christians have no idea where their Bible comes from and sadly don't question anything.

Because of our relationship of trust while he was in high school, I was able to explain that I never intentionally hid any of this from him. I never imagined talking to high schoolers about the JEDP theory, and at that time I was even fuzzy about what it was. I told him there were books we could use to examine each of the problematic passages he was raising. We even looked some up so Bill could see that there are scholars who are aware of these alleged contradictions but have intelligent ways of looking at these passages without just discrediting the Bible. But this experience showed me that we can't assume that people in our churches won't ask the harder questions about problematic passages. We can't just assume that everyone believes what church leaders say. We need to recognize that a flood of critical information is entering mainstream culture. We can't assume that all the PBS or Discovery Channel specials aren't impacting people. We can't assume that the universities aren't teaching things which challenge and can confuse those raised in the church.

WE MUST NOT HIDE THE DIFFICULT AND BIZZARE PARTS OF THE BIBLE

We really need to understand that it isn't a bad thing to admit to the people in our churches that the Bible has some very strange things in it. We quite often skip or make light of some of the more difficult things to understand or try to explain them in such shallow ways. We lose our integrity and respect when we do. The Bible is filled with things like a talking serpent and a talking donkey, people marked with 666, pillars of fire in the sky, a guy who has Hulk-like strength as long as he never cuts his hair.[17] Imagine someone reading these things who has grown up in a culture that regards the Bible as mythological. Many of these stories would seem to fit right in with fictional works like the Lord of the Rings or the Chronicles of Narnia. Are we ready to explain these stories?

NO ONE EVER TOLD ME THAT NOAH GOT DRUNK AND NAKED

How about all the R-rated murder, genocide, and gory violence in the Bible? There are children being slaughtered, human sacrifices, suicides, incest, rapes, adultery, nudity, and plenty of drunkeness.[18] We generally don't like highlighting these things, but it's all in there. I remember reading for the first time the account of Noah getting drunk and passing out naked (Gen. 9:20–23). I was never taught about that in any Sunday school I went to. You always picture Noah as a cute old Santa Claus-like man who lived happily on a boat with animals. Our daughters have a Noah and the Ark toy set, and that's exactly how it looks. But reading that Noah got drunk and passed out naked actually made the Bible more credible to me as I was reading it for the first time. It showed the humanness of Noah and that he made mistakes. He wasn't just a cartoon character. I just taught about this in our church and joked a little (in a respectful way), saying that I couldn't blame him. After all that time being stuck in an ark that stank

> IT SEEMS MORE PEOPLE ARE DOING THEIR HOMEWORK ABOUT THE BIBLE OUTSIDE THE CHURCH THAN THEY ARE INSIDE THE CHURCH.

of urine, he got out and said, "Whew! I'm glad I'm out of that ark!" and got carried away with too much wine in celebration. (Please don't be upset by my saying that. I'm just being honest to prove a point.) We need to be

THE CHURCH IS FULL OF FUNDAMENTALISTS WHO TAKE THE WHOLE BIBLE LITERALLY

open and honest about the difficult passages and odd stories in the Bible. It seems more people are doing their homework about the Bible outside the church than they are inside the church.

DOING OUR HOMEWORK *AND* BUILDING TRUST THROUGH RELATIONSHIPS

I hope that at this point you won't just dismiss all of this, thinking, "Well, it's not our job to do our homework about various vewpoints being taught today," or, "That's the Holy Spirit's job to make it clear to people," or, "The Word of God will not return void, so all we need to do is quote verses from the Bible," or, "Of course they don't like us or what we preach from the Bible, because they are blinded by Satan and unregenerate." I agree, of course, that God's Word is powered by the Holy Spirit, and that God's Word will not come back void. I fully understand that the Spirit opens unbelievers to truth. But if we really care about people, we will go to the extra effort to be teaching and not just quoting verses. If we really desire the people of our churches to "correctly handle the word of truth" (2 Tim. 2:15), then we must teach people to become students of the Scriptures themselves. If we care about people, we have to be honest and open about the difficult passages of Scripture, because doing so builds trust and credibility, and when PBS and the History Channel show television specials on the Bible that talk about other ways of looking at the Bible than what we teach, the people in our churches won't be caught off-guard.

WHAT THE WORD *LITERAL* MEANS IN RELATION TO THE BIBLE

The word *literal* conjures images of people who dogmatically think we should accept everything in the Bible as literal. But figurative language isn't literal. If we say that someone is green with envy, we don't mean his skin is green. Similarly, the Bible says things that aren't meant to be taken literally. They should be understood as figurative language used to convey truth. For example, Jesus said some true things about himself using figurative language. He called himself bread (John 6:35) and a gate (John 10:7). He called people sheep (Matt. 10:6). Obviously he didn't mean these things literally. The Bible uses figures of speech such as similes and metaphors to make comparisons. When Jesus said, "The kingdom of heaven is like a mustard seed, which a man took and planted in a field" (Matt. 13:31), he didn't mean that the kingdom literally is a mustard seed. When the Bible says, "The trees of the field will clap their hands" (Isa. 55:12), it doesn't mean that the trees literally will clap actual hands. Jesus used hyperbole to make a point when he said, "If your right eye causes you to sin, gouge it out" (Matt. 5:29). He did not mean that you should actually pluck out your eye. Other times the Bible uses anthropomorphisms, describing God in human terms: "For the eyes of the Lord are on the righteous and his ears are attentive to their prayer, but the face of the Lord is against those who do evil" (1 Peter 3:12). But this doesn't mean that God has a physical face with eyes and ears. The book of Revelation and parts of the books of Daniel, Isaiah, Ezekiel, and Zechariah are written in apocalyptic form, using visions, symbols, and numbers to communicate. Because most of the apocalyptic works were written during times of persecution, the writers used symbols that were understood by the persecuted but not by the persecutors. These apocalyptic sections of Scripture had true meaning but were not meant to be taken literally. So as leaders in the church, we have to be careful how we teach and what conclusions we make. The people in our churches follow our lead and will learn from our teaching how to study and approach the Bible.

SADLY, MANY PEOPLE DON'T KNOW BASIC BIBLE STUDY METHODS

I'm not saying anything that one can't learn in a basic class on how to study the Bible. But some well-intentioned Christians don't know basic Bible study methods, and they can easily jump to rather bizarre conclusions. Don't assume everyone understands biblical hermeneutics.

I was a guest preacher at a large church, where I was asked to talk about the afterlife. I talked about some of the Bible's descriptions of heaven and hell, going into the mysterious passages where the New Testament uses the word Gehenna rather than Hades. Hades seems to be a temporary place, but Gehenna is the eternal place where the unsaved go after the soul has been reunited with the body (John 5:28–29; Rev. 20:10–15). I explained that Jesus used the word Gehenna when referring to the eternal hell. Everyone living in the area of Jerusalem in Jesus' time knew Gehenna as the name of a garbage dump in a narrow valley right outside the walls of Jerusalem. I explained that at that time, they burned garbage day and night, and even animal and human remains were thrown into this dump. The bodies of executed criminals and individuals denied a proper burial would be dumped there. It was known as a horrific place, with a horrible stench from the fire and smoke and worms eating dead flesh. In Mark 9:47–48 Jesus talks about hell using a term which is the translation of the Greek word *geenna*, which in turn is a transliteration of the Hebrew *ge hinnom*, meaning "valley of Hinnom" or "Gehenna." He even quotes Isaiah 66:24—"where their worm does not die, and the fire is not quenched"— which describes the scene after a battle when dead bodies were being eaten by worms and burned.

So I said it was natural to use the garbage dump of Gehenna to symbolize the horror of hell. Jesus didn't necessarily—and most probably didn't—mean that hell would have literal worms and literal flames. He was making a point using symbols and images that his listeners would be familiar with. Whatever it may actually be like, hell is not somewhere you want to be. I showed photos of today's Valley of Gehenna garbage dump in Jerusalem and lightly joked how I had walked through hell to take these photos. I made it clear that I believe Jesus taught about hell as a real place of eternal existence but that we don't know what it actually will be like there.

IS HELL IN THE CENTER OF THE EARTH?

When I finished preaching, the head usher, whom I had met earlier, approached me. Though he was kind as he spoke, he disagreed that we don't know exactly what hell is like or where it's located. He shared that the Bible clearly says not only that hell will have fire but also that it's in the center of the earth. I asked him, "You mean our earth?" and he said, "Yes, hell is in the core of our earth where the magma center is." He said Jesus was not talking about the garbage dump as a metaphor for the horror of hell. He quoted Numbers 16, where the earth opened and swallowed people, and Isaiah 5:14, where the grave opened up like a cavern to take people below the earth. He quoted the passages in Revelation about the abyss, and talked about lava and geologists' descriptions of the earth's center. He was not a crazy person; he was sincere and intelligent. But he was taking Bible passages so literally that he concluded that hell is below the ground. I asked him how he reconciles all the flames and fire with Jesus' claim that it would be a place of darkness (Matt. 8:12; 25:30), but he didn't answer.

What was most disturbing to me was that this was a large Bible-teaching church. The head usher must have been around awhile and experienced whatever leadership training or membership class they have. Didn't they teach people how to study the Bible? I believe this church focused on high-felt-need application in its teaching, but perhaps they never really taught Bible study and interpretation methods.

I had a similar experience in another church when I served as a guest preacher and mentioned that there are different viewpoints on the end times, including amillennialism, premillenialism, and postmillennialism. Later I talked to someone who told me that some people in that church actually got upset that I mentioned viewpoints other than a pretribulational, premillennial rapture. They said that this view is the correct interpretation of Scripture, so I shouldn't have mentioned the others. I even talked to a man from this church who kept quoting 1 Thessalonians 4:16 and saying, "The Bible says it is a pretribulational rapture, period!" He said, "If we stray from a pretribulational rapture as the literal interpretation, then the church will fall apart and become liberal because people will think they can wait till the tribulation starts before they'll clean up their acts and they'll just live sinful lives now." Again, these are all wonderful people who truly love God. But their conclusions, which they see as fact, and their desire to have no other views mentioned don't seem to be healthy things. They are shut off to any discussion, and imagine how those outside the church would view their closed beliefs on what is not a core issue? (Not the return of Jesus, but how he will return.)

While I was in seminary, one of my professors showed the class a newspaper article about a father who punished his teenage son by beating him severely with a club. The father was arrested and brought to court. In his defense, the father quoted Proverbs 13:24: "Those who spare the rod hate their children." The article said that his wife was called to testify and was asked why she didn't intervene. She responded with Ephesians 5:22: "Wives, submit to your husbands." This is an extreme example of what can happen when people don't understand biblical hermeneutics and incorrectly take the Bible literally.

SOMETIMES WE TAKE THE BIBLE LITERALLY, SOMETIMES WE DON'T

All of the Bible is inspired (2 Tim. 3:16), but not all of the Bible is to be taken literally. Our job is to understand as best we can what parts of the inspired Scriptures are literal and which are metaphorical or figurative truth. Plenty of the Bible is literal, such as Jesus' rising from the dead. When you read all of the resurrection accounts, it's clear that they are written not as metaphors or parables but as descriptions of a historical event. But what about other parts? If we believe that all of the Bible is inspired, then our job is to study the Scriptures with great prayer and humility and to distinguish between the literal and parables, metaphors, hyperbole, and other figures of speech. We need to teach people in our churches about the origin of the Bible and how to interpret its various genres. Too much is at stake not to.

WE'RE NOT IN A "THE BIBLE SAYS IT, I BELIEVE IT, THAT SETTLES IT" WORLD ANYMORE

An old saying goes, "The Bible says it, I believe it, that settles it." It's still used quite often by some Christians who take a dogmatic stance on an issue based on a single Bible verse. But we are living in a culture in which we can't make such statements with integrity anymore. It's more effective to say, "The Bible says it. I believe the Bible is inspired. I take into consideration who the Spirit used to write it, to whom it was written, and the cultural context it was written in. I read the context of the verse, not just the verse itself. I study various commentaries to see what a variety of scholars say about it, praying the whole time I'm studying. And that forms my best understanding of it." We often do more damage than good when we just throw Bible verses at people without explaining them. When Jesus quoted a verse from the Hebrew Bible, he was speaking to people who knew the Hebrew Scriptures. When the New Testament writers used a verse to tell about a prophecy being fulfilled, their readers were already familiar with the passage and its context. But people in our emerging culture don't have that kind of knowledge of the Scriptures. So we need to explain things to them, not just "shoot Bible verses at people like bullets," as one person said. We should be like the Bereans, who "received the message with great eagerness and examined the Scriptures every day to see if what Paul said was true" (Acts 17:11). They did their homework.

Several years ago I was walking downtown and a man handed me a tract about hell and the Bible. I started walking away and then turned around. I was calm and nice, but I put myself in the shoes of all the others he was handing this tract to. I could see a pile of the tracts accumulating in the closest trash container, so I asked him, "Why are you confident that what this tract says is true? The tract says I am going to hell, but you don't know me. How do you know that I'm going to hell?" He looked at me and said, "I am only telling you what the Bible says," and then, "The Bible says it, I believe it, that settles it." I could see this was a dead end, so I asked why he felt that the Bible is true but other religious books aren't. He just looked at me and again said, "The Bible says it, I believe it, that settles it." And then he suddenly turned around and without saying anything walked away very fast, almost at a slow trot. I'm sure he was sincere, but if I hadn't been a Christian, I would have walked away thinking, "Those poor Christian fundamentalists. They don't even know why they believe what they do."

A FAMINE IN THE LAND OF HEARING THE WORDS OF THE LORD

Despite misperceptions of what Christians believe about the Bible, exciting and positive things are happening. Recently I was at a church attended by thousands of people from emerging generations. Up to half of the people in this large church are from non-Christian backgrounds. When I looked at the Bible-study notes for the sermon, I found information about cultural setting, historical context, and the audience for whom the text was written. When I looked at the classes being taught in this church, which I was told are heavily attended, I found a lot of theology classes.

In the church I recently helped to launch, we've done something similar by starting a "school of theology." Don't let the name fool you. It's just some basic classes on biblical hermeneutics, world religions, church history, and related subjects. We chose the name School of Theology because we wanted to unapologetically say that these classes are for serious study and to help fulfill our vision statement, which is "to see God transform us into a worshiping community of missional theologians." We're just in the beginning stages, and the first night we offered some classes, I wasn't sure what to expect. I wasn't teaching, but I showed up to see how it went.

As I approached the church building, I turned the corner and saw a line of people stretched around the building, waiting to sign in and pick up the class notes. I remember thinking, "Look at this! We're a new church primarily of people in their twenties, and here are all these people lined up outside, waiting to learn about hermeneutics, church history, and world religions." Standing in line was a non-Christian who had been coming to our church. She was there for the hermeneutics class. I stopped to say hello, and I could see from her response how excited she was about theology and the Bible. Even as a non-Christian!

When I attended Multnomah Biblical Seminary, the founder, Dr. Mitchell, would look at his students when he asked a question, and if he saw a blank stare, he would jokingly say, "Don't you folks ever read your Bibles?" He would quote from Amos—"'The days are coming,' declares the Sovereign LORD, 'when I will send a famine through the land—not a famine of food or a thirst for water, but a famine of hearing the words of the LORD'" (8:11)—and he would apply it to people today. I really am convinced that emerging generations hunger for the Scriptures. I believe that the emerging church needs to revere, teach, study, and discuss the Bible. The more we do so, the more we will be able to talk to people in our emerging culture about the Bible and address issues thoughtfully, and the more the stereotype that Christians are fundamentalists who take the whole Bible literally will lessen.

I emailed Dustan after reading his comments about the virgin birth on his blog and asked him if he wanted to meet and talk about that. He is a busy guy and could easily have said no, but he said he'd love to hear why I don't think that the story of Jesus' birth was simply based on pagan virgin-birth accounts. Will Dustan change his mind? I don't know. That's between him and God. But I will be doing some homework so I can have an intelligent conversation with him about it. I probably will even buy the book he referred to on his blog, so I can read what is convincing him otherwise and try to understand why he came to the conclusion that he did. And I will pray, recognizing that it's not the homework but the Spirit of God that draws people to Jesus. I will be praying that even if Dustan disagrees with me, he will at least know that not every Christian fits the stereotype.

WHAT CAN WE LEARN FROM THIS MISPERCEPTION?

What I love about being missionally minded in our emerging culture is that it forces us to really study the Scriptures to know why we believe what we do. Interacting with people outside of the church should cause us to hunger to really know what we believe. Of course, we need to focus on becoming loving, Spirit-filled ambassadors (2 Cor. 5:20). Our love, not our knowledge alone, is what will make a difference. Without love, we are only clanging cymbals, as Paul put it (1 Cor. 13:1). So let me suggest what church leaders can do to help eliminate the stereotype that Christians are fundamentalists who take the whole Bible literally.

We need to teach people in our churches basic Bible study skills

I imagine you have picked up on how much I believe we need to set the pace in teaching people not only how to study the Bible but also how to view many of the theological questions of our day. I believe we should be offering classes in our churches on how to study and understand the Bible so that the people in our churches are equipped not only theologically but also to have normal, respectful, and intelligent discussions about the Bible with those outside the church. In appendix 3 I recommend some books to help with this.

Also, we who are in leadership shape how people view the Bible by the way we teach and preach. We need to explain in our teaching and preaching how we distinguish between what is literal and what is figurative. We need to share how we have come to our conclusions, explaining the cultural and historical contexts of the passages we are using instead of just jumping to the application. I believe people, both inside and outside the church, are hungering for this type of information. Many find the Bible boring, and I think it's quite often because we aren't teaching the historical context and making it come alive that way. When we teach people how to understand the Bible in its historical and cultural contexts, we bring life and meaning to it. Yes, I know it is the Holy Spirit who makes the Scriptures clear (1 Cor. 2:10–14), but we have our part to play in how we teach.

The people in our churches represent to those outside the church what a Christian is. Therefore we need to teach and set an example for others in a way that doesn't reinforce poor exegetical and hermeneutic skills. The Scriptures themselves say, "Not many of you should presume to be teachers, my brothers and sisters, because you know that we who teach will be judged more strictly" (James 3:1 TNIV). So we need to approach our teaching and preaching with great prayer, humility, and preparation.

We need to be careful not to teach our opinions as what the Bible says

Over and over again I have read and heard preachers and fundamentalist Christians say "God says …" and then give personal opinions instead of what Scripture actually says, or quote a verse and build an opinion on it without taking into consideration the context or the audience. We need to be careful any time we tell people "God says …" and then say things that are more our opinions than fundamental doctrines we can know with certainty.

We need to be careful how we handle our positions on theological topics outside of the core fundamentals, such as whether we have a young earth or an old earth, the use of alcohol, the mode and subjects of baptism, and the role of women in ministry. Wonderful godly people differ in these areas, and we need to understand that these are not fundamentals. The cliche that we should "major on the majors and minor on the minors" is true. When we consistently slip in our opinions and say, "God says …" that is a dangerous thing. When we have personal minors we make majors, that's an unhealthy thing. When we take subtle or not so subtle jabs at those who have different opinions on non-core issues, that is un-Christlike and only shows how Christians fight and bicker with each other. When we are seen fighting and pointing fingers at each other, why would someone want to become like us? I am not talking about differences in core theological beliefs, since there are times when we need to make distinctions from others when we have core differences. But when Christians battle and point fingers, it generally is about Calvinism versus Arminianism, or a literal six-day creation, or end-times views. One day we will know all truth, and I wonder if we will be ashamed at how much we focused on minor issues and at what we said in tearing down other Christians.

We need to teach how to have fundamental beliefs without being a fundamentalist

I believe that as leaders we should be teaching why we hold to some fundamental doctrines, but we can do so without being fundamentalist. I have been in ministry serving with youth and young adults for over fifteen years. I have been immersed in non-Christian circles with those who have grown up in our emerging culture. I am convinced that there is no resistance to teaching or believing in fundamental truths. In fact, I see attraction and even relief when they hear rational and heartfelt reasons for having some core theological beliefs. But when we move from having some fundamental core beliefs to being a fundamentalist and becoming hard and dogmatic about minor doctrines and develop judgmental attitudes about external nonbiblical issues, we lose respect, credibility, and our voice.

What I'm trying to stress is that we can confidently say we have certain fundamental beliefs and that emerging generations are even drawn to our heartfelt and humble explanation of our beliefs. I believe there is a hunger for truth today, and we don't have to be afraid to say that God has revealed truth to us. However, we need to be careful in how we say that and how much truth we say we actually have, prayerfully and humbly admitting some things are a mystery we may never know in this life. We can humbly hold fundamental beliefs without being "one of those fundamentalists."

We need to be prepared for a new wave of questions

Because of the wealth of information available to people today, we need to be prepared to answer new challenges, such as Dustan's raising the issue of the virgin-birth stories that predate Jesus or the several questions Bill asked from his green notebook after he took an English literature class. How will we answer these issues intelligently? How do we talk about the origin of Christianity and the canonization of the Bible? Are we ready to say why we trust the Bible as being inspired? Are we ready to talk about the evolution debate in a way that is honorable to Jesus and respects science at the same time? Are we ready and not afraid to reexplore some theological questions we thought were all clean and tidy, but as we get asked about them, they don't seem as clean and tidy as they once did? We live in a thrilling time of all types of theological questions being asked today. May we be ready to engage in some wonderful and challenging discussions in the years ahead.

We need to use the Bible with love

In the beginning of this chapter I quoted Penny, who believes that fundamentalists use verses as weapons to shoot people down. I understand why she thinks that. I listened to her stories of how the Bible was used more to hurt her than help her. True, the Bible is referred to as a sword in Ephesians 6:17 and Hebrews 4:12. But in context, those verses are about positive help and the proclamation of the gospel, not attacking others. Yes, Scripture is referred to as a hammer in Jeremiah 23:29. But in context, this verse is about God speaking against false prophets, and not about using the Bible against someone who is earnestly seeking him, wondering if he is real, or just minding their own business. The Bible presents a message of hope, healing, love, and forgiveness of sin through the gospel. We need to be sure we aren't subtly misusing the Bible as a hammer or a sword when it should be used as words of hope, healing, and guidance.

I read on a blog an interesting observation about Christians and their use of the Bible:

> "The Bible Verse of Crushing Self-Righteousness Mode." This is the mode for the user who wants to crush another person by pulling a verse of the Bible out of context, without any supporting commentary or reasoning, and use it to justify why "I am right and you are wrong and the Bible says so!" In this mode the words of the verse that are being used magically appear on the side of the Bible Hammer in "Flaming Letters of God's Wrath" to help fry the opponent (many times referred to as "the enemy" or "the deceiver") to a crisp. The second mode is "The You Are Not a Real Christian/Smiting Mace of Judgement Mode." This is for the user who has judged his opponent as not being a true Christian (true being defined as one of the following: goes to the right church, reads the right version of the Bible, has the right political views, thinks the same thoughts, sings the same songs [or doesn't sing at all], etc., etc., etc. [you get the picture]) and wants to smite the dev ... er, I mean the other person with God's True Light of Vanquishment.

In this mode the Bible Hammer glows with a terrible, blindingly bright white light that reveals the True Light of God's Love to the opponent.[19]

How sad that in our culture the Bible is known more as a weapon for beating, bashing, and shooting people than for being sweet like honey (Ps. 19:9–11), for reviving the soul (Ps. 19:7), for giving light for direction (Ps. 119:105), for providing guidelines for walking in freedom (Ps. 119:45), and for its wisdom (Ps. 119:98). There are so many beautiful and wonderful things about the Bible. I believe we can move from being known as fundamentalists who take the Bible whole literally to being known as a community that takes the Scriptures and theology seriously yet holds beliefs with humility and prayer, and is able to intelligently speak and teach from the Bible with compassion and proper biblical hermeneutics:

> The church is full of fundamentalists who take the whole Bible literally

> The church holds beliefs with humility and strives to be thoughtful theologians

Penny and I met recently and talked for almost three hours. We discussed the Bible and what it says about certain topics. Penny had never seen most of the passages I showed her. She expressed interest in the Bible and asked me about translations. When I asked her if she wanted a copy, she enthusiastically said yes. A week later, I bought her a Bible and dropped it off at her workplace with a note. We will be meeting again soon, and the adventure of discussing the Scriptures will continue with one who likes Jesus but not the church.

It is the Spirit, not us, who draws people to God, but we need to do our homework, be available, be friends with those outside of the church, and be praying. People are ready to learn what is in the Bible, if only we'll take the time to be with them so that they trust us. We need to be ready to discuss it with compassion, love, and intelligence. During a famine of hearing the Word of God in our land, may we become caring people who lovingly give the beautiful Scriptures to people in emerging generations who I believe are starving for the inspired words within it. May we be careful not to misuse, poison, or ruin the beauty and even occasional bizareness of the beautiful and mysterious inspired Word of God.

LOOKING AT YOUR CHURCH THROUGH THE EYES OF EMERGING GENERATIONS

1. Does the teaching and preaching in your church include background information such as the cultural and historical contexts of the text, the audience, and other significant information?

2. How well does your church distinguish between subjective opinion on minor issues versus the key core doctrines? Do you feel your church focuses too intensely on certain minor doctrines? Which ones?

3. How open and honest is your church about the difficult and even strange passages in the Bible? Do you feel equipped to answer the hard questions?

4. What opportunities does your church provide for people to learn how to study the Bible and understand the various genres and why it is not wise to use verses out of context?

5. What are you doing, or what could you be doing, to help break the stereotype that all Christians are fundamentalists who misuse the Bible?

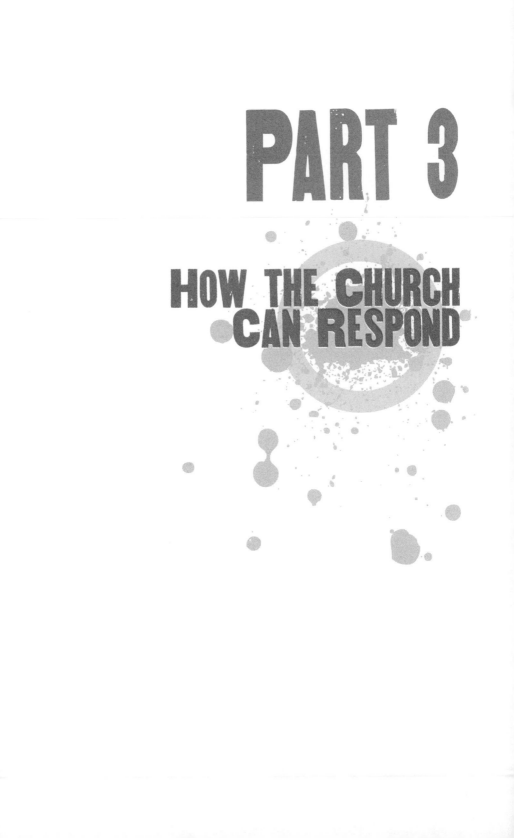

PART 3

HOW THE CHURCH
CAN RESPOND

WHAT THEY WISH CHURCH WERE LIKE

11

I would be totally into going to a church if the church revolved more around the person of Jesus than around the personality of the pastor. I'd be totally interested in going if the church were more about helping and loving other people than about criticizing and condemning other people.

—GARY

I hesitate to write this chapter. When I speak about the topic of this book in workshops, I don't cover the material I include in this chapter. I close by saying that I also asked all the people that I interviewed, "If you were ever to go to a church or return to a church, and if you could shape it, what would that church look like?" Everyone in the workshop perks up, and you can sense the anticipation in the room. This moment often feels like the climax of the workshop. I put the question, What do they wish church were like? on the screen, and I even play it up a bit by saying, "Okay, here's what they say they wish our churches were like." And then I stop.

I turn off my laptop and fold down the screen. And then I say, "Actually, I'm not going to tell you what they said. Instead of my telling you what people in my town said, you need to go out in your community and befriend people and ask them yourself." I always sense an immediate letdown. "What? Tell me what they wish church were like. I want to know what they said!"

The reason I stop there and don't share anything further is that I'm hoping that pastors and church leaders will go out and dialogue with emerging generations in their communities. While this takes effort, time, and prayer, the insight that pastors and leaders would gain by interviewing people themselves would be far more beneficial to them than my telling them what I learned in my community. And I'm always afraid that if I give pastors and leaders the information in this chapter, it will lessen their motivation to pursue relationships with those in their communities.

IT DOESN'T MATTER HOW YOUNG OR HIP YOU ARE

Don't think that if you aren't young, you shouldn't be outside the church office, building relationships with younger people. I am convinced that younger generations want to have relationships with those who are older. You might not go to clubs and concerts together, but you certainly can have a friendship. And from friendship comes trust, and from trust comes dialog about spirituality and even church. Your age and wisdom do make a huge difference with younger people.

When I was in my twenties, the three people who had the greatest impact on me were much older than me. The first was a pastor in England named Stuart Allen, who was eighty-three years old. He was about as unhip as you can get. He didn't know anything about contemporary bands and was removed from contemporary culture, and his preaching was not too lively. In his tiny little church, he would play the organ (in a musical style I was not fond of) and then walk to the pulpit so slowly that it seemed to take him five minutes to get there. But none of that affected how God used him in my life. He went out of his way to spend time with me so that I saw Jesus in his life. I was invited to belong to the little church community, and the people opened their arms and their lives to me without judgment or pressure to become like them. Stuart loved me and invited me to his home, despite the fact that I dressed in all black and wore human-skull bolo ties. (I still wear mainly black.) My haircut was a very tall pompadour with shaved sides that looked like a bleached mohawk. I was immersed in the music scene, and probably most pastors, especially eighty-three-year-old ones, wouldn't have wanted to hang out with me at that time. But Stuart saw past my appearance and listened and patiently answered my questions. We met in his home every week. God used him to change my life.

The second influencial person was my father-in-law, Rod Clendenen, who was in his late sixties when I met him. And the third was Dr. Mitchell, a professor at Multnomah Biblical Seminary, who was ninety-two when we met.

So please don't think that people in emerging generations don't want to be in relationships with older people. Believe it or not, they respect the wisdom of those who are older and are looking for good examples to follow. But they are turned off by and tune out people who are out to convert them by subtly trying to change their dress and the music they listen to so they'll fit in with your particular Christian subculture.

GETTING THEM TO GO TO CHURCH ISN'T THE GOAL

Our goal should not be to get people to "go to church." We should be inviting people to participate in the life of the church community and to participate in the activity of God, not merely inviting them to attend our worship services. Though in most cases getting people to participate in worship gatherings is a step in the process of their coming to trust Christians and the church, the goal is to see the Spirit of God transform them into disciples of Jesus whether or not they are going to your weekly worship gathering.

We need to understand the difference between "belonging, then believing" and "believing, then belonging." We need to understand that in most cases in our emerging culture, belonging precedes believing. In today's culture, people don't come to have trust and understanding until they feel they belong. Then the Spirit moves in them, bringing them to a point of belief.

THREE THINGS YOU SHOULD KNOW BEFORE YOU READ THIS CHAPTER

Before I share what I learned from those I interviewed for this book, as well as observations I've heard during my travels across the country, let me mention three things you should keep in mind when you read the rest of this chapter.

1. We shouldn't change to match what people wish church were like

When I ask individuals outside of the church what they wish church were like, it's not at all with the intention of changing the church to conform to what they want. I remember years ago asking a teenager what type of youth ministry he would go to, and he said he would love it if the church served kegs of beer at the youth meetings. Naturally, I didn't jump right up and comply with his request. We have to be careful that we don't become so "seeker friendly" that we lose the holy distinctiveness of the church. The church is a supernatural community that gathers to worship, to learn what it means to be a disciple of Jesus, and to serve God together. So our purpose is not to change things just so that people outside the church will like what we are doing. That misses the point entirely, and in my opinion it is dangerous to simply conform to what people want instead of to what the Scriptures give guidelines for.

I am, however, all for designing our worship gatherings in a way that resonates with our hearts and culture while expressing our worship as believers. I don't see that as compromising; it's simply being wise. The early church met in homes, while most churches today meet in formal buildings and sit in rows. The early church greeted each other with a "holy kiss," while today we exchange a handshake or a hug. Culture does change our forms of worship, but culture should not dictate or change the heart of worship or water our worship down. Throughout church history, various expressions of worship developed in different cultures. But we don't change our unapologetically gathering to worship God, learn from the Scriptures, experience times of repentance, celebrate communion, and serve and encourage each other. (Ironically, these are exactly the things many outside the church are looking for.)

Nevertheless, I still find incredible insight when I ask those outside the church what they wish church were like. I try to see what's behind their answers, looking for patterns and for factors that shape their thinking and values. I listen to how the church has wounded them and to church experiences that have been bad for them, and I try to understand why their experiences were bad for them. I always look for ways that we may have wronged people or have made poor impressions on them. Some of their criticisms and impressions may very well be valid, so we should be eager to hear what they say while at the same time recognizing that we don't automatically change based on the desires of people outside the church. As leaders in the church, we are directed by Jesus — the head of the church—and by the guidance of the Scriptures, not by people outside the church.

2. When asked what they wish church were like, they described the worship gathering

As you read this chapter, keep in mind that the answers of interviewees reflect that most people in our culture view church as a worship gathering or a building we meet in, and not as the people who gather. Probably the way I asked the question, along with people's definition of church, provoked mainly descriptions of the worship gathering. I hope that one day both those inside and outside the church will define church as the people, and not as the weekend worship service. But that must start with church leaders teaching that we must "be the church" and not just "go to church." (See chap. 8 in *The Emerging Church* for a fuller discussion.) I feel our evangelism has gone far astray because we focus so much on "inviting people to church," and thus we have incorrectly defined church to those outside the church.

Obviously, the worship gathering is but one part of the life of the Christian and of the weekly rhythm of a church. In previous chapters, I made observations and presented people's comments on the church's character, leadership, attitudes, and beliefs, areas that would be included in a more comprehensive answer to the question, What do you wish church were like? so hopefully you'll look at those chapters as extensions of this one.

3. God uses a wide variety of churches to reach and disciple emerging generations

There is no one type of church that emerging generations are drawn to. I have visited relatively small emerging churches that have a beautiful sense of community and good dialogue. I also have been to several emerging churches whose numbers are in the thousands of people. In larger gatherings, I always ask, "Are these just young Christians who transfer to this church because you have hipper music or a charismatic speaker, or are new believers coming to faith here?" The answers vary, but a significant number of nonbelievers come to faith in Jesus through very large emerging churches. Some churches focus on the arts in worship and give careful attention to aesthetics. But I recently visited a large emerging church that didn't have a single piece of artwork on the walls. So as frustrating as it may be, there really isn't any one model of church to follow. So much depends on the personality, temperament, and giftedness of the church's leaders. So much depends on the community, and on whether the church is starting from scratch in a living room, is an alternative worship gathering in an existing church, or is launched with a couple of hundred people from another church. There are lots of expressions of church that emerging generations are being drawn to.

So keeping these three things in mind, here are some of the responses people I interviewed gave to the question of what they wish church were like.

WHAT THEY WISH CHURCH WERE LIKE

1. I wish church were not just a sermon or a lecture but a discussion

Virtually the first thing every single person I talked to said is that they wish church weren't just a sermon but a discussion. They uniformly expressed that they do not want to only sit and listen to a preacher giving a lecture. And it's not because they don't want to learn. They expressed a strong desire to learn the teachings of Jesus and to learn about the Bible. Rather, they feel they can learn better if they can participate and ask questions.

Let's look at a few comments from those who like Jesus but not the church:

> *Why aren't church leaders paying attention to what we are doing in university? All the emphasis in churches is on the pastor's one-way sermon. But in university, we don't like listening to the lectures in the big 100-level classes. They are the least favorite. The large classes are the ones which are hardest to pay attention in and the hardest to learn from. We learn best in upper-level classes, which are the smaller ones, and in the labs where discussion takes place and our voices can contribute to the learning experience. The church has it backward focusing their teaching all in a lecture. I would like church to be small enough to have dialogue and not just sit in a lecture.* ALICIA

Teaching in church is totally important. But not just having the pastor beat into our heads what he personally believes from up on a stage and everyone then just has to accept that. I definitely would want to be challenged, but in a way that honors and respects what I believe too. I would want the forum to be able to talk back and discuss what they are saying and ask questions. But in the churches I have been to, there isn't the opportunity for this. It is more the pastor or preacher speaking to you, and you just have to sit there and listen.

DUGGAN

I'd like church to be more like when you go to a philosophy meeting where people can dialogue and intelligently grapple with Scripture texts together. Not just sit there for an hour listening to one person telling like-minded people what they want to hear without questioning or talking about it.

PENNY

Over and over I heard similar answers from other people. What is really important and exciting to see is that they all want to learn about, study, and discuss the Bible. It's thrilling to hear their enthusiasm about the Bible and the teachings of Jesus.

Listen to Alicia, who voiced strongly her feeling that large meetings with a lecture are not the best way to learn:

There is a place for larger meetings in a church, just like there is a need in universities for the freshman in the general education classes. So I am not against them. But the church needs to provide a lot more than that if they want to be serious about seeing someone like myself want to be part of one. Didn't Jesus spend most of his time in smaller settings with smaller groups? With his twelve disciples? I bet that is where they learned the most from him, not when he was in the masses with larger crowds.

ALICIA

What is interesting to note is that most of Jesus' teaching involved dialogue. Likewise, the early church met in homes in groups of probably twenty to fifty. In this smaller setting, there was bound to be lots of discussion and participation even though there was a teacher. I believe, as Alicia stated, that learning best occurs not in a one-way lecture format but through a mix of teaching and discussion. So I believe that they are right in saying that dialogue would help them learn about Jesus all the more.

I sensed a strong bias against big meetings from most of those I talked with. But it wasn't about the size of the group. It was more about the loss of the ability to dialogue. It was also about the fear of having only one pastor preach and not being given the opportunity to question that person's teaching.

Listen to Dustan's thoughts on this:

> *If I were to go to a church, I wouldn't want it to be where one person did all the talking and teaching, but more of a rotation. So one person doesn't become a superstar in the eyes of everyone there. The teacher or leader should be a servant, not someone who gets all this status from being on a stage. I think there should be an intellectual look at the Bible and definitely some teaching, but also a lot of time for open questions and discussion. That's why I think the meetings should be smaller. Every once in a while a big meeting is cool, but not as the norm.*

DUSTAN

I can understand what Dustan and the others are saying. Having been on-staff at a megachurch for over twelve years, I've seen how people can become passive listening to a preacher. Without a forum in which to raise questions and dialogue about the Scriptures, it is easy for people not to have to think too deeply for themselves. But that doesn't have to be the case, even in large churches, if the leadership sets the right culture in the church. I know several emerging churches that have thousands of people from emerging generations attending large worship gatherings in which someone preaches in a one-way format. But the leadership also has created a culture in which people are given permission to ask questions and dialogue and are given opportunities outside of the larger church meeting to do so.

When you hear of larger churches that are effectively reaching emerging generations, you'll likely find that they emphasize additional smaller gatherings in which dialogue and discussion can occur. One large emerging church I have visited has hundreds of smaller "house churches" (their term) that meet during the week. These smaller settings are where interaction and dialogue take place, and the leadership emphasizes that the smaller gatherings are part of the fabric of the church, rather than just a side program. Another large emerging church offers theological and biblical classes throughout the year, promoting them as a major part of their church. The classes include the sort of discussion and interaction that those I interviewed would desire.

I know that many church leaders will say that this isn't anything new, since their churches also have classes or small groups. But I'm not talking about just having classes and small groups as add-ons to the larger gathering. These deeper theological classes and house churches are more than just typical small groups, and they are promoted as being just as important as, if not more important than, the larger worship gathering. The smaller meetings provide in-depth teaching involving homework, assigned reading, and lots of interaction. The house churches generally have leaders, but the groups are oriented around communal discussion about the Scriptures.

In the recently launched church I am part of, we pray that God will move hundreds of people to trust in Jesus, but we want to be very careful about how we grow. We are doing our utmost to have Community Groups throughout the week in which people dialogue, study Scripture, and ask questions in smaller settings. During sermons, we try our best to pause and ask questions, even with several hundred people in a worship gathering. As often as possible, we hold Think Tanks, settings in which people can raise any question and can challenge anything, and can express their opinions and be respected and not shut down. Because we're a new church, we're striving to do whatever we can to build these values in from the beginning, since it may be harder to do after we're more established. We are trying to have a culture in which people can dialog and know that they can be heard and ask questions and give input and opinions.

2. I wish the church would respect my intelligence

I remember a conversation I had with someone who was raised in a church but left when she reached her twenties. She wasn't critical or cynical but was sincere as she spoke to me about her story. She attended a large church and participated in the children's and youth ministries through her formative years. She said she learned a lot and made great friends. But as she entered her twenties, she says, "I left the church, because I grew out of it." That statement might sound arrogant, but if you knew her or could see her heart, you wouldn't come to that conclusion. She said that the teaching was repeated every three or four years, perhaps with a different name for the series, but pretty much the same thing repackaged. She said that the lyrics to most of the songs were more akin to a "teenage romantic crush" than worshiping God's transcendence and majesty. She explained that the music and the projection of the lyrics on the screen came across like a Disney children's video, and she almost expected to see a bouncing ball above the words to help teach people the songs. She was bothered by the preacher's simplistic outlines and how most of the time he ignored problem passages and controversial issues. It was all exciting as a teenager, but then she seemed to outgrow what the church had to offer her. She was involved in serving in the church, but she really wanted to learn, and there was no place in the church for her to do so at the level she wanted. She found that buying theological books and commentaries and staying home to read them was more helpful than going to the worship gatherings.

Now, I know that we can't experience the body of Christ in isolation and that abandoning the church is not the answer. We all need to be part of a local body, and with her zeal for learning, this young woman probably would make a great teacher. But she said that when she talked to the pastor to explain her feelings, she felt he wasn't very understanding, and she said he wasn't willing to add any theologically deeper classes to the more pragmatic ones the church offered. The pastor wasn't convinced that many people at this church loved teaching, so there wasn't any need to go into the historical background or cultural context of Scripture. He explained that people just wanted their "felt needs" met, that they wanted to see how the Bible deals with their day-to-day activities. She concluded that the people were more interested in their lives than in learning about God and the life of Jesus. She sincerely wanted deeper teaching; she wanted the opportunity to grow. And so, she said, "I left the church to find Jesus." At the time I talked with her, she was exploring some smaller mainline churches where she felt she could have more intelligent conversations about theology, but she hadn't yet found a church to be part of.

Her experience isn't an isolated one. Listen to these comments:

> *I learned more about the Bible in a secular university in English literature classes than I ever learned in any church I went to.*
>
> ALICIA

> *If I were to go to a church, I would want it to be going into the culture, the history, and what the social constructs of the day were so we can understand the meaning of the biblical writers all the better. I'd like the church to respect my intelligence and be challenging my thinking and allowing me to wrestle with what the teacher says, sharing my disagreements if I have some, and to have the ability to ask questions.*
>
> GARY

I get so excited hearing these comments, because they show that people today really desire to learn about Jesus. How ironic that many said they don't feel the church is a place to learn about Jesus to the degree they want! We are in a wonderful time of hunger for spiritual depth. Unfortunately that hunger is being fed by television specials on the origin of Christianity and on Jesus, specials whose perspective is usually framed by the Jesus Seminar–type of viewpoint and those who don't hold to an orthodox view of Jesus. We are losing our chance to be a voice to emerging generations about who Jesus is. May our desire to reach those who like Jesus but not the church cause us to provide a deep level of teaching, not only for application but also for academic learning. People are saying, "We want to be taught the Bible to learn about Jesus. But teach with intelligence, and don't expect that we won't ask questions or challenge what you are saying. Give us the opportunity to ask questions, and be respectful of our questioning. We want a learning environment, not a watered-down lecture that ignores difficult passages and oversimplifies the teachings of Jesus." What more could we ask for?

3. I wish the church weren't about the church building

In a similar vein, the people I interviewed commented on not limiting "church" to the church building, which is interesting because "church" isn't a building. Yet they seemed to have the impression that Christians see the building as church, and they desired to move beyond that:

I wish church were not always about being in the church building. It seems the church wants us to always come to them, but they don't want to come to us. Why don't we meet here, like in this coffeehouse we are at? It would be more conducive for discussion here than in some church building. Why not meet in a dance studio? Why not meet in a bar? Didn't Jesus meet with people in all kinds of places?

ALICIA

Make the gathering a roundtable discussion, an uplifting motivational dialogue. Meet in people's homes, in coffeeshops, places vibrant and alive. I'd like to meet with about twenty people in a bar, drink a few pints, and discuss the Bible. That would be a church I would go to. Make it a discussion: What do you understand of this paragraph from the Bible? What does it mean to you? Make church a book club with soul.

PENNY

What I find so refreshing about these comments is the desire to meet to discuss Jesus and the Bible. But they express some resistance to meeting only in the church building. They desire to break out of the walls of the building and have "church" in other places—in homes, bars, coffeeshops, and dance studios. Comments like these get me thinking logistically, because it's easier to set up meetings in the church facility. But it's also possible to mix meetings in the church facilities with meetings and discussions in other places. Some people get defensive and say that a pub or bar is no place for discussion of the Scriptures to take place. But often these same people have no problem with the fact that C. S. Lewis and J. R. R. Tolkien met weekly in an Oxford pub to discuss life, literature, and theology. If Jesus were living among us today, I wonder if we wouldn't find him hanging out in a coffeehouse or pub, opening the Scriptures and discussing the kingdom of God there. Didn't he hang out with people at a wedding, where he provided the wine? I can imagine Jesus in a coffeehouse or pub just as easily as in the classroom of a church building. To be honest, I find it refreshing to think of bringing theological and kingdom discussion into places where people hang out. And the fact that people who like Jesus but not the church are interested in that opens up possibilities for new meetings in addition to the weekly worship gathering on a church's campus.

4. I wish church were less programmed and allowed time to think and pray

People I interviewed said they wish that church weren't so programmed and would allow time and space to think and pray. This wish ties in with negative experiences some have had in church gatherings and is similar to their desire for "church" to be more participatory. The feeling is that you go to a church, sit tightly in your seat, listen to the music, watch the preacher preach, and then go home. It all seems overly programmed, allowing no time to really think or pray.

Listen to some of the comments they shared:

> *I don't know why when I go to church they have to constantly say "stand up now," "sit down now." It feels like I am a kindergartner playing Simple Simon, with the pastor telling me what to do in the canned and preplanned program.*
>
> GARY

> *I went to a church where they gave a lot of freedom. After the teaching and during the music and singing, they allowed you to walk to different prayer areas [interactive prayer stations]. This showed they wanted us to take on a more active role in the worship time. Instead of just telling people when to sit and stand, it was more like a school with hands on learning in the prayer areas. It allowed me to go off by myself after the teaching and sit by myself and pray and reflect on my thoughts to God.*
>
> ALICIA

Alicia explained that when she goes to church, she hopes to actually spend time with God and pray. This is a high value for her. She loved having a church that had teaching but also allowed her both time and the space for prayer. This church provided prayer stations with Scripture to read and some interactive exercise with which to respond to the teaching. (See the book *Emerging Worship* for examples of prayer stations.) She went on to say:

> *I really like having a place in the church to go be quiet and pray. Everyone then doesn't have to be all doing the same thing—sit, stand, sing. Having some spaces to go to helped me be part of a worship experience that didn't seem contrived and controlled. It allowed me to, in a way, have a custom*

> *worship time that enabled me to pray all the more rather than be in some*
> *forced situation.*   ALICIA

Listen to what she desires. She wants to learn and also to pray, to worship, to connect with God, to interact with Scripture. What beautiful things to be asking for.

As we experiment in our church's weekly worship gathering and explore ways to provide time after the teaching for prayer, I am constantly amazed at the level of people's desire to pray. No too long ago, we taught a message about trusting in God for the future, and we had a space set up where people could write down what they wanted to trust God with and could write some prayers on three-by-five cards. We had a station set up behind some curtains where people could kneel and place their requests below the cross. The words "trust me" were written in large letters on the table. After the teaching, I explained that those who wanted a space to go to write out prayers of trust could use the station while the rest sat and sang some worship songs. What was amazing was that the line to use this station was so long that I had to go to the worship leader and ask him to extend that part of the gathering another thirty minutes. I stood back and watched the people of the church lining up to kneel and pray and cast their concerns before God, and I thought, What more could a pastor want? But it took planning to give people the space and time to respond to what we were suggesting in the sermon that they do.

5. I wish the church were a loving place

I remember the thing Duggan shared instantly and enthusiastically when I asked what he wished church were like:

> *If I were to go to church, I'd want it to be like a family. A healthy family*
> *where you all are looking out for each other. Where they are glad to see*
> *you and it really feels like a community. A place where they love you, even*
> *when you aren't doing well. Love shouldn't be conditional. I feel that most*
> *churches will only accept you and love you when you obey them and do what*
> *they say. But I think Jesus would accept me and be there for me when I am*
> *doing good or bad. I think church should be loving like that.*   DUGGAN

It was interesting how strong his response was, immediately calling the church a family that is loving and supportive of one another. At the same time, he feels that the church comes across conditionally with their love and acceptance.

> *I'd like the church to be where if I didn't go for a while and then came back, they would be glad to see me because they loved me and not try to guilt-trip me for not being there. I wish the pastors and leaders were like baristas or bartenders. Everyone likes to see a bartender who is nonthreatening, there to listen to you, not to judge you, but to listen and help with any advice. They are glad to see you if you haven't been around for a while.*

How ironic that those outside the church don't feel it's a loving place. Overall they feel it's loving toward those who are like them and are one of them, but not to outsiders.

> *I'd want a church to be an example of Jesus and his love to the outsiders, the outcasts, and the ones who don't normally fit in. The misfits. I'd want the church to love, love, love those who need it the most. The confused, the broken, the ones society even rejects or treats poorly. I'd want the church to accept those who don't necessarily dress or look like normal churchgoers. But the church shouldn't all look the same. I want church to be diverse and accept diversity and love diversity. I'd want to be in a church that is known as a loving people. But a Jesus-loving people too, and that's what makes the church different from just loving people; they love Jesus too.*

Molly pretty much said what Jesus did when he said that the greatest commandments are to love God and love people (Matt. 22:37–39). The two go hand in hand. If people who like Jesus but don't like the church ever went to church, they would want to experience and see love among those in the church. How would someone who comes into our churches see and feel love among us? Would they just get a quick hello from the usher, and then sit down and be ignored? How about someone who looks different from the rest of our church? Would they feel loved? Or would they get the sense from people in our church that they don't belong? How do they find relationships in which they can be loved? This is not an easy thing to answer, but it's an important thing. Jesus spoke of loving even our enemies, yet the church often isn't even known for loving people in its midst. Now, of course, there are lots of churches who truly do love one another. But the overall impression of those outside the church is that we are a closed group.

6. I wish the church cared for the poor and for the environment

Thankfully, over recent years, the church at large really seems to be paying more attention to serving the poor and needy in their communities, getting involved in global AIDS awareness, and being more aware of what products a church buys. Everyone I included in this book expected that a church that they would want to be part of would naturally be involved in helping those in need, just as they assumed Jesus would. So taking action in local and global compassion and social justice issues was overwhelmingly a quality they'd look for in a church. Another common wish is that the church would be environmentally aware. They expect the church to watch what it consumes and to be involved in caring for the environment.

7. I wish the church taught more about Jesus

Another thing people I interviewed said is that they wish the church would teach more about Jesus. How fascinating! I have heard a lot of sermons, so I can understand this. Look at most sermon titles and outlines today. Quite often, there's not too much about Jesus in them, and you might not even hear him mentioned except perhaps in an opening or closing prayer. People in today's culture are respectful of and open to Jesus. They like him, or at least what they know of him, and if they are going to be part of a church, then they want the church to be about him:

> If I were to go back to church, I really would want to learn a lot about Jesus. What did he think of things? What was his message? What did he value? I am not interested in just hearing what the pastor thinks; I want to know what Jesus thinks.

Jesus was this revolutionary guy who had tons to say. I would like church to be about what it means to really be following this revolutionary person. He wanted people to love others and make a positive difference in the world, so if I were to go to church, I would want to hear mainly about what Jesus said in regards to making a positive difference in the world.

ERICA

How wonderful and exciting to hear such interest in what Jesus has to say! But if we were to take an honest outside look at our churches, would we see and hear more about the senior pastor and his or her thinking than about Jesus and his thinking? Would there be more talk about dealing with personal issues or protecting oneself from the evils of the world than about Jesus? Would the head of the church appear to be the senior pastor or the elders rather than Jesus? I know these things may be hard to measure given the realities of leading a church today. But are we paying attention to them?

As we wrestled with these questions in our church, we decided to place a large cross front-and-center where the pulpit and pastor normally would stand, making the symbol of the risen Jesus the focal point of the room, not the pastor or worship leader. When someone speaks or leads the band, they stand on a smaller platform below the cross. We are trying to stress in any way possible that all of us in leadership are serving Jesus, who is the leader of our meetings. When I preach, I regularly point to the cross behind me, sharing that Jesus is why we are here. These might seem like subtle measures, but don't underestimate things like this. I shared in chapter 5 how someone recently became a Christian in our church and said that the placement of the cross spoke volumes to her when she first came in and that she trusted us more as a result. Little things like this do make a difference.

It's so easy to slip into leading our churches on our own strengths, personalities, and human wisdom without recognizing constantly that Jesus is the head of our churches and without consulting him. Yet I believe emerging generations are sensitive to whether churches and Christian leaders follow Jesus or follow our feelings and personal agendas. I know how easy it is to be self-dependent and subtly lose focus on Jesus. In our church, to avoid forgetting that Jesus is the head, we often place a "Jesus chair" at our staff's meeting table, an empty chair that reminds us that he is with us and that we are serving him. Often we stop and pray, "Jesus, please lead us in this. This is your church; we are your servants. Help us to know what to do here."

All of these measures are subtle and may even sound silly, but they do have great meaning, and the beautiful thing is that this is exactly what those outside the church want a church to be—Jesus-focused and Jesus-led. The more we reinforce that Jesus is the ultimate head of our churches, the more credibility we will gain and the more biblical we will become. If someone walked up to an individual in your church and asked, "What is the goal of the teaching here?" would they say, "To help me have a better family and help me not to sin," or would they say, "To help me be a better disciple of Jesus," knowing that these other things will then fall into place? What a joy it is to hear that people outside the church would want a Jesus-focused church if they ever were to be part of one. May we not disappoint them in this.

TOO MUCH TO COVER IN ONE CHAPTER

There were many other comments that I could share, more than would fit in the limited space of this book.

There were comments on the importance of having a good children's ministry. One would expect that younger families, especially, would place a high value on children's ministry, but at the same time, I'm hearing that they don't want to be totally separated from their children all the time and would want to experience "church" together as a family.

There were comments about the value of diversity. They don't want the church to be a "bunch of clones," as one girl put it, who think alike, dress alike, and act alike. They want to be accepted for their individuality and creativity. Although there were comments about wanting to be with other people their age, they also want older people to mentor them and help them learn. When I was in young-adult ministry, one of the most beautiful things was seeing people in their twenties hunger for the wisdom and care of people older than themselves. We set up most of our midweek home groups to have older couples and singles in their forties, fifties, sixties, and even seventies mentoring and shepherding the younger ones.

There were comments about the worship environment. One girl, who had visited an emerging church which focused on the arts, said, "If I knew church was like this, I would have gone a long time ago. I wish more churches would incorporate art like this one did, because they allowed people to create art there; as an expression of worship, it felt much more like community involvement than just the preacher." I told the story earlier of a girl in her twenties who came to our church, and eventually was baptized, after she found out about our church through an art event we hosted downtown. So people in emerging generations value and appreciate art in the worship environment perhaps more highly than other generations.

THEY WANT SOMEONE TO ASK THEM TO BE PART OF A CHURCH

Ironically, talking with many dozens of those who like Jesus but not the church has convinced me that they aren't opposed to being part of a church. I wish you could see their eyes as they talked and hear their hearts. They are open to being part of a church community, but the invitation to do so has to come through relationships of trust. They don't want a stranger walking up to them on the street and handing them a tract. Nor do they want a casual acquaintance putting pressure on them in a weird way to come to their church. If only we will try to understand what keeps them away, we will be surprised to discover their openness to the church.

LOOKING AT YOUR CHURCH THROUGH THE EYES OF EMERGING GENERATIONS

For each item in the list "What they wish church were like" (below), ask yourself two questions:

1. Is this something the church should be about? Why or why not?

2. Is this something your church is addressing? If not, what could you be doing to address it?

WHAT THEY WISH CHURCH WERE LIKE

1. I wish church were not just a sermon or a lecture but a discussion.

2. I wish the church would respect my intelligence.

3. I wish the church weren't about the church building.

4. I wish church were less programmed and allowed time to think and pray.

5. I wish the church were a loving place.

6. I wish the church cared for the poor and for the environment.

7. I wish the church taught more about Jesus.

OUR TWO BIGGEST BARRIERS

12

> I wish I would have known earlier
> that not all Christians are such jerks.
> I had no idea. Maybe I would
> have believed in Jesus earlier.
> — MOLLY

Many skeptical church leaders believe that people from emerging generations have negative impressions about Christians and the church because the cross is a stumbling block. These people, they say, reject the cross, so of course they are negative about the church. Now, it's true that the cross is a stumbling block to people (1 Cor. 1:23); however, we can't dismiss that easily people who like Jesus but not the church. The problem isn't that they stumble over the cross. The problem is that they stumble on the attitudes of some Christians and on the Christian subculture that we have put in their way before they can even get to the cross.

WE HAVE CREATED A NEW CHASM IN THE BRIDGE ILLUSTRATION

I suspect you are familiar with the well-known Bridge Illustration. I don't like to use it too often because this illustration places God on only one side of the chasm, when we know that God is everywhere (Ps. 139:7). Also, it characterizes the gospel as being only about the forgiveness of sin and obtaining eternal life in heaven, when we know it's also about participating in eternal life and living in the kingdom now. But setting aside these concerns, I'm going to use the familiar diagram to illustrate my point in this chapter (see figure).

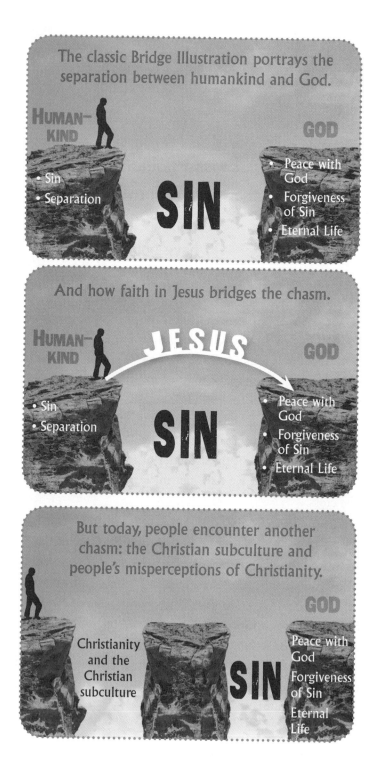

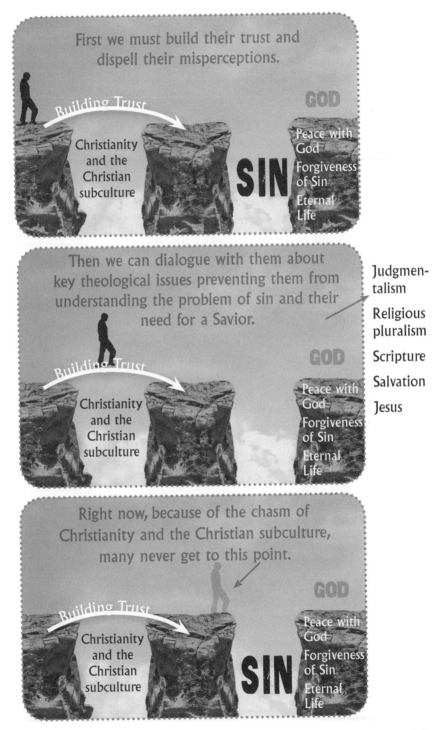

235

In the Judeo-Christian world of the midtwentieth century, the Bridge Illustration worked well. Most people understood the concept of one God, and even if they were not religious, they generally understood what sin is. Most people trusted and respected church leaders, Christians, and the Bible, so when Christians spoke about God and Jesus, people listened more readily. After they agreed that they were sinners and trusted what Christians said, and the Spirit moved them, they crossed the bridge, putting their faith in Jesus.

But in our post-Christian culture, people encounter a second chasm, the chasm of the Christian subculture. We have created this chasm with our rhetoric and attitudes, which have led people today to harbor negative perceptions of Christians and Christianity that prevent them from trusting us and being interested in the gospel. The negative perceptions of the church I have covered in this book create this new chasm. This new chasm keeps them from ever getting to the sin chasm. And because we have become citizens of the bubble, having lost our understanding that we are missionaries in our culture and staying comfortably within our church walls and networks, the new chasm only continues to grow.

We need to bridge this chasm of the Christian subculture by befriending people outside the church, inviting them to participate in community, and dialoguing with them. We need to be the light of Jesus and the living gospel to them, building their trust in us so that they will be ready to listen.

After we have earned their trust and dispelled their misperceptions, we can address ideas prevalent in our culture which keep people from understanding the gospel, such as sorting through religious pluralism, and key theological ideas such as the inspiration of the Scriptures and who Jesus really is. Then individuals can understand what the Bible teaches about sin and salvation and can arrive at the point where most people in the middle of the last century started.

Of course, people might not respond to the invitation to put their faith in Jesus as Savior (Heb. 3:12–13). But I have talked to so many people outside the church who, despite all of the Christian media, evangelistic campaigns, outreach events, and other influences, have never even heard or experienced the gospel. We need to recognize that we have created this second chasm, and we need to make the effort to bridge it by building trust so that people may at least be brought to the point of hearing the gospel and understanding their need for a Savior.

FOCUSING ON THE KINGDOM NOW AS WELL AS THE KINGDOM AFTER WE DIE

Before we go on, it might be good to discuss what I mean when I say "hear the gospel." The core of the gospel is the good news described by Paul in 1 Corinthians 15:3–4, "that Christ died for our sins according to the Scriptures, that he was buried, that he was raised on the third day." This is the Jesus-centered gospel that changes and transforms us. But the gospel isn't only about getting to heaven in the future; it's also about the wonder and beauty of living, serving Jesus, and participating in what God is doing in the kingdom here and now.

There's some refreshing discussion going on about how we can view the gospel as more than just the forgiveness of sin. Please don't misunderstand me. First Corinthians 15 clearly indicates that we are forgiven by the work of Jesus and our faith in him. But the gospel is more than only forgiveness. I'm not suggesting that we add anything to what 1 Corinthians 15 says, since that's the pure gospel and nothing else is. I'm suggesting that as we explain it and live it, we need to do so in a way that gives a more holistic picture of what the gospel does in our lives. Author and professor Scot McKnight uses a helpful analogy:

> The gospel is about God's embracing grace that unleashes our embrace of God and our capacity to embrace others. You don't respond to grace all at once, any more than you fall in love all at once. For far too many, conversion is seen as a birth certificate instead of a driver's license.... Conversion is a marriage rather than the marriage certificate. The question I'm being asked, and I don't mean to be hard on anyone who is asking it, is ... how you get a birth or marriage certificate, and I think the point is a driver's license and a marriage.
>
> The question the gospel of embracing grace asks is not "what can I do to get in?" but "will I be a part of God's work?" Once this is understood, and that the gospel is designed to regenerate our hearts to love God and to love others, then what we are asked to do is as

simple as that: we are asked to love God and to love others. That, my friends, ain't sumfin' that happens all at once.[20]

This discussion is huge and is not the point of this book, but I bring it up because the Bridge Illustration is so focused on the forgiveness of sin and going to heaven. Most people today have no problem admitting they sin. But most don't understand how sin creates the need for a Savior. But when we speak of the gospel as an invitation into a beautiful relationship with God that gives us the privilege of participating with him in loving others and making a difference on earth, people today can relate to it. Again, please understand, I affirm that the gospel is a radical message that entails faith in the risen Jesus (Rom. 10:9), the denial of self (Luke 9:23), and repentance to align with God's will (Acts 3:19). I know that this message is a stumbling block and that there will be those who reject this good news. Yet I am convinced that we have created a new stumbling block with our Christian subculture that keeps people from even getting to the gospel at all.

DIGGING THE CHASM WITH OUR CHRISTIAN SHOVELS

People outside of the church who aren't in relationships with those inside the church might never hear the gospel or get to see it lived out in someone's life. Instead, they'll only get an impersonal tract that focuses on hell or see a street evangelist who many times ends up making things worse. Sometimes when I talk to pastors about this, someone will quote Romans 10:14 — "And how can they hear without someone preaching to them?" — and tell me that their job is to preach the gospel in their church. But people who need to hear the gospel most likely aren't going to their church. On Sundays, they are sleeping in, shopping at the flea market, going out to breakfast — they're anywhere but at a church meeting. I don't know why we think that if we have good preaching or add a worship band or have coffee and candles that they will come. Those things are all good, but people outside the church aren't looking for a church with those things. They aren't looking for a church at all. It is in the context of relationships with missional Christians that they become inspired to come to worship gatherings. But the sad part is so many outside the church don't have a relationship with someone inside the church. I'm always amazed at how many people outside the church say they don't know any Christians personally. It's not that they would mind hanging out with one if a true friendship was built, but the Christians they work with or attend school with don't make themselves known to them or befriend them and spend all of their social time with other Christians. And so we widen the chasm.

The good news is that I know several pastors who are creating missional cultures in their churches, encouraging their people to befriend those who are outside the church and draw them into community with those who are following Jesus. They have found that when this culture is established, large numbers of people from emerging generations come into their churches. When you talk to these church leaders, it's clear that they see themselves as missionaries and that they are creating a missional culture in their churches.

THE HOLY SPIRIT STILL CONVICTS AND CONVERTS

Even though there's human effort involved, ultimately it's the work of the Holy Spirit that draws someone to Jesus. Jesus said to his disciples, "But when he, the Spirit of truth, comes, he will guide you into all truth" (John 16:13). He also said that the Holy Spirit would convict the world of sin (John 16:8–11) and that it's the Father who draws people to him (John 6:44). So clearly it's not human effort alone that draws individuals to Jesus so they understand who he is and place their faith in him. This should excite us and lead us to hope that many will come to faith. I've heard people easily dismiss those who don't like the church, blaming hardened hearts and the stumbling block of the gospel. It really makes me incredibly sad to hear that. I hope we never dismiss God's

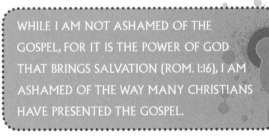

WHILE I AM NOT ASHAMED OF THE GOSPEL, FOR IT IS THE POWER OF GOD THAT BRINGS SALVATION (ROM. 1:16), I AM ASHAMED OF THE WAY MANY CHRISTIANS HAVE PRESENTED THE GOSPEL.

power to change lives. God can draw to himself whomever he wants, and he uses people and churches as part of that.

While I am not ashamed of the gospel, for it is the power of God that brings salvation (Rom. 1:16), I am ashamed of the way many Christians have presented the gospel. Quite often, I have seen the gospel treated like

239

a product on a late-night infomercial or hawked like wares in a street market. But as soon as these "evangelists" sense you're not interested in buying, they dismiss you and it's on to the next potential buyer. I am ashamed to hear the stories of individuals who are treated as nothing more than targets. If the arrow of someone's gospel presentation doesn't hit the target, then the person is dismissed as nonelect. Then it's goodbye, no interest in a friendship or in caring about the person. How do you think this makes people feel? Is this how Jesus treated people?

JESUS CARED ABOUT PEOPLE AND LOVED THE WORLD

One of my favorite New Testament scenes is when Jesus rode into Jerusalem on Palm Sunday. In Luke 19:41–42 he approached the very city that would reject him, knowing he was going to be crucified and foreseeing the future destruction of the temple and of the city. He didn't look at Jerusalem and say, "You had your chance! Too bad! Now you're gonna pay!" No. He looked out at those who rejected him and his heart broke and he wept. Matthew 9:36 says, "When he saw the crowds, he had compassion on them, because they were harassed and helpless, like sheep without a shepherd." Jesus had compassion for the people. Even in his agony on the cross, he looked out at the people who crucified him and said, "Father, forgive them, for they do not know what they are doing."

Are we like Jesus? Or do we just say, like so many Christians and even pastors, "Oh well! They've hardened their hearts. Too bad"? And then it's off to another Bible study or Christian concert, or to read yet another end-times novel or to discuss what the emerging church is or isn't. It is horrifying and heartbreaking to try to comprehend that some people are going to one day experience eternal separation from God. Do we ever think about that at all? Driving down the highway or sitting in a packed movie theater or at a sporting event with hundreds or thousands of other people, do we wonder if the people around us have ever heard or experienced the gospel?

Do we ever weep as Jesus did for those who reject him? Or do we weep only at the emotional solo that someone sings in a church meeting about how we much we are loved? Do we have compassion for those outside the church who aren't experiencing the abundant and full life Jesus promised

(John 10:10), who aren't experiencing the joy of partnering with Jesus to advance his kingdom and help others, who haven't experienced a healthy church and the beauty of being part of a supernatural community?

NEVER FORGET WHERE SO MANY OF US CAME FROM

God loves people and is patient and wants no one to perish but everyone to come to repentance (2 Peter 3:9). This includes highly unlikely people such as murderers (Acts 8:1), tax collectors (Matt. 10:3), the sexually immoral, idolaters, adulterers, male prostitutes, practicing homosexuals, thieves, the greedy, drunkards, slanderers, and swindlers (1 Cor. 6:9–11), all of whom can inherit the kingdom of God if they will be washed, sanctified, and justified in the name of Jesus Christ and by the Spirit of our God. Most of us have come from a background similar to those listed in 1 Corinthians. Most of us admit that Jesus has changed our lives and how far he has brought us. Let's not forget that this same Jesus can also change others. Someone saw past our hardened hearts and befriended us, despite the fact that we were sinners and didn't believe. And the gospel eventually changed us and turned our lives around, despite our background.

I have had to remind myself of these things. In fact, here are some questions I ask myself:

- Am I numb or neutral to people outside the church?
- Do I intercede daily for people outside the church?
- Who am I praying for now who is not a Christian?
- When's the last time I had coffee or dinner or gone to a movie and just hung out with someone who is not a Christian?

I suspect you are reading this book because you do care. But I am always amazed at how many Christians really don't seem to care much about those outside the church. Isn't something going terribly wrong when so many outside the church are getting so many negative impressions of the church and Christianity? Isn't something going wrong when so many people don't even know a Christian? If the gospel really is good news and repentance is about being refreshed, shouldn't we be doing anything possible to help bring this good news and refreshment to others outside the church? Even if they never put faith in Jesus, at least they can't say that all Christians are jerks, as Molly, whom I quoted at the beginning of this chapter, once felt.

GOD IS WORKING OUT THERE TODAY

I love another thing Molly said which gives me hope. She was a practicing Hindu at the time she was befriended by her Christian roommates and eventually began coming to our church. She thought churches would all be homogenous and not allow cultural diversity. She thought a church would judge her because she was a Hindu. She thought that females would not be respected in the church and was surprised to find that they were. As a poet and an artist, she was pleased to see that poetry and art could be used in a worship gathering. One night she put her faith in Jesus and believed in the gospel as the power to change her life and give her hope not just in the afterlife but here in this life. She ended her beliefs in the gods and goddesses of Hinduism and instead believed in the saving grace of Jesus.

Molly said that she is amazed she is a Christian because she would never have guessed that she would become one. But she did because Christians with missional hearts, who befriended her and cared for her not because they saw her as a target but because they cared about her and liked her, lived out the gospel to her.

> I wish I would have known earlier that not all Christians are such jerks. I had no idea. Maybe I would have believed in Jesus earlier.
>
> MOLLY

"Maybe I would have believed in Jesus earlier"! Molly's quote gives me such hope. Not that everyone will put faith in Jesus just because they meet Christians "who aren't jerks." But imagine all the people who at this moment have the impression, like Molly did, that all Christians are jerks. And imagine how many more might experience and hear the gospel if only we could remove that perception. When Molly met some Christians who cared about her and she realized that not all Christians are jerks, she got over that chasm and moved along to wrestling with what the gospel means, and the gospel melted her heart and she placed faith in Jesus. Every time I see Molly and others like her, I get so optimistic about the future.

Every time I go to a church where I see emerging generations coming to faith, it brings me such hope.

I wonder how many Mollys are living on your block right now? If we believe in a future judgment, how can we ever be content with our own salvation and not really care about people like Molly? It's as if we have all fallen off a ship, and some of us, through God's grace, found a lifeboat, but instead of helping others get out of the water, we ignore their screams. We don't want to get in the cold water, and so we sit around, happy and warm, listening to CDs on our iPods and complaining that the people outside the boat are making too much noise. Instead, we should be desperately paddling around trying to help others into the boat, where they too can experience warmth, community, and safety.

I don't know whether this story is true, though I heard it from a speaker who said he talked with the person involved. A pastor kept wondering why he never saw non-Christians in his church. He was new at the church, but after about a year, he became frustrated that new people weren't coming. He took a walk and ended up entering a bar near the church building. He sat down and got into a conversation with someone sitting at the bar. He shared that he was the pastor from the church down the street and that he had been there for a year. The person was interested in talking about that, so they got into a lively conversation about why he was a pastor and what the church was about. When at one point he referred to heaven and hell, the person said, "I don't really think you believe in that." The pastor asked why and the fellow answered, "If you really believed in hell and what you're saying about a future judgment, you would have been in this bar months ago to tell people about it."

Regardless of whether the story is true, it makes a point about the importance of simply being with people outside of Christian circles. I don't feel we need to be focusing on hell, like in this story. But we can be speaking of the joys of following Jesus and participating in kingdom activity, and we can be inviting others to join us. You'd be surprised what God can do if only we make the effort to get out of our church subculture. We can build bridges of trust to people and break their misperceptions of Christianity. We can make changes in our church culture to create a church of missionaries. In the context of relationships, we can dialogue about theological issues, even bringing someone to the point of understanding sin and salvation and who Jesus really is. Yes, the Spirit does the rest, which is why prayer is so important. But we still have to do our part. We still have to make the effort. There is so much hope, so much possibility, and I hope the church will do whatever it takes to fill the chasm we created that prevents so many from experiencing the good news of Jesus.

LOOKING AT YOUR CHURCH THROUGH THE EYES OF EMERGING GENERATIONS

1. Do you agree or disagree that through our attitudes and Christian subculture we have created a stumbling block in addition to the stumbling block of the gospel? Why?

2. What specific stumbling blocks can you list that prevent people from ever reaching the point of stumbling over the gospel?

3. Ask yourself the following questions:

   • Am I numb or neutral toward people outside the church?

   • Do I intercede daily for people outside the church?

   • Who am I praying for now who is not a Christian?

   • When's the last time I had coffee or dinner or gone to a movie and hung out with someone who is not a Christian?

4. What is your attitude toward those who are outside the faith in our emerging culture? Hope and optimism? Or callousness and dismissiveness?

A GREAT HOPE FOR THE FUTURE

13

> When we say, "I love Jesus, but I hate the Church," we end up losing not only the Church but Jesus too. The challenge is to forgive the Church. This challenge is especially great because the Church seldom asks us for forgiveness.
> **—HENRI NOUWEN**
> *BREAD FOR THE JOURNEY*

As I'm typing this last chapter, I'm watching a television program about the origin of Christianity. A professor from the University of California, Berkeley, is being interviewed and is comparing the story of Jesus' birth and death to mythic hero tales (his phrase) such as the story of Osiris and Horus. Osiris and Horus were mythical Egyptian gods more than three thousand years before the birth of Jesus. The professor says their story tells about a god who fathered a "son of god" who was born to a virgin and was later killed and then resurrected. His theory is that the biblical writers used this story to come up with the story of Jesus.

The professor also mentions Mithras, another mythical "son of god," who derives from Persian and Zoroastrian deities from around 2000 BC. The worship of Mithras was one of the mystery religions that were prominent from the first century BC to the fifth century AD. Like Jesus, Mithras was born in a cave to a virgin and was visited by shepherds. His birth date is the winter solstice, which at that time was December 25. The worshipers of Mithras went through a ritualistic baptism in water, and drank wine and ate bread to symbolize the body and blood of the god. They held Sundays sacred. Another story that predates Jesus is the myth of the Greek god Dionysus. His father was the god Zeus and his mother was a virgin mortal, so he too was called "son of god." Like Jesus, Dionysus turned water into wine as a miracle (he was known as the god of wine), and he too died and was "born twice," coming alive again by the power of his father.

WE MUST BE PREPARED TO HAVE SOME ANSWERS

I'm paying attention to this television program because Dustan wants to meet and talk about whether Christianity merely borrowed from these Egyptian, Persian, Greek, and Roman mythological stories. We have corresponded more since the time I wrote about him in the earlier chapter. As we were setting up a time to meet, he wrote:

> *There do exist direct parallels to just about everything in the New Testament in Egyptian, Hebrew, Greek, Roman, and other stories. The early church, from about 300 AD on, was bent on suppressing all other versions of Jesus' story that contradicted the four biblical gospels, as well as all other religions and religious sects that disagreed with the church. The four inquisitions were another reason why Christianity is what it is today. Much strategy and violence went into championing the modern story of Jesus. Anyone believing in "those [other] virgin–birth stories or religions" was labeled a heretic and prosecuted by the church under penalty of death.*

He wants me to explain why I say that all of the Egyptian, Persian, Greek, and Roman stories of virgin births, baptisms, and resurrected saviors that predate Jesus are just myths. He wants to know why I say that Jesus' story is true, especially since the other stories all predate Jesus, even by as much as three thousand years.

Some people might respond to Dustan by saying, "Oh, of course those stories aren't real; only the Bible is real," and end the conversation there. But that wouldn't be respectful of him. Or they might say that I should just explain to him the gospel and tell him that he shouldn't pay attention to the other stories because they are satanic, that he'd better repent and leave it at that. But that wouldn't be respectful of him either. I frequently ask non-Christians to read the Bible or to look into what I'm saying to see whether it is true. I have to be ready to do the same thing myself or I will be a hypocrite. I need to do some research and articulate intelligent answers to people's claims. So I have some work cut out for me, since I have never really studied Dustan's question before.

IT'S EXCITING BECAUSE THIS IS WHAT BEING A MISSIONARY IS ABOUT

When discussions like the one I'm having with Dustan come up, we can be energized by knowing that we're engaged in the lives of people who are asking us questions. We are told in 1 Peter 3:15, "But in your hearts set apart Christ as Lord. Always be prepared to give an answer to everyone who asks you to give the reason for the hope that you have. But do this with gentleness and respect." So when Dustan asks me to give him reasons for what I believe, I need to do some homework so I can give him answers for the hope I have in Jesus, a person who is not just some mythic hero. And what is thrilling to me is that despite his questions and the fact that he isn't part of a church, Dustan is open to talking about Jesus. Jesus is the point of the conversation. Dustan emailed me and said:

> I'm totally into debating this, just because it's SUPER interesting to me. And growing up idolizing Jesus, I'm still fascinated by Jesus and his effect on the world.

Jesus is not just interesting to Dustan, he is "SUPER" interesting. And I love hearing that Dustan is "still fascinated by Jesus and his effect on the world." I'm looking forward to getting together with Dustan to compare the Jesus of the Bible with the mythic hero he is talking about.

My constant questions to church leaders are, Who are the Dustans in your life? Who are you having ongoing relationships and conversations with? Are you training the people in your church to have a missional heart? Are you creating in your church a culture that encourages people to hang out and develop relationships with those who like Jesus but not the church? And when you answer questions, do you do so with "gentleness and respect"?

MORE THAN JUST APOLOGETICS FOR THOSE WHO ARE ALREADY CONVINCED

My great fear is that you would read this book and then do nothing about it. I hope that my sharing with you what I'm learning about the interest people in emerging generations have in Jesus encourages you. I hope this book motivates you to build friendships with those outside the church if you aren't already doing so.

I had a conversation recently with someone who is really into apologetics and has a ton of well-thought out answers. I asked him, "Who are you talking with and hanging out with who is not a Christian?"

He paused and said, "Nobody."

I asked, "There isn't one non-Christian you are talking to?"

He said, "No."

"Then who are you talking to about all of this apologetics?"

He answered, "Other Christians."

So often we love to study apologetics and end up talking only to other Christians about it. The questions we study aren't derived from being out on the mission field. They come from our interest in puzzling questions. But aren't we supposed to use apologetics to explain what we believe to non-Christians who ask us why we believe what we do?

MAY WE NOT GET IN THE WAY OF WHAT GOD CAN DO

It's really an exciting time to be on the mission Jesus has sent us on. It's thrilling to be in various church worship gatherings—on the West Coast and the East Coast, in the Midwest and in the Bible Belt—and see hundreds and sometimes thousands of people from emerging generations worshiping God and lifting up the name of Jesus.

Sure, the overall outlook is not great, but I have great hope, as long as we learn how to get out of God's way. The negative perceptions of people outside the church are hardly ever about Jesus; they are about us:

- Bill Maher, who hosted the television show *Politically Incorrect*, once said, "I'm a big fan of Jesus. I'm not a big fan of those who work for him."[21]
- Movie director Woody Allen is credited with saying, "If Jesus came back and saw what was being done in his name, he wouldn't be able to stop throwing up."
- Most people today are aware of the well-known quote attributed to Mahatma Gandhi: "I like your Christ; I do not like your Christians.

Your Christians are so unlike your Christ." (Gandhi was known to frequently quote the teachings of Jesus and even had a picture of Jesus Christ on the wall over his desk.)

The people interviewed for this book had much the same types of things to say, which is why our calling is to live out our faith in our culture so that people see that not all of Jesus' followers fit the stereotypes.

If we ask God to change us where needed, and if we would only be the church, there is so much hope. Today I just talked on the phone with a young twenty-something who, through a relationship with someone in our church, recently put faith in Jesus at a prayer meeting. I also got an email from Molly telling me what she is learning and how she is growing in her faith and in her excitement about Jesus. Yesterday as I was driving down the road, I happened to pass the girl who was a practicing Wiccan before she was baptized. We just got an email from a mother who is part of our church telling us how one of the friends her daughter brings became a Christian over the past few months and how excited this mom was about that. Last week I got a phone call from a twenty-five-year-old homosexual asking about our church. He was thinking about coming to our worship gathering, having heard about us, but was wondering how we would feel about that. He asked me what we believe, and I explained our theological position without hiding anything from him. I also expressed how much we would welcome him into our church and that I would love to meet with him. He said he would be coming to visit, and I look forward to meeting him.

EVEN THOUGH WE'LL NEVER HAVE IT ALL TOGETHER, WE CAN HAVE A MISSIONAL HEART

I'm not trying to suggest that our church has it all together. Believe me, if you hung around our church long enough, you would see otherwise. We struggle every single day trying to motivate people to serve the mission and on various ministry teams. We are constantly trying to keep people from thinking that the church is the worship gathering rather than the midweek community groups. Sometimes leaders don't show up or we don't have enough ushers or greeters. We have plenty of technical problems, and sometimes messages go too long or don't connect. We have creative ideas for prayer stations that end up bombing. But we are passionate about constantly trying to develop a missional heart, and that's why some people who like Jesus but not the church are giving us a chance. More than just giving us a chance, they're giving the church in general a chance. I don't believe people are looking for churches that are all together. They are looking for churches that care about Jesus and will care about them. So if your church doesn't have it all together, don't be discouraged. If your church doesn't have it half together, don't be discouraged. I hope that if you gained anything from reading this book it's that it isn't about the music or preaching or programs; it's about having a missional heart, fully dependent on God's Spirit, and not being afraid to make changes and take risks for the gospel.

OFFERING AN APOLOGETIC AND AN APOLOGY

People today are open to Jesus, but the church needs to rethink how we come across to people on the outside. While we need to stand strong on what we believe and need not be ashamed of the gospel in any way, we need to make sure we are presenting a biblical picture of the church and not perpetuating negative stereotypes. We need to offer an apologetic to correct misperceptions.

We also need to offer an apology when the church hurts people in the name of Jesus. We need to offer an apology for arrogant and shameful things we've said and for presenting as truth our fallible opinions. We need to offer an apology for straying from the mission of the church and becoming self-absorbed citizens of the bubble. We need to apologize whenever the beautiful bride of Christ is prostituted for a church leader's or a politician's agenda. We need to apologize when we aren't honest with people and become so seeker-friendly that we don't tell them the hard truth about sin and repentance. We need to apologize when we say that we are all sinners saved by grace but show contempt for those who are still in sin.

YOU REALLY CAN'T DISLIKE THE CHURCH IF YOU LIKE JESUS

The church is a beautiful, wonderful living thing. We are the body of Christ. Yet we all are sinners and make mistakes. I hope we will recognize the mistakes we make, repent, and apologize. I hope we will do whatever it takes to remain pure but move ahead on our mission into the culture. I also pray and hope that those who have misperceptions of the church or have been hurt by the church will give us a chance. Because the reality is that the church isn't just an organization or a social club but a supernatural community. We are the bride of Christ (Eph. 5:25 – 27). So when people say they don't like the church, they are saying they don't like the bride of Jesus, which is like going to a wedding and telling the groom that we like him but not his bride. It's insulting to the groom when we don't like the bride. And the church isn't just a human couple; it's a supernatural part of Jesus. Jesus said he would build it (Matt. 16:18). He wants to keep it pure (Matt. 18:15 – 17). The church is his holy people (1 Cor. 1:2). The church is his body (Eph. 1:22 – 23; 1 Corinthians 12). He is the head of the church (Eph. 1:22). Jesus loves the church and gave himself up for her (Eph. 5:25). So when we say we like Jesus but not the church, we have to understand what we are saying.

What I think most people mean is that they like Jesus, but they don't like what people have turned the church into. We need to explain to those who like Jesus but not the church that Jesus loves the church, and that if they truly like Jesus, then they cannot help but also like the church, because it's his church and his bride. They need the church because it's the expression of Jesus as his body. If they put their faith in Jesus, whether they realize it or not, they are supernaturally part of the church. But we need to help them understand the difference between the church and what we sometimes turn it into.

We have a lot to overcome. This should drive us to our knees in prayer and motivate us to avoid ever shaming the church. It should motivate us to be humble and intelligent students of the Scriptures and to strive with all of our being to make the church known as Jesus' bride, whom he loves. We need to be creating new understandings of the church so that we will no longer be seen as a negative, judgmental, homophobic organized religion that oppresses women, arrogantly thinks all other religions are wrong, and takes the whole Bible literally, but instead will be seen as a loving and welcoming family that is a positive agent of change, holds women in the highest respect, is respectful of other beliefs, and humbly strives to be thoughtful theologians.

The church is an organized religion with a political agenda → The church is an organized community with a heart to serve others

The church is judgmental and negative → The church is a positive agent of change loving others as Jesus would

The church is dominated by males and oppresses females → The church holds women in the highest respect and includes them in the leadership of the church

The church is homophobic → The church is a loving and welcoming community

The church arrogantly claims all other religions are wrong → The church is respectful of other people's beliefs and faiths

The church is full of fundamentalists who take the whole Bible literally → The church holds beliefs with humility and strives to be thoughtful theologians

PLEASE DON'T BE A WEAKLING — THOSE WHO LIKE JESUS NEED YOU

If we really care about people outside the church, we won't be weaklings. We will be passionate about our mission to break out of the Christian bubble. I truly believe that many people will change their minds about the church if they meet Christians who break their stereotypes and care about them. People will give the church a chance if we ask them for forgiveness. And I believe people will forgive the church. If they like Jesus, then they need to forgive his bride for wrongly representing the groom.

Let me close with some important words from author Henri Nouwen:

> When we have been wounded by the Church, our temptation is to reject it. But when we reject the Church, it becomes very hard for us to keep in touch with the living Christ. When we say, "I love Jesus, but I hate the Church," we end up losing not only the Church but Jesus too. The challenge is to forgive the Church.
>
> This challenge is especially great because the Church seldom asks us for forgiveness, at least not officially. But the Church as an often fallible human organization needs our forgiveness, while the Church as the living Christ among us continues to offer us forgiveness.
>
> It is important to think about the Church not as "over there" but as a community of struggling, weak people of whom we are part and in whom we meet our Lord and Redeemer.[22]

Countless numbers of people who like Jesus but not the church are open to receiving an apology from the church and even to forgiving the church when forgiveness is needed. But first they need to be in relationship with someone they can trust.

May we not be weaklings but have the strength and courage to escape the Christian subculture and truly be a church on a mission. May we pray fervently with a missional heart, asking the Spirit of God to move in the lives of those we are befriending. May those who like Jesus but not the church understand the Jesus of the Bible and the full wonderful life that his life, death, and resurrection bring. And may they move from liking Jesus to loving Jesus, and from not liking the church to loving the church, recognizing that the church, despite its weaknesses and mistakes, is still the body of Jesus and the bride whom he loves.

LOOKING AT YOUR CHURCH
THROUGH THE EYES OF
EMERGING GENERATIONS

1. Do you feel optimistic about those who like Jesus but not the church? Why or why not?

2. How would you respond to those who would say that people who like Jesus but not the church have hardened hearts and we shouldn't pay attention to them?

3. Is there anything that you or your church is doing that might be getting in the way of God? Is there anything you or your church needs to apologize for?

4. After reading this book, what specific actions do you need to take to change your church or your personal life?

CRITICISM OF THIS BOOK

As I researched and wrote this book, I was able to speak about the topic of this book to pastors and church leaders around the country, and I have sensed an overwhelming agreement that what I've covered here is indeed what emerging generations are saying and thinking. Many times a pastor or leader has shared with me that these are the very things that their own college-aged children are telling them they feel. So I am fairly confident that my observations apply not only to California.

At the same time, I encountered some valid questions from pastors and leaders, which I'd like to address in this appendix. If you have other questions or want to give feedback about this book, please go to the *www.vintagefaith.com* and *www.theylikejesus.com* websites, where you will find a section for this book on the discussion boards, as well as other ways of communicating about the issues raised in this book. I hope to periodically answer questions and respond to feedback through these sites.

1. **Isn't the reason that the people you quote say they like Jesus because they hold only a pop-culture version of him in their minds?**

Yes, for the most part this is true. Most people I talked with who grew up outside of the church understand Jesus as a peacemaker who loved others and died for what he believed in. They think of him as a rebel who fought for the poor and the oppressed and stood against religious hypocrites. They believe he stood up for social misfits and those who didn't fit in the religious circles of his day. They see him as a wise and great spiritual leader, in many ways like Gandhi or Martin Luther King Jr. But most also sense that he had some sort of unique divine connection and knowledge which set him apart from other leaders. They feel he was wise like a spiritual guru and was divinely enlightened in some way, thus possessing a supernatural aspect. Most people I talked to don't dismiss the idea that he was raised from the dead, though they don't think of the resurrection much or see its relevance. They feel Jesus is an approachable friend, someone who would stick up for them and defend them.

So, yes, they like Jesus because they have a limited idea of who he really is. When we read the Bible, we see Jesus the Son of God, the righteous one, the King of Kings and Lord of Lords, the one who bore our sin as a payment on the cross. We know him as the second person of the triune God we worship, and the one who will judge all the earth. While we may take these descriptions of Jesus for granted, for the most part the people I interviewed for this book don't know these things about him. But as I talked with these spiritually intrigued individuals and shared more about the biblical Jesus, they didn't reject these descriptions of him. It was all new to them because they had never heard of these characteristics before. Over many months, lots of wonderful questions and discussion arose as they learned more about Jesus.

So I don't see anything wrong with their liking what they know of Jesus, even if it's colored by pop culture. Our role is to help them discover the biblical Jesus. But we can be thrilled that at least they are open to the pop-culture Jesus. Their respect for Jesus is a great point of entry into discussion. Instead of dismissing them because of their inadequate understanding, we should celebrate their interest in him and use that as a springboard to engage them in conversations about who he really is.

2. Isn't listening to them conforming to the world? We shouldn't care what the world thinks; we need to preach the gospel and leave the rest to the Holy Spirit.

When missionaries go to other countries, they spend a lot of time getting to know the people of this new culture. They want to understand the culture's values and spiritual beliefs. They want to find out what the people think of Christianity and how much they know about it. No one would ever accuse a missionary who does that of conforming to the world. When we listen to people in emerging generations, we are simply being good missionaries who respect people and want to hear what they think so we can understand how to communicate with them better. Jesus spent a lot of time asking people questions and listening to them. He wasn't conforming to the world; he was caring about people.

If we water down our beliefs and hide who Jesus really is, we would be conforming to the world. Ironically, I have found that people who like Jesus but not the church want nothing more than to talk about who Jesus really is and are willing to open the Bible to look at passages that address their questions. I have found that we can talk openly about our beliefs about sin, hell, human sexuality, holiness, repentance, and all the other things we feel would be difficult to talk about with people outside the church. But the key is how we do it. If we just start spouting our viewpoints or Bible verses without their asking for them or before they have come to trust us, they most likely will shut us out. But if people sense we care about them and can have honest discussion and dialogue with them, we can talk about absolutely anything.

I recognize that it's the Holy Spirit who draws people to repentance and an understanding of their need for a Savior. But we need to do our part. To say that all we have to do is present the gospel and then our job is done, to me, is a cop-out, an easy way out of investing time and prayer in building relationships with people. The power of the gospel changes people, but they need to see it embodied in our lives. In our emerging culture, it's all the more important that we be the church so that people will see the gospel at work, not just hear a presentation of it. Though Paul, in the book of Acts, went into places to preach the gospel without first building relationships with his hearers, he lived at a time when open-air preaching and the public sharing of ideas was an effective form of communication. And preaching wasn't the only way he shared the gospel. We also see Paul living as a tentmaker for long periods of time among people with whom he also was sharing the gospel. We should tailor the way we communicate to suit the culture, not because we are ashamed of the gospel but because we want to communicate it in a way that is best understood by the people of the culture we are communicating it to. That's why we need to listen and to discern how best to communicate with different types of people.

3. **Isn't the real reason people in emerging generations are critical of the church and won't come to church because they are sinners and don't want to give up their sin? Aren't all of their objections simply excuses for their sin?**

Most of the criticism I've heard is based on the assumption that the people in emerging generations that I have talked to are sinners, and therefore the real reason they are critical of the church is because they don't want to change their sinful ways. Yes, people have hardened hearts and people don't want to give up sin. But I don't think that's the key issue. I think they're critical of the church because there are valid things to be critical about. If my only view of the church were from an outside perspective, I'd be critical too. I've even been challenged that I should not listen to them because they are expressing worldly opinions. I am always saddened when I hear this, because when someone jumps to that conclusion, they are saying there's no hope for people in our culture. They dismiss those who don't respond to the gospel right away as the nonelect, so we might as well move on; listening to their opinions and to their hearts is not worth the time and effort because they have hardened hearts.

I would lovingly plead with anyone who would say this (and interestingly it's usually staunch hyper-Calvinists who ask me this) to please remember when you were not a Christian. What was your way of thinking then; how did you view life? Likely you were once outside of the church until someone took an interest in you, listened to you and your opinions, and prayed for you regularly until the Spirit of God eventually convicted you of your need for Jesus and gave you the gifts of faith and repentance. I have seen God change the hearts of those who were following other religious faiths, and now they follow Jesus. I have seen God change the hearts of those who were in all kinds of sin, and now they align themselves with the teaching of the Scriptures. I have seen God change the hearts of those who were against the church, and now they are in love with Jesus and are part of his church. God is God and can change anyone he wants to. He has a loving heart and compassion for people. The Bible says, "He is patient ... not wanting anyone to perish, but everyone to come to repentance" (2 Peter 3:9). I hope we can have the same optimism and love for people that God has. I hope that we will let our hearts be broken for those who don't know Jesus yet, that we will love and respect them as human beings created in the image of God, people for whom Jesus died. I hope we will share the good news of Jesus with others and pray for the Spirit of God to penetrate their hearts and minds so they will turn to Jesus, the real Jesus who is friend, Savior, and Lord.

4. **It's depressing to hear people's negative comments about the church. Are these comments really representative of people in emerging generations, or are they just extreme statements?**

It's true that it can be discouraging to hear negative comments about the church. But look at it like going to the dentist. Many people don't like dental checkups because they'll learn what is really happening to their teeth and gums. But after the cleaning, it often feels good to know exactly what is happening, whether it's good or bad. Likewise, we need to be aware of misperceptions about the church and Christianity so we can develop an apologetic or offer an apology for the church when needed. Some criticisms about the church may seem like extreme statements, but remember that the people I interviewed for this book, and the people I talk with regularly in our church context, are not radicals. They are normal folks living in our town and probably are like some of the people in your town. So look at the comments in this book not as radical extremism but as honest reflections from people in emerging generations.

I hope that I was able to paint in this book an optimistic picture. Churches all across the nation are seeing hundreds and thousands of people in emerging generations become part of their communities. The leaders of these churches are aware of the very things discussed in this book and are doing something about it in their local contexts. As negative as some of the comments may be, there is great hope. The Spirit of God is doing incredible things in the lives of so many people all across the country who have become believers.

5. I don't find people like this in my community. Isn't your opinion skewed because you live in California and interviewed people there?

My area is a melting pot of people from all over the nation. When I selected people to interview for this book, I looked for a wide variety of backgrounds in terms of church experience and where they grew up. I also looked for people with various levels of education and working in a variety of occupations.

The prevalence of the media, the internet, music, and travel today means culture is becoming more uniform across the country and even globally. There are still plenty of subcultures within any culture, but you can go, for example, to Nebraska and find teenagers listening to the same music and dressing the same way they do in Santa Cruz, California. No matter where you live today, you will find people with similar views and patterns. If you don't think there are people in your community who subscribe to these views, I would challenge you to go to a local university and talk to students. Go to clubs, bars, and coffeehouses where people in their twenties are hanging out. Rather than just talking to people in your church, talk with individuals outside of your church.

I'm an introvert, so meeting new people is not easy for me. I simply chose a few places where I would regularly hang out to study. Eventually I got to talk with people who work at the coffeehouses I frequent, and I befriended them. When I asked them if they would help me understand how the church comes across to people outside the church, they all immediately said yes. You could do the same thing. I also looked for opportunities to meet and get to know those outside the church. For example, I met the girl who cut my hair by intentionally going to a non-Christian hairstylist. I find that people are wide open to talking about faith and spirituality and giving their opinions. That's the critical key—asking for their opinions and listening to them. We need to be quiet and listen more.

I would be shocked if you didn't find people in your town who think like those in this book. You'll find them if you look for them, and if you talk to them, their comments may be very close to the ones expressed in this book. I understand that certain pockets of the country may be more conservative and have Christian-based populations, but the perspectives voiced in this book are becoming more of the norm in all of North America.

6. **How did you answer the criticisms of the church in your discussions with the people you interviewed?**

I had *long* discussions with most of the people I quote in this book—direct theological conversations—and I have similar discussions all the time with people very much like them. You'll find my best responses to their criticisms and misperceptions in *I Like Jesus but Not the Church*, the counterpart to this book. In that book, I write to those who have either left the church or are outside the church and are grappling with these areas, and to those who are looking for ways to answer these criticisms.

I would encourage you to consider putting together a teaching series or a class on these criticisms and misperceptions, perhaps adding others you come up with. For creative ideas and discussion questions for small groups, ideas for prayer stations, and suggestions for other ways to cover the material in this book in your church, go to the *www.theylikejesus.com* website. Above all, I would encourage you to escape the church office and Christian subculture. Go and build normal healthy friendships with those outside the church and listen to them. Hear their thinking and understand their hearts. Don't just listen to the adventure I'm on; please be on your own adventure in your own community, if you aren't already. I cannot imagine that isn't what Jesus would be doing if he were here walking around our towns today.

RESOURCES

I LIKE JESUS BUT NOT THE CHURCH

The book you are holding in your hands, *They Like Jesus but Not the Church*, was written primarily for church leaders, addressing our emerging culture's negative impressions of the church and suggesting

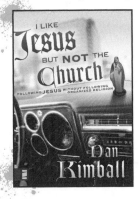

what church leaders can do to correct those impressions. However, the average person needs a book too, one that addresses these negative perceptions of Christianity and the church and helps them wrestle with their questions.

I Like Jesus but Not the Church: Following Jesus without Following Organized Religion is that book. It differs from the one you hold in your hands in that it gives apologetical answers to each of the six negative perceptions as it explores difficult criticisms of the church today. It also differs from *They Like Jesus but Not the Church* because it is for:

- those in the church who are looking for ways to answer the criticisms and negative perceptions of the church and Christianity.
- those outside the church who are struggling with church and Christianity.

Don't let the title mislead you. *I Like Jesus but Not the Church* is a very pro-church book, giving an apologetic for the church and encouraging people who like Jesus to understand why the local church is a necessary part of the life of anyone who desires to follow Jesus. The church may make mistakes, but Jesus loves the church, and it's possible to be part of the church without being a part of "organized religion."

WWW.THEYLIKEJESUS.COM

Resources for a sermon series or class or small group

Because the six perceptions of the church and Christianity discussed in both *They Like Jesus but Not the Church* and *I Like Jesus but Not the Church* are so common, they could be presented in a six-week sermon series, class, or small group study. Go to the website *www.theylikejesus.com* for more information on both of these books and on more resources for using them in your church.

A six-week series could be taught using either the *They Like Jesus* angle or the *I Like Jesus* angle:

They Like Jesus but Not the Church

1. The church is an organized religion with a political agenda.
2. The church is judgmental and negative.
3. The church is dominated by males and oppresses females.
4. The church is homophobic.
5. The church arrogantly claims all other religions are wrong.
6. The church is full of fundamentalists who take the whole Bible literally.

I Like Jesus but Not the Church

1. Jesus wasn't into organized religion.
2. Jesus wasn't judgmental and negative.
3. Jesus wasn't into a male-dominated religion that oppresses females.
4. Jesus wasn't homophobic.
5. Jesus wasn't disrespectful of people of other faiths.
6. Jesus wasn't a fundamentalist who took the whole Bible literally.

The *www.theylikejesus.com* website provides information about the following additional resources to assist you in preparing to teach the various topics covered in these books:

- Outlines for sermons or a class
- PowerPoint slides for teaching
- DVD teaching and small group curriculum using interviews with some of the people interviewed in this book for discussion starters
- DVD clips to use for setting up a topic for a sermon or class
- Graphics and images that can be used for a teaching series or class
- Ideas for prayer stations on each of the topics for use in worship gatherings

SUGGESTED READING

ecause this book is not a theology text, we barely got into the theology behind a lot of the issues we covered. So if you want more biblical and theological insight into the topics discussed in this book, what follows is a suggested reading list.

PART I: WHY EMERGING GENERATIONS ARE CHANGING

Books

The following books remind us of the need to be missionally minded and outwardly focused.

Burke, John. *No Perfect People Allowed: Creating a Come As You Are Culture in the Church.* Zondervan, 2005.

> Addresses issues we're facing in our culture; written by a pastor who understands the realities of emerging culture and takes evangelism seriously.

Frost, Michael, and Alan Hirsch. *The Shaping of Things to Come: Innovation and Mission for the Twenty-first-Century Church.* Hendrickson, 2003.

> Another thoughtful look at why the church exists and how we can forge a missional future.

Guder, Darrell L. *Missional Church: A Vision for the Sending of the Church in North America.* Eerdmans, 1998.

> This book ignited my understanding of the need to view our cities and communities as mission fields.

Henderson, Jim. *a.k.a. "LOST": Discovering Ways to Connect with the People Jesus Misses the Most.* Waterbrook, 2005.

> Another great practical book about personally connecting with those outside of the church.

Hybels, Bill. *Just Walk Across the Room: Simple Steps Pointing People to Faith.* Zondervan, 2006.

A practical book that looks at ways to share Jesus with other people.

Kimball, Dan. *The Emerging Church: Vintage Christianity for New Generations.* Zondervan 2003.

The first half of this book gives the cultural background on how we got where we are today as a mission field.

McNeal, Reggie. *The Present Future: Six Tough Questions for the Church.* Jossey-Bass, 2003.

A great book which forces some self-examination if you're serious about reaching our emerging culture.

Stetzer, Ed, and David Putman. *Breaking the Missional Code: Your Church Can Become a Missionary in Your Community.* Broadman and Holman, 2006.

A great book which scans the horizon to see how churches are changing to be missional in their communities.

Other resources for staying in touch with emerging culture

Magazines and newspapers

- *Outreach* magazine (*www.outreachmagazine.com*). A magazine for church leaders; keeps in touch with all types of evangelistic efforts and all kinds of churches.
- *Relevant* magazine (*www.relevantmagazine.com*). Although I'm not fond of saying we have to be relevant, this magazine is a fun one for reading viewpoints of those in their twenties and thirties on all types of faith and cultural issues.
- Entertainment magazines. I read magazines about the movies, music, and books that are influencing emerging generations. I pay attention to what the most popular films and music are and what messages they are teaching. One magazine I have subscribed to for years is *Entertainment Weekly* (*www.ew.com*). It publishes charts of what people are watching and listening to, as well as reviews. Reading this magazine, I don't even have to see the films or listen to the music to stay in touch with what's going on today.

- Local newspapers. I also read my community's weekly entertainment papers and the local university newspaper, which keep me in touch with the local scene and local culture.

Websites about emerging culture

www.vintagefaith.com. Links and articles about emerging church and culture.

www.beliefnet.com. Articles from the perspectives of all faiths. Reading it will keep you abreast of the variety of spiritual discussion at a national level.

www.thunderstuck.org. A summary of interesting pop-culture and spirituality news.

www.relevantmagazine.com. The website for *Relevant* magazine. News and articles from a Christian perspective written by twenty-somethings who are immersed in our culture.

PART 2: WHAT EMERGING GENERATIONS THINK ABOUT THE CHURCH

I could recommend a dozen or more books for each of these chapters, since they address topics that require theological study. But I will highlight just a few helpful books.

Chapter 5: The Church is an organized religion with a political agenda

Mallory, Sue. *The Equipping Church: Serving Together to Transform Lives.* Zondervan, 2001.

A great book reminding us that the church needs to be organized in a good way, just as any healthy family needs to be, and that the role of the leader is to give away power and control.

Ogden, Greg. *Unfinished Business: Returning the Ministry to the People of God.* Zondervan, 2003.

Another book about the need to break down hierarchical "organized religion" and put ministry into the hands of the people.

Chapter 6: The church is judgmental and negative

Lewis, Robert. *The Church of Irresistible Influence.* With Rob Wilkins. Zondervan, 2003.

Focuses on practical ways churches can be a positive influence in their communities.

Nouwen, Henri J. *In the Name of Jesus: Reflections on Christian Leadership.* Crossroad/Faith and Formation, 1993.

A book which causes leaders to examine whether they are leading with the right heart.

Sanders, J. Oswald. *Spiritual Leadership: Principles of Excellence for Every Believer.* Moody, 1994.

A classic book of self-examination for leaders.

Sider, Ron. *Churches That Make a Difference: Reaching Your Community with Good News and Good Works.* Baker, 2002.

Gives examples of churches that break the stereotypes and are positive influences in their communities through social justice projects and service.

———. *Good News and Good Works.* Baker, 1999.

Looks at how we're presenting a lopsided form of Christianity. Suggests that if we balanced evangelism and social action, the church would be known not for the negative but for the positive difference it makes in the world.

Chapter 7: The church is dominated by males and oppresses females

Blomberg, Craig, gen. ed. *Two Views on Women in Ministry.* Zondervan, 2005.

If you read only one book on this topic, this is the one, because it's written by theologians and presents each viewpoint. However, be warned that you will read each view and then be all the more confused because of the great arguments on each side.

Grenz, Stanley J. *Women in the Church: A Biblical Theology of Women in Ministry.* Inter-Varsity, 1995.

An easy-to-understand book by a respected theologian advocating women in ministry.

Grudem, Wayne. *Evangelical Feminism and Biblical Truth: An Analysis of More Than 100 Disputed Questions.* Multnomah, 2004.

This book takes a very strong stand against women in pastoral ministry. The tone is rather blunt, but if you want to understand the theological defense of the complementarian view, this is the book to be familiar with.

Sumner, Sarah. *Men and Women in the Church: Building Consensus on Christian Leadership.* InterVarsity, 2003.

The author, who has a Ph.D. in theology from Trinity Evangelical Divinity School, shares her journey as a female in the church while interweaving scholarly discussion on this critical issue of the roles of men and women in the church.

Chapter 8: The church is homophobic

Gagnon, Robert A. J., and Dan O. Via. *Homosexuality and the Bible: Two Views.* Augsburg Fortress, 2003.

In this short book, one author presents a pro-gay theology and the other presents a conservative view, and then each critiques the other.

Grenz, Stanley. *Welcoming but Not Affirming: An Evangelical Response to Homosexuality.* Westminster/John Knox, 1998.

A theologically conservative view on homosexuality. If I were to recommend only two books, I would recommend this one and *Loving Homosexuals As Jesus Would* by Chad Thompson.

Helminiak, Daniel A. *What the Bible Really Says about Homosexuality.*

This is a pro-gay book, so I don't endorse its conclusions. However, pro-gay theological arguments are becoming more widely known, and those who hold a conservative view need to be familiar with them.

Thompson, Chad W. *Loving Homosexuals As Jesus Would: A Fresh Christian Approach.* Brazos, 2004.

This is a really great book by a guy in his twenties who struggled with same-sex attraction while growing up in a church. It really is an eye-opening book that will move your heart to think about how poorly the church is prepared to understand and minister to homosexuals. Chad's website is *www.lovinghomosexuals.com.*

Webb, William J. *Slaves, Women and Homosexuals: Exploring the Hermeneutics of Cultural Analysis.* InterVarsity, 2001.

Advocates a theologically conservative viewpoint using "redemptive-movement" hermeneutics. Not an easy book to read, but presents a lot of research.

Chapter 9: The church arrogantly claims all other religions are wrong

Armstrong, Karen. *History of God: The 4,000-Year Quest of Judaism, Christianity and Islam.* Ballantine, 1994.

This is a non-Christian book, but I learned a lot from its neutral perspective on the development of these three major world faiths. I also recommend the follow-up book, *The Battle for God* by the same author. Again, this is not a Christian perspective, but it will familiarize you with the growing perspective of our culture.

Bowker, John Westerdale. *World Religions: The Great Faiths Explored and Explained.* DK, 1997.

Presents a non-Christian perspective, but it's illustrated with incredible photos and drawings, which help us to "see" the various practices and images of global faiths.

Edwards, James R. *Is Jesus the Only Savior?* Eerdmans, 2005.

This book looks at the central question of whether Jesus is indeed the sole Savior of the world. Discusses Jesus as Savior in light of contemporary cultural currents, specifically addressing the thorny issues of religious pluralism, moral relativism, postmodernism, and the quest for world peace.

Halverson, Dean C. *The Compact Guide to World Religions.* Bethany, 1996.

An easy-to-understand guide from an evangelical perspective. This hardcover edition has lots of helpful photos of various practices. This book could easily be used in a class setting.

McDermott, Gerald R. *Can Evangelicals Learn from World Religions? Jesus, Revelation and Religious Traditions.*

This is a fascinating book that presents a case for God's having revealed himself outside of Israel and the church. The author explores four case studies of how Buddhist, Daoist, Confucian, and Islamic concepts have enriched his own understanding of scriptural concepts. Not everyone will agree with his conclusions, but it gives a broader perspective.

Okholm, Dennis, gen. ed. *Four Views on Salvation in a Pluralistic World.* Zondervan, 1996.

This book presents perspectives that every leader should be aware of. Each perspective is presented by a major advocate of that view (Normative Pluralism; Inclusivism; Salvation in Christ; Salvation in Christ Alone).

Rainer, Thom S. *The Unexpected Journey: Conversations with People Who Turned from Other Beliefs to Jesus.* Zondervan, 2005.

A hopeful book telling the stories of people who turned to Jesus from other faiths.

Toropov, Brandon, and Luke Buckles. *Complete Idiot's Guide to World Religions.* Alpha, 2001.

This is not a Christian book, but it's important to read books like this one and then try to read about Christianity through a neutral lens to see how it comes across in light of other faiths, since this is the view that those outside the church have. This book is fun and easy to understand.

Chapter 10: The church is full of fundamentalists who take the whole Bible literally

For teaching Bible study skills

Duvall, J. Scott, and J. Daniel Hays. *Grasping God's Word: A Hands-On Approach to Reading, Interpreting, and Applying the Bible.* Zondervan, 2005.

This book also has a workbook for use in a class setting. It's great for teaching basic Bible hermeneutics that every Christian should know. It would change the culture of our churches if people understood how pastors and teachers come to the conclusions that they do and learned to feed themselves from Scripture.

Fee, Gordon D., and Douglas Stuart. *"How to Read the Bible for All Its Worth"* and *"How to Read the Bible Book by Book."* Zondervan, 2003.

If Duvall and Hays' *Grasping God's Word* is too extensive or expensive for your purposes, these two accessible classics could be used as introductory books for everyone in your church.

Grenz, Stanley J., and John R. Franke. *Beyond Foundationalism: Shaping Theology in a Postmodern Context.* Westminster/John Knox, 2000.

Every Christian leader should read this book to understand some new approaches that are being taken to theology and the Bible.

Smith, Chuck, Jr. *Epiphany: Discover the Delight of God's Word.* Waterbrook, 2003.

This is a great book on how we view and study the Bible. When we started our new church, we bought copies of this book for all of our leaders and had the author give a day-long seminar to our leadership community.

Spong, John Shelby. *Rescuing the Bible from Fundamentalism: A Bishop Rethinks the Meaning of Scripture.* HarperSanFrancisco, 1992.

This is not an evangelical book, and I by no means agree with its conclusions. However, it has been a national bestseller, and this type of view is becoming more accepted today, so it's good to be familiar with it.

Witherington, Ben, III. *The Problem with Evangelical Theology: Testing the Exegetical Foundations of Calvinism, Dispensationalism, and Wesleyanism.* Baylor Univ. Press, 2005.

I suggest this book here because it really is a great look at how there are flaws in all of our categories of theology. It should make us a bit more reluctant to say what is *the* right branch of evangelical theology.

Wright, N. T. *The Last Word: Beyond the Bible Wars to a New Understanding of the Authority of Scripture.* HarperSanFrancisco, 2005.

A great book that takes a refreshing look at how we view the Bible.

For sermon and teaching preparation

The IVP Bible Background Commentary: Old Testament and New Testament. InterVarsity.

Focuses on specific historical and cultural backgrounds of the Bible.

The NIV Application Commentary. Zondervan.

This commentary procedes from "original meaning" to "bridging contexts" to "contemporary significance." If I were to have only one set of commentaries, this would be it.